THE SPY WHO DISAPPEARED

The Spy Who Disappeared

DIARY OF A SECRET MISSION TO
RUSSIAN CENTRAL ASIA IN 1918

by

REGINALD TEAGUE-JONES

[Ronald Sinclair O.B.E., M.B.E. (Mil.)]

Introduction and Epilogue by

Peter Hopkirk

Author of *Setting the East Ablaze:
Lenin's Dream of an Empire in Asia*

LONDON
VICTOR GOLLANCZ LTD
1990

First published in Great Britain 1990
by Victor Gollancz Ltd
14 Henrietta Street, London WC2E 8QJ

British Library Cataloguing in Publication Data
Teague-Jones, Reginald
    The spy who disappeared : diary of a
    secret mission to Russian Central Asia
    in 1918.
    1. British espionage, history. Biographies
    I. Title
    327.12092

ISBN 0-575-04785-2

Typeset at The Spartan Press Ltd,
Lymington, Hants
and printed in Great Britain by
St Edmundsbury Press Ltd, Bury St Edmunds, Suffolk

Contents

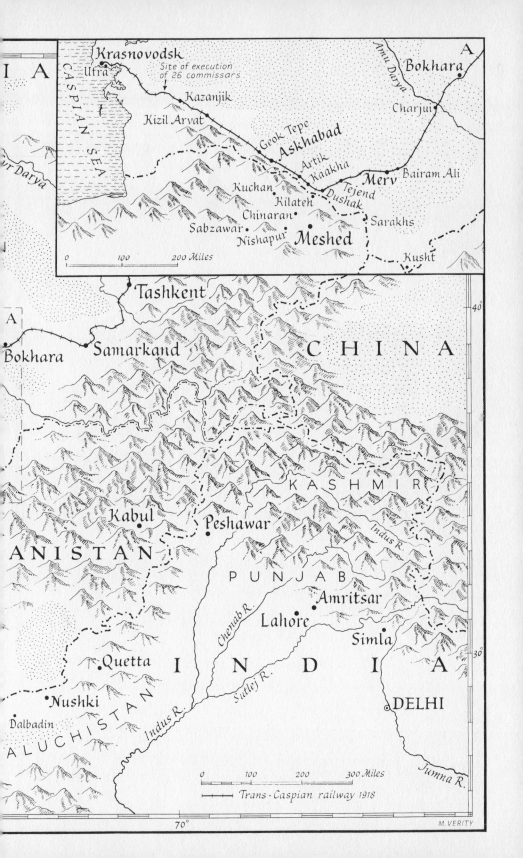

Inset map (top):

CASPIAN SEA

Krasnovodsk

Ufra

Site of execution of 26 commissars

Amu Darya

Bokhara

A

Kazanjik

Charjui

Kizil Arvat

Geok Tepe

Askhabad

Artik

Kaakha

Merv

Bairam Ali

Kuchan

Dushak

Tejend

Kilateh

Chinaran

Sarakhs

Sabzawar

Nishapur

Meshed

Kusht

0   100   200 Miles

Main map:

r Darya

IA

A

Bokhara

Tashkent

Samarkand

CHINA

40

KASHMIR

Kabul

Peshawar

Indus R.

ANISTAN

PUNJAB

Amritsar

Chenab R.

Lahore

Simla

Quetta

INDIA

30

Sutlej R.

Nushki

Indus R.

DELHI

Dalbadin

ALUCHISTAN

Jumna R.

0   100   200   300 Miles

Trans-Caspian railway 1918

70

M. VERITY

Introduction

by Peter Hopkirk

---◆---

Early on the morning of September 20, 1918, at a remote spot to the east of the Caspian Sea, twenty-six Bolshevik commissars were taken out into the desert and cold-bloodedly murdered. Some accounts say that they were shot, others that they were hacked to death. Their corpses were then tossed unceremoniously into a common grave and hastily covered with sand to hide all evidence of the crime.

Because of the turmoil of the civil war, and of the Allied intervention, news of the massacre took some months to reach Moscow. When it did it was to arouse the bitter wrath of Lenin and his fellow revolutionaries, and reduce relations between Britain and the new Soviet government to a new low. For, already incensed at Britain's intervention in southern Russia, Moscow now accused British intelligence officers of being responsible for the deaths of the commissars, at least two of whom were close personal friends of Lenin's. Britain, the Soviet Foreign Minister declared, stood 'publicly convicted of the base, cowardly and treacherous murder of defenceless prisoners'.

Despite vigorous denials by the British Government, the Russians have rigidly maintained this view ever since. Today the fate of the twenty-six Baku commissars has become part of the great revolutionary epic. The supposed role of the British in the martyrdom of the Bolshevik heroes is taught to every Soviet schoolchild. Official paintings, films and other representations of the massacre depict British officers in uniform actually directing it. Visitors to Baku, where the commissars were later reinterred, are told categorically — as I myself was — that they were 'murdered by the British'. Other official accounts of the affair are only slightly less accusatory, claiming — as does *The History of the Communist Party of the Soviet Union* — that the commissars were shot 'on instructions from the British imperialists'.

Even today, more than seventy years later, considerable mystery and doubt still surround the events which led up to the massacre. The British Government, so far as it maintains any interest in the affair (which understandably it has no wish to see revived), has all along insisted that the unfortunate commissars were brutally slaughtered by their own fellow-countrymen and rivals, based on Askhabad, into whose hands it was their misfortune to fall. The fact that this anti-Bolshevik faction, styling itself the Askhabad Committee, or government, enjoyed military and financial support from Britain at the time, did not mean — or so London has always claimed — that the latter was in any way responsible for its actions or excesses.

The reason for the British having such dubious contacts lay in the fact that when the Russian Revolution took place the war with Germany and Turkey was still far from over. The Revolution had led to the collapse of the entire Eastern Front, the break up of the Tsar's armies there, and to the Bolsheviks making peace overtures to the Central Powers. This left the Caucasus and Trans-Caspian regions undefended, and British India open to attack by a Turco-German force advancing eastwards across the Caspian and by the Trans-Caspian Railway towards Afghanistan and the North-West Frontier. It also raised the spectre of Baku, with its vast oil resources, falling into the hands of the Germans and Turks, who were starved of fuel for their military transport and submarine fleet.

At all costs this had to be prevented, although few troops were available, either in India or anywhere else, for this purpose. There was only one other solution, and that was to try to persuade the inhabitants of the region, with British support, to resist the advancing Turco-German forces themselves. British agents and military officers were therefore hastily despatched to Central Asia and to Trans-Caspia to try to discover precisely what was happening there, and who was prepared to resist the invader. (I have already told the story of some of them, including Colonel F. M. Bailey, in my *Setting the East Ablaze*, published in 1984.)

One of the officers chosen was the author of this narrative, Captain Reginald Teague-Jones, who possessed exceptional credentials for undertaking this difficult and dangerous task. Not only was he fluent in Russian, having been brought up and educated in St Petersburg, but he was also well versed in the ways of political extremists. After serving in the Indian Police for several years, mainly on the frontier, he had been chosen for transfer to the Indian Government's élite Foreign and Political Department. In both jobs he had shown himself to be a highly resourceful officer.

In 1917 he was switched to military intelligence, with the rank of Captain, serving at G.H.Q. Delhi as officer in charge of Persian Gulf intelligence. In addition to speaking perfect Russian, he was fluent in German, French, Persian and Hindustani. Later the Bolsheviks were to claim that he had been a British Secret Service agent since long before the war, for which they can perhaps be excused, given his background, which even today is somewhat shadowy. Finally, as he had no personal ties, he was extremely eager to get out into the field and risk his neck at anything which promised both adventure and scope for his unusual talents. Even so, when in the spring of 1918 he set out for Meshed, from where he was to cross into strife-torn southern Russia, he can have had little idea of the extraordinary turmoil and mayhem into which he would be plunged. Least of all could he have guessed the bizarre and alarming consequences it would have for him for the rest of his life.

For at the age of 29, Teague-Jones was to find himself accused by no less a person than Leon Trotsky of being responsible for the deaths of the twenty-six Baku commissars, and being branded by Moscow as 'the accursed representative of bloody imperialism'. Although official British records show Teague-Jones to have been at Askhabad, more than 200 miles away from the scene of the massacre, Trotsky was to describe him as its 'direct practical organiser'. Elsewhere he claimed that the commissars 'were shot without investigation or trial, on a lonely spot . . . in Trans-Caspia, on September 20th, 1918 by Teague-Jones, the chief of the British military mission at Askhabad, with the knowledge and approbation of the other British authorities in Trans-Caucasia.'

It was a chilling accusation, especially coming from a man of such fearsome reputation, who wielded the power of life and death over millions, and was reputed to have agents and assassins everywhere. The unfortunate young officer must have felt very much as Salman Rushdie, the novelist, did when Ayatollah Khomeini publicly sentenced him to death and called on all Muslims to see that this was carried out. Preferring not to risk Moscow's vengeance, Captain Teague-Jones, like Rushdie, promptly vanished from view. Despite repeated accusations against him by the Russian Government and Soviet historians, which continue to this day, he never came forward to defend himself. All he did do, before changing his name and disappearing, was to provide the British Foreign Office with a brief account of the circumstances surrounding the killing of the commissars, and a denial of any implication in their murder himself.

It was only after his death, some seventy years later, on November 16, 1988, that the full truth about his disappearance began to emerge. In an obituary in *The Times* on November 23 it was disclosed that for all those years Teague-Jones had sheltered behind the identity of one Ronald Sinclair. In his hundredth year, the year of his death, he had even published a travel book under his assumed name, although it avoided any mention of his wartime exploits described in this book. The secret of his identity he kept successfully even from his closest friends, as well as from his publisher, none of whom, until they read *The Times* obituary, had the slightest suspicion of who he really was. It appears, however, that there was a little more to it than just that. Subsequent examination of his papers suggests another possible explanation, quite apart from any fear of Bolshevik vengeance, for his change of name and apparent disappearance. This, however, I shall keep to the end of the book, together with a number of other mysteries which surround the affair.

But first Teague-Jones, alias Ronald Sinclair, must be allowed to give his own account of what happened from the moment he set out across Beluchistan and Persia for Meshed and southern Russia. It is compiled primarily from a journal, written in 1920 or there-abouts, which in turn was based on diaries which he kept at the time, together with notes, telegrams and personal memories which he had preserved. From this journal, Teague-Jones had himself produced a narrative, as though for publication, called *Adventures with Turkmen, Tatars and Bolsheviks*. Written some time in the mid-1920s, it tells much the same story as the journal, often in the same words, though with a few significant variations, which are examined at the end in my epilogue. If anything, *Adventures* is less candid, for the author omits passages hurtful to his colleagues and superiors, or possibly damaging to their reputations.

After careful study of the two texts — that of the journal and that of *Adventures* — it was decided by the editor and publisher to take the story from the former, while borrowing certain descriptive and explanatory passages from the latter. However, while care has been taken to preserve accuracy and not to omit anything of significance, the narrative has been edited and put together primarily with the general reader in mind, rather than the specialist historian. Eventually it is hoped the latter may be able to study the originals of both the journal and *Adventures* in the library of one of our national institutions.

Here then, told for the first time, is Teague-Jones's full personal account of the extraordinary events leading to the massacre of the Baku commissars. Only partially told hitherto, it is certainly one of the most remarkable stories to come out of the Russian Revolution, and one over which historians of the period, both British and Soviet, are likely to wrangle for many years to come.

THE MISSION

April 1918

From the Journal of
Captain Reginald Teague-Jones

The Land that Allah Forgot

◆

Boarded the 9.30 train for Nushki. The train dragged its weary way all day through the most godforsaken country imaginable, and Nushki was reached at 5 p.m. Here one changes trains, and I found myself installed in a closed goods van.

Din Muhammed pitched my camp bed and arranged my boxes all around me, one heavy trunk reposing on a deep shelf over my head. It was beastly hot, the temperature being much higher than in Quetta. The train started at about 10.30 and I was soon fast asleep.

My slumbers were very rudely broken at an early hour in the morning. I felt a terrific crash and gradually realised that we had had an accident. I found myself tied up in an inextricable knot with the debris of my camp bed at the wrong end of my goods van. The heavy trunk which had been on the shelf over my head, had been flung the entire length of my bed, and by a miracle had just missed falling on top of me.

After much struggling I succeeded in freeing myself from my bed, and jumped out of the van. The train was at a standstill, it was pitch dark and there was a babel of yells and jabbering from the crowd of frightened passengers who were tumbling out of the train in scores. From the guard, who now appeared and asked me if I were all right, I learnt that the train had broken in two halves while going down a gradient. The first half had travelled a little way ahead of its tail half and had pulled up at a wayside station. No sooner had it stopped than the tail half crashed into it.

Cries from a group of natives down the train indicated that someone had been hurt. I went down and found that most of the trucks were loaded with sleepers and that crowds of natives had been travelling without tickets by getting in among the sleepers and remaining concealed there. One of these poor devils had been caught in the collision and had been crushed.

Assisted by a European sergeant, I worked for an hour in my pyjamas moving the heavy sleepers. None of the natives wanted to help us. It was useless trying to save the man and the moment the pressure was released he expired. A second man was also badly crushed and did not look as though he would survive. The rescue work took us until daybreak and I then managed to get a cup of tea and have my camp bed straightened out again. Fortunately the damage was not difficult to repair and after a short delay the train crawled on to Dalbadin.

29.4.18   Spent the day in Dalbadin. There was a small detachment of Indian infantry here, as also a company of Sappers and Miners who were working on the new railway. The officer commanding was a Colonel and a very nice fellow. One of the first questions the O.C. asked me was whether I knew a certain Major Bingham. I did.

One of the original 'Conspirators' from Delhi, Bingham was now also bound for Meshed, his duty consisting not so much in active intelligence work, as in laying the foundation for a possible future military mission. Bingham believed in travelling comfortably, and I remember him telling me that his motto when campaigning in the East was to take as much kit as far as you could and when possible always stick with it. On this occasion he was certainly adhering to his principle. His total impedimenta amounted to no less than twelve regulation camel loads.

Bingham had disappeared from Delhi very quietly. I now discovered that he was some ten days ahead of me with his caravan. What I also discovered was that he left an atmosphere of dark blue pessimism behind him the whole way. The O.C. Dalbadin asked me with ill-concealed anxiety as to whether the situation was really as bad as it had been depicted by Major Bingham. According to Bingham, the enemy were at our gates with a vengeance. The Turks had simply raced through the Caucasus, were already preparing to leap across Central Asia, and might be expected to appear in hordes any fine morning in Sistan. There was absolutely nothing to stop them. Afghanistan would rise at a signal from the Turk and Beluchistan would follow suit. None of us poor devils on the East Persian Cordon stood the ghostliest chance of ever coming back alive.

The wretched O.C. who was cut off from all regular news had only just heard of the big German attack on our line and naturally believed Bingham. He was vastly relieved when I assured him that things were nothing like as bad as they were painted and that even if the Turk did get into Central Asia across the Caspian, there was sufficient desert between him and us to swallow up bigger forces than he would ever be able to put into the field on this front.

I now continued my journey in the train. The landscape consisted in desert, with the Mekran Hills looming up to the south. The outstanding feature was the snow-covered mass of the Huh-i-Taftan, 13,034 feet high, dimly visible through the haze of the desert. The only interesting phenomenon was the 'moving sandhills', a long chain of sandhills some twenty to thirty feet in height extending for several hundred miles in a straight line from north to south. The curious fact about them is that these sandhills gradually move southwards until they eventually reach the coast.

The explanation is a very simple one. At this particular locality there appears to be an atmospheric channel with a prevalent wind blowing from the interior of southern Afghanistan directly south to the sea. The light desert sand raised by the wind collects in sandhills which assume the natural form of a crescent with the two horns pointing to the south. As the wind continues, the sand is constantly blown from the exposed, or northern, slope of the crescent, over the ridge and falls on the sheltered or southern side. Consequently there is a constant drifting of the sand in a southerly direction.

It was with great relief that I finally reached a tiny spot in the desert known as Mashki Chah, at that time the actual railhead. In Persian *Chah* means a well, which in these parts is generally little more than a water-hole scooped out a few feet deep in the sandy bed of some dried-up stream. While in Simla I had heard considerable discussion as to the ultimate terminus of the railway. The Sappers argued that it was impossible to have the terminus exactly at the frontier owing to the absence of water. They favoured Mirjawa as the terminus from the point of view of local conditions, but Mirjawa was really over the Persian frontier. The political department were averse to crossing the frontier into Persian territory. When I passed along the line this vexed question had not yet been settled, but subsequently the line ultimately not only traversed the frontier, but

1.5.18

continued for a considerable distance into Persia. Apparently our authorities considered that it was as well to be in for a pound as for a penny.

Descending from the train, I was agreeably surprised to find a Ford box car with a native driver waiting for me. He had come all the way from Saindak to fetch me. The question now arose of dividing my kit, as it was impossible to take more than half of it in the car; the rest would have to follow by camel. I accordingly singled out the more portable articles and with Din Muhammed sitting on the kit behind we started off, leaving Gulab Hussein and Naubat to come on with the rest of the kit on camels. It seemed strange to have my same two orderlies who had so often travelled with my camp camels on the frontier, doing exactly the same thing here in this strange land so very far from their own country.

I soon discovered that my Indian driver was a very raw hand at the game. His knowledge of motoring was even more elementary than mine. What was much more serious, he did not appear to have the vaguest knowledge of the road. As a matter of fact there *was* no road, nor was there even a track, save for the numerous goat tracks which criss-crossed the entire country and which were of course no use to anyone. I had a large-scale degree sheet and a compass with me, but this map was nearly responsible for leading me astray. Running across the map a dotted line represented the Indo European Telegraph Line. This was shown running from S.E. to N.W. I therefore decided to make straight north until we came across this telegraph line.

We started off with this idea, but by the time we had done about ten miles and got ourselves into extremely difficult country, we realised that either we were lost, or else the map was wrong. It turned out that the map was wrong. We were fortunate in finding a solitary Beluch shepherd, who directed us, so that we finally came out on the main road, otherwise a very indistinct track to Saindak. We reached Saindak that evening, and were hospitably received by a couple of subalterns who were forming a supply base there. The next point ahead was Robat and as news had come through that the General Officer Commanding the East Persian Cordon, General Dale, would shortly visit Robat, I decided not to wait for my orderlies and the kit at Saindak, but push ahead the next day in the Ford car.

The distance to Robat was sixty miles. We started on the journey soon after daylight, and made fair progress, the average speed being about fifteen miles an hour. The road was very bad and very uninteresting, save for the fact that it ran practically parallel to the Afghan frontier, and in close proximity to it the whole time. This was the nearest I had ever been to Afghan territory and I made a point of crossing the line just to say I had actually been in Afghanistan.

The only vegetation in the surrounding wasteland, apart from camel-thorn and a poisonous succulent which the natives call *ak*, was occasional clusters of stunted tamarisk trees struggling for existence in the dried-up water-courses. Here was subsistence for neither man nor beast. The regular form of transportation was the camel, but during the hot weather months a seasonal disease prevailed which was fatal to camels, and with the approach of summer the tribes-people regularly evacuated all their animals to less pestilential regions.

But war takes little account of such factors. Indian units of the East Persian Cordon had to be supplied and this was done by a system of regular camel convoys involving very large numbers of baggage animals. The tribesmen were reluctant to bring their beasts into the heat-stricken area and demanded exorbitant payment. This had to be met, but the casualty rate in every convoy was exceedingly high, and the terrible wastage of animal life was only too evident in the thousands of bleaching skeletons which marked this southerly section of the long caravan trail to Meshed.

The first halting place on this march is Kirtaka, which boasts a well of water and a *caravansarai* [inn]. Further on, the road became much better, and we were able to run at the terrific speed of thirty-five miles per hour, faster than anything had travelled in Eastern Persia in previous centuries.

We reached Robat at 2 p.m. Our arrival practically coincided with the arrival of General Dale with his Brigade Major and two large cars. To my surprise and amusement I also met Lt Ward.

I had first noticed this young subaltern in Delhi H.Q. He was poring over maps, and seemed to be keeping very much to himself. All anyone knew about him was that he had arrived with some instructions from the War Office. Ward himself did not vouchsafe any information about himself and the next day he had gone, as I understood, to Peshawar on some business. I now discovered that he was bound in the same direction as myself. I was very pleased to find that I should have a companion, but very disturbed to hear from Ward that there was no means of transport ahead and that we should have to wait from ten to fourteen days at Robat before we could move up with the next convoy. Then we should only be able to advance in slow stages with the transport camels.

I had counted on pushing up by double marches if not treble ones all the way to Meshed. However I consoled myself with the feeling that a short conversation with the G.O.C. would soon put matters right. I therefore seized the first favourable opportunity to introduce myself to General Dale, explain the urgency of my mission, and request his assistance in transport. To my disgust I met with passive opposition. General Dale failed to appreciate the urgency of any mission, or the importance of any individual other than himself. He appeared shocked at the idea of my suggesting he let me have a motor to help me on my way, although he had one spare car with him.

I pressed my request and Dale became obstinate, until he definitely refused. I impressed on Dale that I was not a mere junior staff officer but an independent Political Officer directly under the orders of Simla and I would immediately inform Simla how I had been refused assistance in the matter of a car.

I thereupon sat down, wrote out a long report on the road as far as Robat and ended up with a confidential letter describing the attitude of the G.O.C. I there and then sent a wire on my own responsibility to Sistan. I asked the Consul to send me down eight riding camels to the Persian frontier at Kuh Malik Siah.

From this time onwards I took Ward completely under my wing. Like myself he had failed to impress General Dale and had reconciled himself to the idea of moving slowly up with a caravan of transport camels. Ward was from the first an enigma to me, but I must admit, a very pleasant enigma. His complete kit consisted in a Poshtin coat purchased in the Peshawar bazaar, a small tin uniform case containing a change of khaki underclothing and a few odds and ends, a .32 Colt automatic, which he kept slung round his waist, and a couple of boxes of stores which he was taking up to Meshed for Colonel Redl, the Military Attaché. He had no servant and no cooking pots. How he proposed to live on the journey I have not the slightest idea, but knowing Ward I do not suppose he had ever given the question a serious thought. Perhaps he trusted to bumping up against some good Samaritan, and in this case I was to be the good Samaritan.

For the moment the one question was to get on from Robat as soon as possible. In wiring to Sistan for camels, I had stipulated for just sufficient to carry myself, Ward, Din Muhammed and the few articles of kit I had with me. The bulk of my baggage with Gulab Hussein and Naubat I left to fate and the promises of the local transport authorities to see it safely despatched up the line by the next up-going convoy. This meant that it would be some eight weeks on the road before it reached Meshed, but this did not worry me, as I had all the most necessary paraphernalia with me, including the precious Din Muhammed.

Having sent my telegram to the Consul at Sistan, there was *3.5.18* nothing more to be done and I reconciled myself to the fact that I would now have to wait several days in Robat until the camels arrived.

Robat is a pestilential godforsaken spot, the dust-impregnated atmosphere of which is rendered still more depressing by the myriads of flies. Never have I seen so many. I used to think they were bad enough on the N.W. Frontier, where the horses and water donkeys standing just outside one's door attracted them from far and near, but Robat in this respect stood quite alone. If in Frontier posts one slew one's flies in thousands, in Robat one slew them in tens of thousands. It was practically impossible to drink tea. One threw out the dregs of the first cup, and as one poured out the tea from the pot, the flies went in with it. They covered one's arms and one's neck, blackened the paper one was writing on and literally drove one to desperation. We were nearly all wearing nets over our faces, and when sitting about put them over our hands as well.

The one amusement of the day was a ride to a water-hole in the rocks some three miles away, where the water was actually deep enough to bathe in. We made the most of this while we could, for water was going to be worth more than gold to us for some weeks to come.

General Dale and his Brigade Major proceeded on their way to Kwash, leaving behind them a Sapper Officer, Major Packenham Walsh, a very cheery fellow who was in charge of Sappers and

Miners. The idea was to try and make a road good enough for wheeled traffic as far as Birjand. Packenham Walsh was not very optimistic about it, as he explained that the difficulty did not consist in clearing the track, but in making a road which would not be washed away by the first rain, whenever that might be.

5.5.18 Received a reply from Prideaux, the Consul in Sistan, that he was sending transport, horses and camels, to a point one stage south of Sistan and had wired the local agent at Kuh Malik Siah to arrange camels locally there for the first part of the journey. This sounded more like business and we decided to ride out the following day to Kuh Malik Siah and hurry up the arrangements.

6.5.18 Borrowing mounts from the cavalry, Ward and I started off for Kuh Malik Siah to interview the agent. Packenham Walsh had told us of the existence of a motor transport officer named Abbott-Young, who had his 'headquarters' at Hurmuk, a deserted spot in the desert some six miles beyond the village of Kuh Malik Siah. Packenham Walsh said that Abbott-Young was an excellent fellow and if it was possible to induce a car to run, he would certainly help us as much as possible. I therefore decided to pay a visit to Hurmuk.

We sent a wire to Abbott-Young informing him that we were coming and asked him if possible to send a car to meet us at Ziarat Diwan Shah, which is the customs post for traffic entering Persian Beluchistan from Eastern Persia. After a hot but otherwise pleasant ride, as we were traversing country we had not seen before, we reached Diwan Shah and to our delight we found a box Ford car awaiting us. Leaving our horses, we went on in the car and soon reached Hurmuk, a veritable little hell of its own, but with the one saving feature that it had a fairly good water supply, obtainable from water-holes dug in the sand.

Abbott-Young proved a thorough Sahib. He was in control of a sort of movable repairing shop in company with a couple of British N.C.O. mechanics and some ten or twelve half-trained native drivers. His description of his drivers made one realise that someone ought to have been shot for allowing them to be passed out for active service. The drivers hated the locality and knew nothing about cars. They indulged in sabotage and deliberately crocked cars and laid them up indefinitely. Such was Abbott-Young's most unenviable job. I often wonder how he got on eventually. Doubtless

24

when the dirty part of the work had been overcome, some senior officer would be sent out from Simla to complete the work and would in due course get all the kudos.

Abbott-Young very kindly placed one of the only two workable Fords at our disposal to take us back to Robat. On the way back we stopped at Diwan Shah and the local British Trade agent gave us tea and promised to have the necessary camels at Hurmuk and ready for us the following day. We then motored back to Robat and found that Gulab Hussein and Naubat had rolled up with the heavy kit.

Ward and I set off from Robat at 5 p.m. in the Ford car, Din *7.5.18* Muhammed and the kit having started ahead on mules. We bumped along the shingly track as far as Hurmuk, where we were relieved to find the camels actually waiting for us. We wasted no time in commencing the loading up, but found the Sistani camel men very useless hands at it and had to do most of the work ourselves. It was only after much cursing and shouting on all sides that we finally got the camels loaded up by 9 p.m. We then drank some very muddy water and Ward and I led the way, picking our tracks by the light of the stars and the corpses of dead and decaying camels, and plodding along at the camels' regulation pace of two and a half miles per hour.

This proved one of the most trying nights of the journey. I was alone on my camel with a bundle of bedding and before we had gone far, the ropes wore loose, and the saddle and myself with it slid off completely over the camel's tail. For the next half hour I was engaged in a struggle trying to fix the girth. Even in daylight, with that particular animal, it would have been difficult, but in the dark and single-handed, it was a very tricky problem. With the camel kneeling, the moment I began to tauten the girth the brute let out a throaty roar and lurched to his feet. Possibly the rope was chafing him somewhere, but in the dark it was impossible to tell. I got him, protesting loudly, back to his knees and this time I tautened very gradually, but he plunged to his feet again before I could finish the job and secure the rope. For a third time I got the growling slobbering creature down on his knees, then, holding the end of the belly-rope as tightly as I could, I climbed quickly into the saddle and he immediately swung himself up onto his legs again.

By daybreak I was absolutely tired out, for, not taking into *8.5.18* consideration the heat and lack of water, I had been travelling and working ever since 5 p.m. and it was now 5 a.m. and all I had had to eat was a small lump of bully beef without bread. Ward also seemed pretty exhausted.

It was now a question of finding a halting place with some drinkable water, where we could get a little rest and allow the following camels to catch us up. We eventually came to a water-hole, but great was our disappointment to find the water undrinkable as there were several dead camels lying in it. We therefore had no alternative but to push on once more and try our luck again. Fortune favoured us, for at 8 a.m. we came upon another water-hole and although the water was filthy and had been contaminated by camels and other animals, there were actually no corpses lying in it and we drank of it.

There was also a very small shelter just by the water-hole which proved a godsend, for to our great discomfort a dust storm began to get up. We crept into the shelter through a hole in the wall, the camels drank their fill and knelt down in the shelter of the wall and the sand storm broke on us. Both Ward and I were so weary that we fell asleep the moment we lay down and slept through the storm until the indefatigable Din Muhammed awoke us at 9.30 and cooked us a breakfast.

9.5.18   At 11 a.m. we started off again and travelled very steadily. I had a better camel now and we padded on without another break until 9 p.m. We were assisted by the weather. There was a strong wind which caused the sky to be overcast, presumably by dust, as there were no clouds. What struck me particularly was the fact that although there was a strong wind blowing, there was no sand in the air. It might have been higher up and probably did account for the sky being overcast, but to us the air was perfectly clear and although we were travelling through the desert, the ground appeared to have been swept so clean that not a grain of sand was raised by the wind. All the sand had been swept into sand dunes and these appeared to hold it.

The next few days passed in uneventful fashion. The track continued to lie through desert and it was very rare that we met a single soul. The *hauzes* [water-holes] for the most part contained water, and dirty as it was we used to drink it eagerly. The only thing we allowed to prevent us drinking the water was when we saw a dead camel or donkey actually in contact with it. This we could not stand. All the water-holes were full of dead insects, particularly the huge dung beetles which are very prevalent in this part of Persia. Of wild life we saw practically none. A very few vultures, kites and crows and birds of prey were met with occasionally, but with two exceptions we saw no game birds and only once did we sight a solitary Persian gazelle.

In spite of the monotony neither Ward nor I were really ever dull. Ward was a most amusing companion. He appeared to have a most intimate inside knowledge of both London and Paris and used to relieve the monotony by singing countless very improper but most amusing French songs. By birth an Australian, he had joined the North Staffords as a ranker and with them had seen what little experience he had of the Frontier. He very often used to talk about Afridis, and appeared to wish to give one the impression that he knew a good deal about the tribes. He certainly knew a smattering of Pushto, but it was a very thin smattering. Gulab Hussein, with whom Ward had tried to practise at Robat, stated to me in confidence that he did not understand what the Sahib was talking about.

During the war Ward had obtained a commission in the K.R. Rifles. What his war service was I cannot remember, but I should unhesitatingly say that he had done well, for he was undoubtedly a very gallant fellow. He was very reticent about his present mission and, noticing that he did not wish to speak, I did not press him for any explanation.

He was absolutely helpless on the journey as he knew nothing of the language and could only threaten the camel men with his revolver, which he always carried about with several spare magazines in cowboy fashion. Our travelling kit consisted in a thin khaki undervest, khaki breeches and riding boots. I had a thin uniform jacket and a khaki shirt rolled up in my haversack for such times as one might enter a civilised area and I used to shave every two or three days. Ward allowed himself to go unshaven for a week at a time and appeared to take a delight in making himself look as much like Captain Kettle as possible.

The morning of May 17th found us within a good day's march of *17.5.18* Nasratabad, the capital of Sistan. At a small place called Chahn Muhammed Reza we found a couple of Sistan Levy *sowars* [cavalrymen] awaiting us with horses. We called a halt and I seized the opportunity to shave and generally make myself more respectable. I suggested to Ward that he make himself a little tidy. To pull Ward's leg I said that I had been told that the Consul had his wife living with him. I didn't believe it myself, nor did Ward, and he refused to shave. He therefore continued in his torn vest, covered with weeks of dust and perspiration.

As we approached Nasratabad the country became greener, owing to numerous water-channels, off-shoots of the gigantic lake known as the Hamun. We cantered into the straggling town and were conducted to the Consulate. Entering the compound gate we found ourselves in a nice green garden and I chaffingly alluded to the mythical consul's wife. Ward was not in the least perturbed until we were ushered into a delightful cool drawing-room. When we saw the chintz-covered armchairs, the little tables with silver ornaments and other bric-à-brac both Ward and I exclaimed simultaneously, 'Good Lord there is a wife after all.' The Consul next appeared, Colonel Prideaux, looking very spick and span and cool in spotless white clothes, which emphasised all the more our own dirtiness. He looked curiously at Ward, who was profuse in his apologies for his appearance and craved some soap and water. I had fortunately produced my shirt and drill tunic, so looked more or less dressed and clothed in my right mind.

Prideaux very kindly offered us the use of his wardrobe and it was ludicrous to see Ward sauntering forth half an hour later in whites made to fit Prideaux, who stood six feet high and could not have weighed less than fifteen stone. Ward himself was only about five foot seven inches and slightly built. We were introduced to Mrs Prideaux, a very charming lady, who gave us afternoon tea. The four of us dined together that night and then I looked as ridiculous as Ward, for I also borrowed the Consul's white dinner clothes. The trousers reached almost up to my armpits and the coat down to my knees.

One of the first questions Prideaux asked me was whether I knew a Major Bingham. Did I think Bingham's opinion was sound? The Consul sincerely hoped not, because Bingham had created such a blue wave of pessimism and depression around him, that Prideaux was contemplating seriously sending his wife down to India. I told them to disregard anything that Bingham might have told them and they appeared very much relieved. I found Prideaux very helpful. Hearing that I was in a hurry to get on my way, he offered to send us on in his own car as far as Neh, and also undertook to wire Birjand asking them to send and meet us. I very gratefully accepted the offer and it was accordingly arranged for us to start off across the Hamun the following morning. The car would meet us on the other side.

The next morning we crossed the Hamun on *tutins* [rafts made of reeds] which were poled across just as one poles punts on the Thames. It took us four hours getting across. The pleasure of the trip was marred by the myriads of mosquitos. Fortunately by this time experience had taught us never to go anywhere in Eastern Persia without face nets. *18.5.18*

From the Hamun to Neh was a very uninteresting run, but at Neh we pitched our camp in a most delightful Persian garden, under the shelter of some fruit trees, with *bulbuls* [Persian nightingales] singing all night.

From Neh to Birjand is about 120 miles. We did this on cavalry horses which we obtained in Neh. *20.5.18*

In Birjand I heard that the G.O.C. was there. The G.O.C. now appeared to be quite well disposed toward us and very surprised that we had got up the line as quickly as we had. I laid stress on the fact that it was entirely due to the assistance of the Consul who had managed to spare us his car. I followed this up by expressing the hope that the G.O.C. would let us have one of his cars as far as Meshed. The General hummed and hawed, said he would consider it and finally agreed to let us have the car as far as Turbat-i-Heideri. I was very pleased at this, and began to make plans to get away the next day.

The next morning I went round to his office to make final arrangements about my departure. To my disgust I found him in a great rage. It appears that he had just received a telegram from the Chief of the General Staff in Simla giving him a thorough hauling over the coals for not having given me more assistance when I first asked him at Robat. The telegram was apparently a real stinker and called on General Dale to give his reasons in writing, requiring him to send all details of his available cars at the time and what they were all engaged in. The G.O.C. was furious and in his wrath quite wrongly imagined that I had *now* wired Simla complaining that he was not helping me in getting to Meshed. I sweetly explained that I had merely mentioned being held up at Robat in a confidential letter I had written from Robat.

After this explanation General Dale cooled down somewhat, but went back on his promise to let me have the car even as far as Turbat-i-Heideri, finally agreeing to let me have it as far as Kain. I was very disappointed, naturally, but the old man was adamant and it was no use arguing. A more petty display of spleen I never saw.

General Dale seemed to me quite unfit to be a general in an independent position. His chief peculiarity lay in the fact that he was a religious maniac. Many were the stories told of how he would convene religious meetings for the men and staff at a moment's notice and invite 'all Christians' to attend. The men used to hate it and him. One day a Persian traveller arrived in Birjand, who let it be known that though a Persian he was really a Christian. This came to the ears of the G.O.C. who decided to hold a special prayer meeting in his honour and put on one of his officers to translate the Lord's Prayer into Persian. The prayer meeting duly took place and the Persian was subsequently entertained at tea by the General and then went on his way rejoicing. It was not for some time afterwards that circumstances arose which prompted those responsible to the conclusion that they had entertained unawares a very dangerous anti-British spy and agent who was working for Kiazim Bey in Afghanistan.

22.5.18   We left Birjand at 8.30 the next morning and I was not sorry to shake the dust of the place from off my feet.

The ride from Kain to Turbat-i-Heideri was dull and uninteresting through flat barren country. Though on cavalry horses we completed the distance in easy stages. We could easily have doubled our marches, but we had to consider our commissariat, in the shape of Din Muhammed with his cooking pots and the camels. As it was, we arrived in Turbat comfortably on the afternoon of May 27th.

27.5.18   Here we at last caught up the much talked of Major Bingham. We were very pleased to meet each other again and together went off on a tour of inspection round the bazaar. This was of the closed-in variety so common in Persian towns. Here for the first time Russian influence began to be really manifest. Large numbers of the population were wearing Russian high boots and *kaftans*, a large proportion of the articles for sale in the shops were of Russian manufacture, and a few shops had Russian notices up. I called on the Russian Consul, a man of uncertain aspect named Maximov, with the reputation of being an arch-intriguer, and also on Madame X, the wife of a previous consul. I found the lady dressed in full Cossack war paint, *cherkesska* [Circassian coat], *papakha* [fur cap] and dagger complete, and she presented on the whole rather an imposing figure. She enlarged on her present misfortunes, but said that she intended remaining in Turbat as she had her own house and fruit garden, which was better than living under the Bolsheviks.

Bingham and I paid a visit to the local boys' school which also served as a sort of democratic club. Bingham was in a 'sleuthy' mood and plied the wretched principal of the school with countless questions regarding propaganda and satisfied himself at any rate that Turbat-i-Heideri was an absolute nest of anti-British and German propaganda, not to mention Persian and Russian intrigue. I am afraid I did not take things so seriously, particularly as I was beginning to know Bingham and his extraordinary habit of suspecting everything and everybody of some deep laid plot.

The next morning we started off after an early breakfast. Our *28.5.18* mounts were fresh and both Ward and I felt we should like to have done the whole trek into Meshed without a stop. (Bingham had remained behind and was coming up with his whole caravan.) The ride was pleasant but uneventful and we reached our camping ground early in the afternoon. It was a delightful spot — an open stretch of magnificent turf. A 40-lber tent was pitched near by and an officer of the 28th Lancers gave us some tea. The cavalry subaltern was going off to Nishapur, and on parting I said, 'Give my love to Omar Khayyam'. I have always wanted to go there and visit the tomb of the old astronomer-tentmaker. 'Oh,' said the subaltern quite seriously, 'I don't know him, but he's our local contractor there isn't he?'

The next day marked our final trek into Meshed. We started off *29.5.18* at daybreak. The weather was delightful and the going good. It was beautifully cool, and we were rapidly forgetting the intense heat of the desert we had left behind us. By midday we had crossed the summit of the last range of hills and before us lay the Meshed plain. In the distance a large expanse of vegetation marked the town of Meshed and one caught the glint of the sun on the domes and minarets of the great mosque. At the side of the road, on the top of a

31

hill, was a small shrine from which pilgrims would offer up prayers of thanksgiving that Allah had spared them from the dangers and difficulties of the long road and brought them at last within sight of the sacred city, the goal of their pilgrimage.

Descending the hill, we walked our horses until we reached the level of the plain below. We then trotted for miles along the dusty road shaded by rows of trees on each side. The hills were left behind and in a couple of hours we were actually in the outskirts of Meshed. We walked our horses along the road, inches deep in fine dust, which encircles the crumbling mud walls of the city. The sun beat down upon us with almost the same heat as in Sistan. Both we and our horses were covered with clotted perspiration and dust. We finally turned into the town through an ancient mud gateway. A Punjabi sentry and a little group of *sepoys* [Indian soldiers] marked the barracks of the Indian detachment. We passed a wide square with throngs of what appeared to us to be highly civilised people, and two minutes later our *sowars* pulled up in front of a large Persian doorway surmounted by the British Royal Arms and the wording 'British Consulate-General'. We had reached our destination.

We dismounted stiffly from our dusty, sweat-soaked horses. The date was May 29th, one whole month since I had left the railhead and forty days since leaving Simla.

The Holy City

◆

Meshed, the capital of the great province of Khorassan, is famous as the holiest city in Iran and an important centre of pilgrimage for all Shiah Muslims.

Its history began when, in A.D. 809, the Caliph Haroun-al-Rashid was leading a military expedition through Khorassan to crush a rebellion in his distant domain of Transoxiana. While staying in a country residence near the village of Sanabad, the Caliph fell ill and died with great suddenness. His body was interred in the garden belonging to the house and a tomb was erected over the spot. The famous Caliph M'amun, on his way from Merv to Baghdad, passed by Sanabad to visit his father's tomb. He was accompanied by his son-in-law and heir presumptive, the greatly revered eighth Shiah Imam, 'Ali Riza'. History records that, after eating some grapes at Sanabad, the Imam fell violently ill and succumbed shortly afterwards.

The Caliph, greatly affected by this second tragedy, ordered the Imam's body to be interred beside his father's grave and had a single mausoleum erected over both tombs.

However, the Shiah community, shocked by the sudden demise of their popular Imam, refused to believe that his death had been a natural one and suspected that the Caliph, impelled by jealousy of Ali Riza's great popularity, had had the Imam poisoned. In the course of time the Imam's tomb became a place of pilgrimage, while the village of Sanabad acquired great sanctity and came to be known as 'Mashad' — the place of martyrdom.

Through the centuries, Meshed, like most cities in Asia, had its periods of prosperity and decline and repeatedly suffered devastation at the hands of Mongol and other invaders. Shahrukh, who succeeded Tamarlane, did much to reconstruct and embellish the city and his consort, the famous Gauhar Shad Khatun, built the beautiful mosque which bears her name and ranks among the outstanding architectural jewels of the Islamic East. Subsequently, Meshed lapsed into relative obscurity, until now, it seemed, it might once again find itself playing an active role in far-reaching events.

There was nothing particularly impressive in the outside appearance of the consular doorway, other than the shield with the Lion and Unicorn, for high walls and massive doorways are the general rule in Persian cities, where a desire for privacy is linked with need for personal security. But when, seconds later, the heavy double doors swung slowly back on their hinges, the view which met the eye was unbelievably lovely.

To me, in that moment, the printed English wording on the shield, 'British Consulate-General', welcome as it was, seemed quite inadequate. There should have been added those oft-quoted words of Persia's illustrious poet — 'If there be a paradise on earth, it is this, it is this, it is this!'.

After the dazzling glare of the sun on the monotonous khaki of the sand and mud walls, we found ourselves in a beautiful English garden. An avenue of large elms and chenars led through lawns and a fruit garden to the building of the Embassy, which was almost entirely shrouded in foliage and flowers. To the right as we entered along the avenue was a paddock with a cow grazing in it. On the left was a well-stocked fruit garden. Then came the house, with a wide verandah running round it, covered with roses and hung with baskets of flowers. Beyond extended the rose garden with arches and pergolas ablaze with colour, then the badminton and tennis courts and, beyond that and behind, a combined orchard and kitchen garden with every conceivable kind of fruit and vegetable.

At the door of the Embassy we were met by Colonel Redl, the Military Attaché, who introduced us to his wife. We were accorded a very kind welcome, and rooms were placed at our disposal.

Redl struck me at once as being an extremely nervy man, a fact which became more and more obvious as one knew him better. Ward went in and had a tête-à-tête conversation with him, after which I went in and interviewed him. From him I understood at last the nature of Ward's mysterious mission.

Ward, though an excellent fellow, was an adventurer of the first water. It appeared that after having obtained a commission in the Rifle Brigade, Ward found himself in London and paid a visit to the War Office, where he found a brother officer working in the Russian Intelligence Section. How far the inspiration originated with Ward, I cannot say, but Ward's proposal was to penetrate into Trans-Caspia and destroy the Central Asian railway by blowing up the big bridge between Krasnovodsk and Askhabad and so frustrating any Turkish advance through Trans-Caspia into Afghanistan.

It was a daring plan, and that no one could deny, least of all the War Office, who seem to have been very much impressed with the idea. As regards the technical question of actually destroying the bridge, Ward claimed to have had experience in dealing with explosives. Where he obtained this experience no one appears to have asked, but his word was taken for it, and there it was. Ward was accordingly despatched with War Office blessing right round the world via Canada and Japan so that no one should suspect that his ultimate destination was Turkistan. I remember his disgust as he told me how after misleading everyone including his relatives and all his best girls as to his destination, he received a letter while in Montreal addressed, 'Lt K. Ward, en route Turkistan, Montreal.' The letter turned out to be a bill from his agents in London!

Ultimately Ward arrived in Delhi, where I first met him. He disappeared to Peshawar for a very hasty course of instruction in explosives, incidentally hurriedly brushing up his Pushto. It appeared that he had a case of explosives coming along somewhere behind him and at his urgent request Redl sent a wire down to the railhead to hurry it up.

Ward's awful secret having been let out, there was of course no further question of secrecy between him and me. While admiring him for the way he had kept his affairs to himself, I could not help feeling that he had no possible chance of carrying out even a small portion of what he had gaily undertaken to do. In the first place he had no knowledge of any language save a very elementary knowledge of Pushto and some extremely risqué French songs. Secondly, while being quite practical in many ways, he lacked experience and seemed quite incapable of fending for himself out in the wilds. I am convinced that had I not taken him in tow at Robat, he would never have found his own way up to Meshed.

35

The next personality I now met was Colonel Grey, the Consul-General. 'The very model of a modern Consul-General', Colonel Grey was a charming man, tall, well built, with a grey moustache, clear-cut aristocratic features, and speech and bearing denoting the best type of English gentleman. He had spent some time in the Persian Gulf and was an excellent linguist, speaking fluent French, Persian and Arabic. His weak point was his nervousness which reflected itself in his temper. He could not stand Redl, and Redl loathed him. To do them both justice, they concealed their dislike for each other, but even to the outsider it must often have been obvious.

Though I personally got on equally well with both parties, I could quite understand the irritating effect which such diverse characters must have had upon each other. Of the two, I must say that Colonel Grey commanded more of my sympathy. Redl's flippant remarks would at times simply invite trouble. It was a problem to me why Redl continued to live in the Consulate, save that to a certain extent the arrangement suited both parties. Thus Mrs Redl, a nice homely little woman, but very fond of scandal, occupied herself in a most capable manner with all the affairs of the household. Without her, Grey would have been compelled to rely upon his Persian servants, or else import a housekeeper. Redl as Military Attaché really had his own house, and a very charming house it was, situated beyond the Consulate garden, with a very delightful garden of its own. The house was unfurnished, however, and I think Redl preferred putting up with occasional skirmishes with C.G., as Grey was called, to the the trouble of furnishing an empty house. Redl had a great saving feature in his dry humour and was very good at telling an amusing story. He spoke extraordinarily bad Russian for an interpreter in that language and, as far as I can remember, equally bad Persian.

Another British officer who was destined to figure prominently in coming events was Captain Sydney Jarvis, formerly an engineer employed in Russia by a large British firm. Jarvis had come down from Moscow shortly before my arrival in Meshed. Redl had been impressed with Jarvis' experience of Russia which he himself lacked, and particularly with the fact that Jarvis had had recent experience of the post-revolutionary elements in Russia and had even had to talk to Bolsheviks. Redl had urged that Jarvis be kept in

Meshed and it was understood that he would return shortly from Tehran.

The foreign colony in Meshed were too numerous to be treated of separately here. The leading light was undoubtedly Madame Nikolsky, the wife of the Russian Consul-General. The latter was himself a small insignificant little figure whose weakness was only equalled by his inborn love of intrigue. His wife, however, more than made up for her husband's failings and was a very masterly woman indeed. Our general impression was that she overawed him and certainly generally seemed to get her own way. She would inevitably appear late at dinner when invited to an official function and on one occasion did not hesitate to express her annoyance when, after arriving about one hour late, she discovered that the remainder of the party had not waited for her, but had gone on with the meal.

The British, or rather Indian, garrison at this time comprised a small detachment of the 19th Punjabis and a squadron of the 28th Lancers. These troops had been pushed up the line from Birjand when it became apparent that the Russian troops were going home and that their defection would throw open the road for a Turkish advance. They had come up at short notice and with a totally inadequate supply of clothing and equipment. They were consequently in very difficult circumstances indeed. The horses of the cavalry had no spare shoes at all, while the men themselves were largely without foot gear and were obliged to purchase *givas* [canvas Persian shoes]. The fault for this disgraceful state of affairs lay entirely with General Dale. Numbers of telegrams had been sent to General Dale describing the desperate state of the troops but no response was made and the detachments at Meshed rapidly became immobile.

The question occupying the minds of both the Turks and ourselves at the beginning of June 1918 was firstly whether the Bolshevik authorities in Trans-Caspia would attempt to oppose a Turkish advance eastwards of the Caspian, and secondly, if the Bolsheviks did not attempt to oppose such advance, whether the British would be able to interpose any obstacle independently of the Bolsheviks.

The Bolsheviks did not know themselves what attitude to adopt. At one moment they were all for fighting the Turk. The next moment, the peace party, prompted of course by Turkish and German money, would refuse to countenance any further fighting.

Information also reached us that there were a number of German, Austrian and Turkish agents in Askhabad, who appeared to be on good terms with the Bolshevik commissars, but what their actual game was we were not in a position to know. Our intelligence from the other side of the frontier was disgracefully scanty and did not speak at all well for Redl's organisation. It was in fact a puzzle to me what Redl had been doing all this time, sitting in an important centre like Meshed, yet in total ignorance of what was really going on just over the frontier.

Colonel Grey was well informed on the internal situation in Meshed and Khorassan in general, but I was surprised to find that he too knew practically nothing about current events in Trans-Caspia. Indeed, he admitted frankly that he devoted his entire attention and interest to conditions and happenings in his own bailiwick and regarded developments in Russian territory as none of his business.

He confessed that he was disappointed when I had explained the nature and scope of my own mission. He had hoped, he said, as a political officer, I would remain and assist him with the many problems he was faced with and assured me there was plenty of enemy activity to keep me fully occupied locally without my having to cross into Russian territory.

I consoled him somewhat by saying that, from what I had already heard, it would be unwise to dash off into Trans-Caspia without careful study of the situation and preliminary preparation.

My study first unexpectedly involved the Centro-Soyuz, or Central Russian Co-operative Society in Moscow. Its activities were now brought to our notice in the following manner. About the beginning of June a party of eight Russian Jews came down from Askhabad and gave out that they were purchasing agents for the Centro-Soyuz, in which capacity they were to buy up large quantities of grain, raisins and cotton. After staying several days in Meshed they dispersed into the various neighbouring towns such as Nishapur, Sabzawar and Kuchan. It was from the last named town that we next had news of them — and the situation in Kuchan was by no means satisfactory. The Kuchan Governor was refractory and refused to acknowledge allegiance to the newly appointed Governor-General of Khorassan, who was strongly pro-British, and whose presence in Meshed went far to keep in check any outward development of pro-Turkish intrigue.

The local British trade agent in Kuchan, a respectable little Armenian named Hofsepiants, had apparently made these Centro-Soyuz agents a very reasonable offer of a quantity of grain and raisins, but the agents had declined to purchase on the plea that they were not out to buy at present but were just inspecting the market. Meanwhile they had actually purchased a large *sarai* [warehouse] in Kuchan and rumour had it that they were expending very large sums in reconstructing it. It was suggested that they were really rebuilding the *sarai* to hold troops. Whatever their real occupation, the movements of these two Jews seemed to have given rise to considerable suspicion and the Consul-General asked if I would go out to Kuchan and have a look into the situation. This I did willingly. I took with me six *sowars* of the 28th Cavalry, and Ward accompanied me.

It was impossible to push on too fast because of our mules. So we went slowly, Ward full of his bridge, the destruction of which was, of course, the sole raison d'être of his tremendous journey halfway round the world. We discussed all sorts of possibilities in connection with its destruction. We worried over this question a great deal, particularly since Simla had been showing every indication that they were very much perturbed at the continuous reports being received of Turkish progress in Trans-Caucasia.

Ward realised that there were going to be bigger difficulties in his way than he had anticipated. It was very doubtful whether any person would be able to travel through Trans-Caspia with explosives unless he had friends and confederates over there who would work in with him. The question therefore was to find these confederates. Now the only possible elements other than the Bolsheviks, whom we ruled out as impossible, were the Armenians, of whom there were about 700 armed in Askhabad, or else the Turkmans who possessed practically no arms at all.

Redl pinned great faith on the Armenians, though all he knew about them was information he obtained from a local Armenian trader named Karibian who was in touch with Armenian elements in Askhabad. The 700 armed Armenians (which number I was sure was exaggerated) in Askhabad comprised most of the armed police or town militia, and Karibian was informed by certain of them that

18.6.18

they could rise and seize the town provided the coup were followed up by British assistance. These Armenians I regarded as broken reeds from the first, though Redl appeared inclined to place faith in them. The Turkmans I knew nothing about and saw no means of getting into touch with them, short of a visit to Trans-Caspia.

It was this question of establishing contact with 'someone' in Trans-Caspia without delay which kept my mind busy during the journey to Kuchan. I had hopes of finding out some means of working the plot in Kuchan, where there were a lot of Armenians with trading relations with Askhabad. If Armenians must be definitely ruled out, then I evolved a wild plan of buying some Kurdish brigands to accompany me and run a consignment of bombs or other explosives through the hills by contraband paths and get them to a spot on the railway. It would then be up to Ward, or whoever went through, to do the actual blowing up. It sounds a wild scheme now and it sounded a still wilder one then. Nevertheless I was in deadly earnest and fully resolved that before I left Kuchan I would have some plan cut and dried. I had decided quite definitely that if I could find the right kind of Kurdish brigand — and the hills round Kuchan were infested with them — then by means of a goodly sum of money which I felt confident of getting, and the promise of some plunder into the bargain, I would be able to get through the mountains with explosives.

Ward was very taken with this idea and at once began concocting a long wire in a wonderful cipher of his own back to Meshed requesting Redl to order up another consignment of explosives in case the first lot had gone missing. This we sent off on arrival in Kuchan. It transpired afterwards that Ward's telegram had arrived quite undecipherable, so that nothing had been done!

Thus planning and arguing, Ward and I made our way along the Kuchan road. We halted at midday at a small tea shop and reached Chinaran at sunset. Here I broke the rule which I had adhered to right through the journey from India, namely never to enter a *caravansarai* [inn], as Redl had told us that the *caravansarai* at Chinaran was quite clean and that we could put up in it without any fear of disease or vermin. We mounted some wooden stairs and, pending the arrival of Din Muhammed with mules, sat down to rest on some large wooden benches intended to serve as beds. There was no other furniture and the walls were bare save for a few roughly scratched caricatures drawn by Russian Cossacks who had doubtless frequently been moving up and down this road. We had not been sitting more than five minutes when I felt something crawling across my hand; vermin — and swarms of it. We immediately struck a light and stripped our coats off. They were full of vermin, but they had not had time to get to our other clothing. So much for Chinaran. We slept the night on the mud floor of the roof.

The next day we were off at daybreak. The next stage was uneventful and we camped at a nice little meadow with a brook running past it. Some mud-walled enclosures served as stables for our horses and mules. *19.6.18*

We broke camp at daybreak and reached Kuchan in the early afternoon. Our arrival caused considerable excitement in the town. We were the first British officers who had been there since the war, and the six *sowars* of the 28th Cavalry looked quite impressive with their lances and red and white pennants. The population did not know what to think of it. *20.6.18*

Hofsepiants very kindly put us up and provided stabling for our animals. Hofsepiants was a willing little man and very pro-British. He was, however, perturbed at the Turkish advance through the Caucasus. He seemed unable to believe that the Turks might penetrate as far as the Caspian, but the letters he had recently received from that part had made very pessimistic reading. He was out to help me in any way possible. I told him under a promise of great secrecy that I wished to go through to Trans-Caspia in disguise if necessary and hinted at the necessity of taking explosives with me. He ruled out the Armenians at once, saying that it would be too risky, as they were absolutely under the thumb of the Russian Bolsheviks and someone would almost certainly give me away. The idea of the Kurds struck him as being more feasible and he promised to get me into touch with one or two Kurdish headmen and robbers by the next night at the latest.

The conversation then turned to the two Jews, Vaksin and Khabat. He showed me the house in which they were staying and I decided to call on them quite openly and see what they looked like. I accordingly went round that same evening. They were both at home and both very surprised and obviously frightened at my visit. I told them that I had come from Meshed to enquire into the

41

economic situation and understood that they were interested in the same questions as myself. They told me that they were really only looking round and that they had so far not been instructed to effect any actual purchases. I mentioned the *sarai* and they made some excuse for having purchased it, though as far as I remember they stated that they had not yet definitely purchased it. I made a mental resolution that they were lying and resolved to go round and have a look at the *sarai* that night. The two Jews were very relieved when I went, though they had plucked up courage considerably when they found that I had not come to arrest them.

I told Hofsepiants the result of my interview and between us we concocted a very nice plan of action. The next day was his birthday and he proposed to celebrate it by inviting a number of friends. Among the number would be Vaksin and Khabat. Having got them to his house he would keep them there while I went round and searched their premises for incriminating documents. This plan sounded all right, particularly as Hofsepiants said that he knew their servant and would try and buy him to give me a free entrée to the house in his masters' absence.

21.6.18   The next day was a very busy one. I intended wasting not a moment or an opportunity of spreading British prestige. I argued that every little we did was to our advantage and a set-off to the activities of the Turks who were damnably active everywhere. The Armenians were for us to a man and from all reports the Kurds were sympathetically neutral. In the morning I spent a considerable sum of money in buying up all the spare bread in the bazaar and making a free distribution of it to the poor and starving. Altogether I fed over five hundred people.

That night the guests duly turned up. Hofsepiants said that he had successfully squared the Jews' servant who would let me into the house and that he would keep them amused in my absence. We were just sitting down to the meal when, according to plan, my host's servant entered with a telegram. I opened it, found it was in cipher and asked permission to leave the table and decipher it at once in the next room, which was my bedroom. In this room was my host's black sombrero hat and overcoat. What better disguise for a conspirator? I put them on and jumped through the window. Making my way to the Jews' house I knocked at the door, but though I knocked repeatedly no servant came to open the door and sadly I had to acknowledge that I had been done. The servant must have repented and decided not to play up. He had also probably told his masters all about it into the bargain.

I hurried back and rejoined the party by way of the window. Ward was very relieved to see me back again, but it was not until I had sat down that I realised that he had been holding a loaded revolver under the table-cloth the whole time! I really believed he would have shot either or both the Jews if they had shown the slightest inclination to leave the room.

The dinner party turned into what in those days I should have called an orgy. The actual meal consisted for the most part in very substantial and extremely palatable *pilaff* and the drink was chiefly *kishmishovka*, a rank type of fire-water faintly resembling vodka and made from *kishmish* [the local raisin]. This was my first introduction to the drink and I was called upon to consume no less than eight glasses of it. Many nonsensical speeches were made and everyone drank everyone else's health. I was half hoping the Jews would get drunk, but though they drank copiously they seemed used to the drink and did not become very affected by it. The party finally dispersed tottering and belching at 1 a.m.

The next day we spent in wandering round the bazaar. There *22.6.18* was very little to see and I was glad when evening came. After dark I paid a surreptitious visit to the *sarai* purchased by Messrs Khabat and Vaksin. I managed to open the outer door and get into the courtyard. Ward and I soon found ourselves poking around inside.

The *sarai* was an unusually large one and struck one at once with the advantages of its structure from the point of view of turning it into a fort. It had the usual high walls round it, and what would in an ordinary *sarai* have been housing for mules and horses and store rooms for grain were large rooms with stone floors and wooden window frames. These improvements had only just been put in, in fact some of the window frames had not yet been fitted. The laying of the stone floors alone must have cost large sums of money and they would have been quite unnecessary luxuries had the accommodation been intended only for grain, raisins, or cotton. One corner of the *sarai* had been built up and looked for all the world as though the owner intended posting a machine-gun there. Outside, the *sarai* looked like a typical frontier outpost, save that there were as yet no loopholes. The situation, too, was admirable for the purpose, as the *sarai* was in an isolated position on the very outskirts of the town facing along the main road.

Ward and I were busy pacing out the dimensions of the inside buildings when we heard voices and looking up found the two owners of the *sarai* standing watching us from the entrance. They looked rather scared, but they had us at a distinct disadvantage. Obviously bluff was the only decent way out of an awkward situation.

'Hello Mr Khabat,' I said, 'come and look at this *sarai* and tell me what you think it would cost to hire for our trade agency.' Khabat looking rather sheepish muttered that this was his *sarai*, but that there were doubtless other ones to be rented in the neighbourhood. I apologised profusely for trespassing on their domain, but passed it off by congratulating them on having acquired such a valuable piece of property, which when finished would be an ideal spot for people to live in. The last shot told and Khabat looked most uncomfortable. Laughing to ourselves, Ward and I tactfully withdrew, leaving the Jew looking far from happy.

Late that night I received my first Kurdish visitor. This was a young Khan, relative of the local Governor, but *not* a loyal subject of his. His father had been murdered and all his heritage plundered by the Governor and the youth had come at dead of night to ask the British to help him get his own back. I talked to him very severely — told him the British did not help mere youths who could not help themselves, advised him to bide his time and, while reminding him that the Governor would most certainly hang him in the morning if he learnt of his visit to me, warned him that the British would almost certainly do the same if he failed them when they had need of him. I softened it down a little as he was leaving and told him that the Governor's days in power were numbered and that if he behaved himself there might be a chance of his getting his own back again. Exit visitor No. 1.

My next visitor was a Kurd robber chief named Khuda Verdi, more commonly known among both friends and enemies as 'Khuddu'. This was the real article, a cut-throat bandit whose usual line of business lay in running contraband between Trans-Caspia and Persia, but who was always open to undertake 'odd jobs'.

Khuddu was one of the most picturesque and typical bandits I have ever met. He had a cruel wolfish face, a long plum-coloured *kaftan*, open sufficiently to show the hafts of two Circassian daggers in his waistband, wonderful leg wrappings and leather moccasins, with a gigantic sheepskin *papakha* on his head and a pole five feet long and four inches thick in his hand. He spoke out like a man. He said that he understood that I had a kind of sympathy for people of his kidney and he had come round to ask if I would help him to wipe out one or two individuals whose official prominence placed them rather beyond his reach.

I assured him of my entire sympathy, but regretted that circumstances for the moment prevented my taking an active part in liquidating the officials mentioned. I added that from what I had heard of the local Governor he was certainly a burden to the people and I would try and bring pressure to bear in Meshed to have him removed from Kuchan. (Incidentally the Governor was removed shortly after my visit, for the Governor-General sent a detachment of scallywags from Meshed who escorted the Kuchan Governor all the way back to Meshed, where he was deprived of his governorship and disgraced. Khuddu also was destined to figure again. In 1920 he entered into negotiations with the Bolsheviks who gave him money and arms to organise a detachment of cut-throats to harry the British detachments on the frontier.)

Khuddu and I did not come to any agreement, or decide on any definite plan of action. The situation was far too uncertain to permit of that. From talking with Khuddu, however, I came to the conclusion that venturing into the hills with a party of cut-throats and a few mules laden with explosives was risky, but might be feasible as far as the frontier. One the other side however, the Kurds would be out of their own territory. They would be treated as raiders and the most I could expect them to do would be to dash to the railway, leave me and the stuff there and rush back over the frontier as quickly as they could. What would my position then be — stranded on the railway line in the desert in hostile territory with a heavy load of explosives which I could do nothing with? I should be picked up by the first party of wandering Turkmans and either killed outright or taken into Askhabad and exhibited as a curio, or as a spy who had been fool enough to get himself caught. All this, mind you, provided I were not murdered in the Persian hills by the Kurds themselves.

The game was obviously not worth the candle and I abandoned the Kurd scheme forthwith. There remained only one other plan and that was for me to go into Trans-Caspia in disguise if necessary and

45

see for myself how the land lay. Having decided this, there was no further purpose to be served in remaining in Kuchan and we arranged to leave the following morning.

23.6.18   The next morning both Ward and I were nearly total wrecks. Poor Ward had developed a tremendous boil on his face which must have caused him excruciating pain and which prevented him talking much. I was still feeling the after-effects of too much *kishmishovka* and was not at all strong. However we started off after a very early cup of tea. Din Muhammed had made good progress, as he always did when left to himself, and we did not catch him up till 2.30 by which time we were very ready for something to eat. We eventually found him halted under a willow tree with a good *tiffin* ready for us. The horses had a good feed and we started off again quite fresh, reaching Chinaran at 7 p.m. The map showed we had done a full fifty miles, though I could scarcely believe it.

24.6.18   The next day we were up early and soon covered the thirty-five odd miles into Meshed. I immediately reported to both Grey and Redl and put forward my suggestion that I should go through into Trans-Caspia myself. Redl was afraid to say yes straight away and accordingly wired Simla. Jarvis also volunteered to go to Askhabad, and it was decided that, provided India agreed, he should start off first, as he had already been there on his way through from Moscow, and that he should return as soon as possible. India wired their approval and we began to make our arrangements for departure.

Jarvis duly started off and we anxiously awaited news of him. No news came and no telegrams were received from him. Meanwhile rumours of Bolshevik excesses continued to filter through and there were repeated indications that the Bolsheviks were throwing in their lot more and more with the Germans and Turks.

30.6.18   When, at the end of the month, Gulab Hussein and Naubat Khan arrived with my kit, I decided to waste no more time, particularly as Simla were urging us to get a move on. I resolved to leave immediately.

Trans-Caspian Trader

I decided to dress myself as a sort of Persian Armenian trader and *1.7.18*
for Gulab Hussein to go as a pure Persian. I had gone 'native' on
other occasions and in other places and had got away with it. I
foresaw little difficulty in the matter of language; my Persian was
sufficiently fluent. So too was Gulab Hussein's. He was himself a
Shiah Moslem. Gulab Hussein went down the bazaar and
purchased what we considered the most typical kit and least likely
to attract attention. I also went to the Russian consulate and
obtained passes for ourselves. In the passes I purposely had
ourselves shown as British subjects, but resolved only to use these
in case we got into serious trouble, or if we found the general
atmosphere favourable to British nationality.

I set out with Colonel Redl's blessing and the best wishes of the *3.7.18*
little Meshed community and felt happier than I had felt for many
long weeks. At last I was nearing my goal, Russian Turkistan.

Starting the mules off with the muleteer, Gulab Hussein, and
Din Muhammed in the early afternoon, I followed after them on
horseback about 5 p.m. The last purchases I made in the bazaar
were two cones of Persian sugar which I took in case it might be
useful to make presents to people, knowing that sugar was a scarce
commodity in Trans-Caspia. The road was good and I had no
difficulty in finding my way until I reached the hills and it grew
dark and I found myself wandering about what appeared to be
uncultivated fields. It was some time before I found the faithful Din
Muhammed cooking dinner over a fire. He had not expected me to
be so late, and was beginning to be a little anxious. Dinner was
ready and an hour later we were all asleep, with the horses picketed
close beside us.

We were up at daybreak, the mules loaded up and were on the move in half an hour. I had four mules, one of which was lightly burdened and carried Din Muhammed as well, and two ponies, one for myself and the other for Gulab Hussein. It was very pleasant riding in the early morning. We left the hills — they were only low ones — and after an hour's steadily plodding ahead we reached a gorge, forded a stream and found ourselves among another system of foot-hills. By 11 o'clock the sun was getting very warm, the ride was monotonous and hot and this was by far the least interesting portion of the journey. We kept the pace up, however, much more so than the muleteer liked.

We halted for lunch in a delightful orchard. We had now entered a pleasant valley, green with fields of growing corn and clusters of fruit trees. We lazed on the grass under the trees, while the animals grazed and rested, and started off again about 4 p.m. Our road was a winding one, leading round one hill, over another, down into a valley and up over another hill and so on endlessly. But the hills were no longer barren and the country was green instead of brown.

As we approached the village of Kilateh, we noticed hundreds of skeletons of horses and mules lying by the roadside and clustered thickly around the village. The muleteer explained that these were the remains of the horses which had come down with the first exodus of Russian refugees from Trans-Caspia. The wretched refugees had come down in hundreds and their horses had been unable to find fodder, for the grain famine was at its worst and the drought had left not a blade of grass anywhere. The animals died off in hundreds and very few could have got down to Meshed, as the skeletons clearly showed.

Din Muhammed stopped at the village and bought a couple of chickens and some milk. We then followed our invariable custom, left the village behind and camped out on the hillside a couple of miles further on. 'Camping out' was of the very simplest. We carried no tents and the only luxury I permitted myself was my camp bed. The reason I carried this was really only in case I should at some stage of the journey find myself compelled to sleep in a *caravansarai*. My bedding consisted of a Kashmiri blanket and a green canvas valise. I preferred to have the valise, not only to keep the blanket clean, but should we have at any time struck wet weather, with the valise and bed together, I could have constructed a temporary shelter under which Din Muhammed could have cooked the meals without any trouble.

My kit was very light on this trek, the only cumbersome article besides the cook-box being a black tin uniform box. I had brought this with me as I wished to see whether it would be possible on a subsequent trip to take a largish box of explosives with me along the railway without having trouble with the authorities and without their inspecting the contents. It was therefore a very simple matter halting for the night and dossing down anywhere. Although somewhat chilly at night, the temperature was really very pleasantly cool and the Kashmiri blanket was quite sufficient without other coverings.

Another feature of my equipment were my *chagals* [canvas water bags], which I had brought up from Quetta and had used a good deal on the journey through the desert. I now had three of them with me. It was quite unnecessary to have them at all at this stage of the journey because there was plenty of water in the streams, but I took them in case of accident, or difficulty at the Russian frontier. I quite expected to be searched and although I had had no previous experience of the Bolsheviks, I did not expect that they would be any better than my own Indian policemen. In other words, when you are being searched, the less people find on you, the less you are likely to lose. Now I had come on this journey with a plentiful supply of money consisting of Russian paper notes of the Romanov variety, popularly known as *Nikolaevsky*. The lining of my coat was stiff with notes, but the bulk of the money was in the third *chagal*. To anyone looking at it it appeared exactly the same as the other two, save that if you tilted it up no water came out.

The next day we were off again at daybreak. The road led up *5.7.18* over a range of hills higher than anything we had crossed so far and I discovered a beautiful level plateau among these hills which I marked down as an excellent spot for a landing place for aeroplanes, should we ever have any in use up there. We now came to the really high mountain ranges lying between Khorassan and Trans-Caspia. In character they resembled the Black Mountains. We found walking quicker than riding, but we had plenty of time and there was no cause to hurry, as we could not get any further than Khakistar that day in any case.

We halted for the midday meal right up on the hillside at a spot where a waterfall gushes out of the rock, several hundred feet up a sheer precipice. The water was icy cool and I seized the opportunity to have a bath in a pool among the rocks. We now began the descent. We scrambled on foot down a stony path, little more than a goat track and in places very trying for horses, though easily passable for mules and hill ponies. Down, down we went until we came into the stream bed. This we followed until the sides of the valley became steeper and closed in on us and we found ourselves in one of the most wonderful gorges I have ever seen. The only way through the gorge was by the stream itself. This was not more than twenty feet broad and in many places less. The walls of the gorge came down sheer to the stream and at times one went from daylight into semi-darkness. We waded down the stream for about an hour. Then we emerged from the narrows of the gorge and came out into the village of Khakistar.

This point marks the real geographical frontier between Persia and Russian territory. The actual political frontier is about five miles further on in the level valley, but this is the gate, or one of the very few gates, from the north into Khorassan. A more wonderful spot cannot be imagined, for a handful of men could hold up an army corps, and there is no alternative route, no way round. Whoever wishes to enter Khorassan at this part of the frontier must enter through this gorge.

The village of Khakistar is nothing more than a small cluster of buildings huddled together on the right bank of the stream. The latter is quite shallow and has the appearance of a typical trout stream. On the other side are one or two paddocks with poplar and other large trees overshadowing them.

Khakistar is important as the customs post for this trade route. There is also a post office and telegraph, the latter communicating with Meshed. At the time of my arrival there, a quarantine post had also been established for the examination of persons arriving from Russian territory, where cholera was said to have broken out. The quarantine arrangements were in the charge of a little Persian doctor. He had only just started his quarantine post and already had one or two victims, whom he explained he would have to detain the regulation five days. To aid him enforcing this measure he had a squad of Persian *tufangchis*, 'regular ragamuffins' is the best term I can think for them, for they were both ragamuffins and at the same time were regulars detailed from the Persian garrison in Meshed.

I had a cup of tea with the doctor and the local customs official, who seemed to think it was his duty to examine my baggage. I told him he could if he liked, but that I should treat it as an unfriendly act. He was not serious about it and nothing further was said. Going out for a stroll I wandered down to a tent which was pitched on the other side of the stream. Here I met a lady named Madame Popova, the sister-in-law of a very charming woman whose acquaintance I had made in Meshed. This lady had just come down from Askhabad and was virtually a refugee.

Hearing who I was, Madame Popova implored me not to go to Trans-Caspia, adding that she had seen Jarvis there and had heard that the Bolsheviks were on the point of arresting him. Popov, her brother was also with her, and now came out of the tent looking very unshaven and travel-stained. He confirmed what his sister had said, stating that Jarvis had been staying in Askhabad at an hotel and had called on various people in the town. He, Popov, had seen Jarvis and had warned him to be on his guard. He was doubtful whether Jarvis would be able to get out in time. Popov added that if Jarvis were arrested anything might happen, as there were a number of German agents in Askhabad who appeared to be influencing the local Soviet, and they would certainly have any Englishman shot if they could possibly manage it.

All this was very perturbing and for the moment I did not know what to do. I had just decided that I would stay where I was at Khakistar until Jarvis turned up or until I could get some news of him, when who should come along but Jarvis himself. I had just time to shake hands with him when up came three *tufangchis* and informed him that he was in quarantine and must stay on the other side of the stream and that I must keep away both from him and from the Popovs, who were also in quarantine. This was too much, so telling Jarvis to stay where he was I made straight for the little doctor. I forget exactly what I said, but I succeeded in impressing him with the importance of Jarvis and how urgent it was that he should go straight to Meshed. He gave way and Jarvis came over and put up in the same room as myself.

Jarvis then told me all about things. He had got to Askhabad without any trouble and no one had paid any attention to him. He had called on the local Soviet and reported his arrival in a perfectly friendly manner. The Bolsheviks had been very anxious regarding the presence of our troops in Meshed and were apparently under the impression that we had half an army corps there with which we meant to invade Trans-Caspia. While letting them continue to believe in the presence of large numbers of troops (I thought of our miserable little detachments with their insufficient equipment) he assured the Bolsheviks that we were not hostile, but very interested in knowing what the attitude of the Trans-Caspian government would be towards the Turks, supposing the latter succeeded in reaching the Caspian. The Bolsheviks had replied to the effect that there was no likelihood of their doing so and that, as regards Trans-Caspia, there was no fear of their ever getting over.

The Soviet were obviously very guarded in what they said and Jarvis was of the opinion that they were hand-in-glove with the Germans and Turks, who were undoubtedly very busy in Trans-Caspia. The Germans were frantically buying up cotton and were trying to get the entire stocks out of the country across the Caspian. The Turks were busy in propagandising the Turkman and other Moslem elements, and altogether the place did not seem very healthy for an Englishman.

I decided nevertheless to continue on my journey, but to make straight for Krasnovodsk and to avoid Askhabad altogether. Jarvis had reconnoitred Askhabad and was in a position to report on the situation there. I would thus be able to examine the whole length of the railway and in Krasnovodsk I would endeavour to queer the Germans' pitch regarding the cotton. It would have to pass through Krasnovodsk and it might be possible to discover some means on the spot of spoiling their game.

From now onwards I began to dream of cotton. I saw myself arriving at Krasnovodsk to find trainloads of cotton lying down by the docks and saw myself with Gulab Hussein pouring oil on it and setting fire to it by night. I developed this idea until I saw myself destroying the entire port of Krasnovodsk by fire and decided that if necessary I would do this and thus render the destruction of the bridge and all the trouble with explosives unnecessary. Henceforth I went on with the journey feeling that at last I had something definite and practical in view and that my visit to Trans-Caspia would have more far reaching results than I had at first anticipated.

The next morning we were up at daybreak. Jarvis told me there was no hurry as the distance to Kaahka on the railway was only twelve miles and that the daily train did not leave till 3.30 in the afternoon. He added that the officer on the frontier was quite a good fellow and no sympathiser with the Bolsheviks. Jarvis himself was leaving for Meshed, so I arranged to send Din Muhammed back with him with instructions to cook for him until I returned. I left the Popovs with four more days of quarantine to do, much to their disgust. I would like to have freed them, but did not want to overdo my bluff with the doctor.

6.7.18

An hour later we reached the little shanty representing the Persian frontier post. I got my own and Gulab Hussein's pass signed and then we moved on to the Russian post which was half a mile further on. I was just a little anxious here, this being my first meeting with the Bolsheviks. I stopped and dismounted as we came up to the post. A couple of Cossacks were lounging about outside and I asked to see the officer in charge. A young fellow came out and I introduced myself as an Englishman and produced my English pass. I had no trouble. The officer wished me a pleasant journey, we shook hands and I started off again. We left the foot-hills behind us and now for the first time I stepped on the soil of Trans-Caspia. One could see one was in Russia by the cottages with their thatched roofs and gardens full of sunflowers. Some reaping and binding machines and large country carts showed that one was again in a civilised country.

We reached Kaahka at 2 p.m., having gone slowly as it was very hot, and found to our disgust that the train had left at 11 a.m. and that there was no other train till the next day. The station was closed, so we went off into the 'town'. There did not appear to be any eating houses, so I went in search of a room for the night. I eventually found a very third-rate hotel where I got a small room, into which I dumped my things. Gulab Hussein decided to remain overnight in a *sarai* with the mules. It was impossible to get any food, so I contented myself with several glasses of tea.

The proprietor was a Caucasian, probably a Tatar, and started talking about the war. For some reason he concluded that I was an Austrian and on that assumption started criticising the Allies. It was

53

very interesting, but most disheartening. He regarded the Great War as practically finished and the Allies defeated. The Turks were doing wonders in the Caucasus and would almost certainly take Baku. They would then drive out the British from Persia. Talking of the British he asked if I had seen anything of them in Meshed. I said I had and gave him a graphic description of several thousand 'Horse and Foot' camping all over the place, with hundreds of heavy guns coming up the line from India. He seemed impressed and could only shake his head and say '*Wah Wah.*' He told me that the train would leave the next morning at 10.30, and that I had better get down to the station in good time so as to get some soup at the buffet before the train started.

7.7.18   I took my Tatar friend's advice and accompanied by Gulab Hussein, looking a fearful villain in his Persian cap, carried our kit down to the station. The kit consisted in *chagals* and the uniform case, all the rest having gone back with Jarvis and Din Muhammed.

We were far too early and the station was completely deserted. We placed our things near the buffet door and while Gulab Hussein went off to explore the surroundings, I seated myself on Ward's trunk to await in patience the opening of the refreshment room.

The sun was now already well above the horizon and its rays lit up the distant Persian hills and glistened on the shining steel rails that seemed an incongruous and intrusive imposition thrust upon this primitive landscape. So this was the famous Central Asian Railway. I was disappointed. No railway anywhere could look more commonplace, yet to me the very name spelled Romance. As a child I had revelled in the travels of Marco Polo, of Anthony Jenkinson, of Vambery and Burnaby, and had been thrilled by the tragic adventures of Colonel Stoddart and Captain Conolly.

As a schoolboy in the Imperial Russian capital, I had attended parades and watched the Tsar, surrounded by Grand Dukes and Generals, take the salute, as Turkmans and Cossacks walked, trotted, and finally dashed at full gallop down the enormous parade ground. Youthful impressions are strong and lasting, and to travel to Central Asia had thereafter remained one of my greatest ambitions. And now I was there and this was it!

It did not require much imagination to picture Kaahka before the coming of the railway: a small oasis, or perhaps a mere waterhole in the surrounding desert. A long chain of such oases linked together had formed the great caravan route that was the legendary Golden Road to Samarkand. The builders of the railway had found their task much simplified, for the trail had been beaten out by the flat padded feet of millions of camels through the long course of history and the water-holes even now continued to play their role, since locomotives, any more than camels, cannot work without water. And this was a thirsty land.

And as for Romance, from where I now was sitting, some hundred miles along the line to the south-east was Merv. For centuries, as 'Merv, Queen of the World', it had ranked among the foremost cities of Central Asia until the Mongol hordes descended upon it. They laid waste the vast irrigation system, massacred the population and razed the entire city to the ground. Only one single monument, the ruins of the great mosque, still marks the ancient site.

Merv remains traditionally the centre of one of the principal Turkman tribal communities and is famous as the home of those most attractive of all oriental carpets, the highly-coloured 'Merv Tekke', popularly known in the trade as 'Bokharan' rugs.

Beyond Merv lay an area of swamp and after that, another hundred miles of desert, the Kara Kum, 'Black Sands', stretched to the banks of the broad mud-coloured Amu Darya, the Oxus of the Ancients.

At Charjui the river was crossed by a fine steel bridge, reputedly one of the largest in Russia, and beyond the river stretched the mainly desert lands of the Emirate of Bokhara with its ancient capital of romantic mystery and evil repute.

Before the Russian Revolution Bokhara was regarded by Muslims as the holiest city in Central Asia and was difficult of access to all but True Believers. It was famous for the great number and grandeur of its mosques and colleges. Colonel Charles Stoddart and Captain Arthur Conolly had journeyed there in the first half of the last century as emissaries to the court of the ruling Emir. Their mission ended in disaster, for after long months of imprisonment and torture they were finally executed.

Beyond Bokhara the track, still following the old caravan route, turned north and then eastwards to Samarkand, a city of glittering turquoise domes and minarets, of mosques, religious colleges and tombs. Outstanding among them stood the ruined mosque of Bibi

Khanum, Chinese princess and favourite wife of Tamarlane, also the tomb of Tamarlane himself.

Then farther, still northwards, towards the very heart of the continent, the track led on to Tashkent, the former administrative capital of Russian Turkistan, a sprawling military centre, with a large native population and currently the headquarters of the Tashkent Soviet administration.

In the opposite direction from Kaahka, eighty miles to the north-west and still on the old caravan route, lay Askhabad, provincial capital of Trans-Caspia, its correct Persian spelling, Ashkhabad, signifying 'Abode of Love'. Beyond it the track continued in a straight line linking a chain of cultivated oases inhabited by Turkman communities, each with its scattering of Russian officials. The only place of any historic interest was Geok Tepe, where the Tekke Turkmans on 24th January 1881 made their last desperate stand against the invading Russian army under General Skobelyev. The Turkmans were finally routed and fled with their families into the surrounding desert, where they were ridden down by Skobelyev's pursuing Cossacks and slaughtered to the last man, woman and child.

The only other point of interest was Kizil Arvat, important for its extensive railway depots and repair shops and with a fixed community of Russian railway workers. For the whole distance from Kaahka to just short of Kizil Arvat the railway continued to run parallel to the mountain range of the Kopet Dagh, which formed a great natural barrier between Trans-Caspia and Persia, a dozen-odd miles away to the south. Beyond Kizil Arvat the mountains receded and the track headed out across the waterless wasteland until it reached its western terminal on the Caspian at Krasnovodsk.

I might have gone on day-dreaming in the sunshine, but at this point I was rejoined by Gulab Hussein, who returned from his stroll with nothing of interest to report and with a very poor impression of Kaahka. The station was quite quiet and no one seemed to be stirring. At 9.30 a man came along and opened the buffet. A quarter of an hour later smoke issuing from the doorway showed that the *samovar* had been lighted, so I went in. After waiting a short time the attendant, a very uncouth looking *mujik* [peasant] served me with some excellent soup. At this same moment there was a loud clanging of a bell and the daily train from Tashkent came panting and hissing into the station. Through the open door of the buffet I saw crowds of people both sexes clustered on the roofs of the Pullman cars and the next moment the buffet was raided.

Never have I seen such a sight. It might well have been a scene from one of the London musical comedies. There were Russian peasants in red shirts, Armenians and Persians, Cossacks and Red soldiers, Sart traders and Bokhariots, Turkmans in their gigantic *papakhas*, while among the crowd were a number of pretty young girls and women in the latest Paris summer fashions. All this medley came crushing into the buffet and clamoured for glasses of tea, hunks of black bread and platters of soup. Somehow or other they all seemed to get served and Asiatic and European, Mongol and Muscovite sat down literally cheek by jowl, and satisfied their hunger.

I hurriedly finished my soup and went off to look after my boxes. I found a scarlet-shirted porter looking very suspiciously at my black uniform case and it was obvious that he did not like the appearance of it at all. He asked what was in it and finally requested me to open it, passing several remarks for the benefit of those around that for all he knew the box might contain bombs. I smiled to myself as I thought that it was just as well that it didn't, and after a frantic search in all my pockets I eventually found the key and satisfied the man that the contents were quite harmless. The box was then labelled and put into the goods van in quite a civilised manner. Seizing my *chagals*, Gulab Hussein taking one and myself the other two, we purchased our tickets and took our places in the train. I was fortunate in obtaining a place next to the window, whence I could keep an eye on the bridges and culverts.

We started off about 11 a.m. and it was not long before I realised that I had made a great mistake in not coming supplied with bread. All the other passengers appeared to have brought a supply on board with them; however it was too late to rectify the error then. Four hours later we arrived at Askhabad. It was very hot and the atmosphere inside the train was stifling. I had not intended to get out at Askhabad, but decided to see if I could get some bread at the buffet. No such luck. There was not a scrap to be had. All I succeeded in purchasing was a bottle of Narzan water.

57

There seemed to be a certain amount of excitement going on in the town and we saw detachments of mounted men moving along the streets. One detachment appeared to be entraining for somewhere and we were told that they were en route to Kizil Arvat to impress the population there. While we were waiting at Askhabad, a number of Red soldiers boarded the train and started pulling the luggage about. They did nothing beyond making themselves extremely annoying to the passengers and they fortunately passed my luggage over and missed me as I was walking about the platform.

I was very relieved when we left Askhabad and were once more on our way towards Krasnovodsk. I kept a very careful watch on the line the whole time, but beyond a few small culverts saw nothing of any interest and certainly nothing worth blowing up. I was beginning to feel anxious about the big bridge, which had not yet hove in sight, and I concluded that it must be somewhere in the vicinity of Krasnovodsk. Unfortunately it now grew dark and became impossible to see anything.

We eventually pulled into Krasnovodsk at midnight. Gulab Hussein wearily and stiffly slid from the train, collected our uniform box from the luggage van and after a very great deal of difficulty succeeded in depositing it in the left-luggage office. We then betook ourselves to the restaurant and tried to find something to eat. Alas all we could find was again a bottle of Narzan and a glass of tea. Feeling decidedly miserable we endeavoured to find an unoccupied corner of the waiting-room in which to lie down and sleep. We found no unoccupied corner, but managed to squeeze in between some other people and eventually went off to sleep.

8.7.18   The next morning we were up early, but were not early enough for Krasnovodsk. It was a real case of the early bird catching the worm. All we found in the bazaar was a very small piece of bread, which Gulab Hussein and I shared between us. Later we found some caviare, but without bread it was not very attractive. Thoroughly disgusted with Krasnovodsk I decided to catch one of the first boats across to Baku. There at any rate we might find something to eat.

I first of all delivered two letters which I had brought from Meshed to the address of Doctor Arkannikov and also to a man named Nikolai Nikolaevich Semov. I found the doctor all right and introduced myself. He was quite a nice fellow and lived in a house near the station with his wife and daughter. I told him I was going across to Baku and would call again on my return. I failed to find Semov in his office, but left word that I would look him up on my return. Semov was the manager of the steamship line Kavkaz-i-Merkury, and I had been advised to get into touch with him as he was anti-Bolshevik and a trustworthy man on whom I could rely to help me if necessary.

I next went to the shipping office and purchased tickets for myself and Gulab Hussein to cross to Baku by the ship leaving that afternoon. I had to buy separate tickets for the food, which I was told would be supplied on board. I was delighted to hear this and would willingly have purchased a whole book of food tickets had it been possible. By this time we were getting very hungry, but as another hunt around the bazaar disclosed nothing more interesting and palatable than dried salt fish, we gave it up as a bad job and contented ourselves with the thought that we would have as good a meal as we could possibly get on board.

At 2.30 in the afternoon we boarded the boat, a wretchedly small steamer called the *Tuman*. I immediately began reconnoitring to see what was going on in the cooking line, but could see nothing but a large *samovar* in full blast. People seemed to be buying glasses of tea and then going away to the corner and producing the inevitable hunks of black bread from their own private store. I made enquiries and produced my precious food ticket, but was told rather gruffly that there was no food on this ship. All the regular steamers had a restaurant service, but this was a supplementary boat and did not boast any arrangements for feeding. Very sadly I broke the news to Gulab Hussein and then we burst out laughing. There was nothing else to do. We had a glass of tea and comforted ourselves with the thought that tomorrow we should be in Baku and would be able to eat as much as we wanted.

That night a storm arose and gave us a fearful tossing. We *9.7.18* floundered about all night and eventually dropped anchor. We remained at anchor in mid-Caspian the whole of the day until evening, when the sea became calmer and we were able to proceed on our way. Fortunately we were all feeling so seasick that we lost all desire to eat and so passed another very miserable day. I should now be thoroughly thankful when this journey was over. I was still wearing my tiny Persian cap and the sun gave me a splitting headache which somehow would not leave me.

10.7.18 The next morning we arrived in Baku, and after landing, we made straight for the Hotel Europe where we ordered breakfast. With the exception of the plate of soup on Kaahka station and a tiny scrap of bread at Krasnovodsk, we had been travelling five days without any real food and both Gulab Hussein and I felt that we could not have gone much further. The hotel was quite a good one, but all they could give me was an omelette. I think I ate four large omelettes in succession. I was waited on by two Armenian waiters, who hearing that I was English immediately began asking when the British were coming to save them. Rumours were already rife in Baku that the British had arrived in force at Enzeli and were preparing to come across to Baku, and my arrival caused no small stir.

My first object was to get into touch with the British Consul and find out as much as I could regarding the situation in the Caucasus. I was informed that the Consul was a certain MacDonnell and that he was in the habit of coming to the Hotel Europe every morning. I therefore seized the opportunity to have a wash and shave and generally made myself look more respectable. I also went round the shops and bought myself a straw hat. It was a long time before I could find one and I eventually had to pay Rbls 400 which was about £10. The hat was a shop-soiled one and was the only one left in the shop. Returning to the hotel I met MacDonnell and he gave me a graphic description of the situation.

The one fact that was really important was that the Turks were making steady progress towards Baku. They were at that time only some forty miles away and the opposing forces were showing every sign of disintegration. In Baku there were about five different governing bodies, none of which could pull together. There were the Bolsheviks, the Centro-Caspian, the Armenians, the Caspian Fleet and the anti-Bolsheviks. The latter and the Armenians were all for fighting. The Bolsheviks were opposed to fighting. The Russian military commander, Bicherakov, was himself at the front and his supporters in Baku were doing their best to collect and send him assistance. The Bolsheviks were going about endeavouring to prevent any assistance being sent. Notices were placarded in the town threatening with death as traitors to the Revolution all and everyone who dared to wear any badge of rank, even a corporal's stripe, or join the forces fighting the Turk. The Armenian committees were in a state bordering on panic, while to crown everything the Caspian Fleet, consisting of a couple of gun-boats, the *Kars* and *Ardagan*, and one or two armed steamers, decided that they were really the decisive factor and every now and then would send ashore ultimatums and threaten the town with bombardment if their terms were not accepted. Meanwhile the British Mission of Dunsterforce was for the time being held up and powerless to act, since its crossing to Baku was being opposed by the Azerbaijan Bolsheviks backed by the Caspian Fleet. The situation was indeed a pretty kettle of fish.

MacDonnell arranged for my papers to be visa'd and the next *11.7.18* morning Gulab Hussein and I left for Krasnovodsk.

My visit to Baku had been a very short one, but it had sufficed to give me a clear appreciation of the general situation and it was now of vital importance to get the news back to Meshed and India without delay.

It must be remembered that Baku was at this juncture completely cut off from the rest of the Caucasus and the telegraph to Enzeli was not working. My information was therefore the most recent that India could get and I resolved to try and make the journey back to Meshed in record time. Fortunately on this occasion the Caspian behaved itself and the crossing took only the normal twenty hours.

Cotton Conspiracy

12.7.18 We reached Krasnovodsk at daybreak. As the little steamer tied up
alongside the wooden jetty, the sun, a great ball of fire, emerged
from a sea of mist across the Trans-Caspian steppe. Crowds of local
inhabitants thronged the landing stage, eager to hear the latest
news from Baku. Had the town fallen? Was it still holding out?
Were the Turks near it? Many of them were Armenians, anxious for
news of their relatives. For their compatriots, the Turkish advance
had spelled disaster, and one could see in their eyes a haunting fear
of worse to follow when the enemy captured Baku.

The Russians were more phlegmatic and seemed to have
resigned themselves to whatever Fate might have in store for them.
'Chto boodyet — poost boodyet' ['What will be — well, let it darn well
be!']. But their eagerness to hear the latest developments betrayed
that they too were not free from anxiety as to what the immediate
future might hold in store for them.

As they thronged round the gangway, greeting and embracing
their friends and relations, Gulab Hussein and I slipped unnoticed
ashore. I had not a moment to lose if I intended to catch the next
day's train to Kaahka, as before leaving Krasnovodsk I was
determined to try and do something about the cotton question.

On my journey through from Kaahka to Krasnovodsk, I had
seen bales of cotton piled up on every wayside station. At
Krasnovodsk the railway sidings were filled with truckloads of it,
while in addition there were several huge dumps of neatly piled
bales, both in the railway sidings and down by the quays. In Baku I
had learned of the presence in Astrakhan of a German mission,
whose problem it was to secure as much of the Turkistan cotton
crop as they could get hold of. They had completely won over the

Soviet authorities and the Baku Soviet were co-operating with them to the extent of sending over available shipping to Krasnovodsk for the transport of the cotton across the Caspian.

In Baku I had had no chance of going further into the matter, but I felt sure that I would be able to learn more about it in Krasnovodsk. I was anxious not to lose a moment in my dash back to Meshed, but I was prepared to remain one day in Krasnovodsk for this cotton question, if necessary, and calculated that with an extra effort I might make up for the delay by doubling my marches through the hills into Persia.

So far my only connection in Krasnovodsk had been Dr Arkannikov. He and his wife had given me a cordial invitation to stay with them on my return from Baku and I made it my first duty to go round and call on them. I would at any rate not have to spend the night on the floor of that crowded and filthy railway station.

Now I had to get in touch without delay with Nikolai Nikolaevich Semov. I had hopes that he might be able to make some suggestions and possibly even take some action regarding the cotton. I had been assured that he was absolutely reliable and that for very good reasons he hated the Reds like poison.

I instructed Gulab Hussein to leave our few belongings at the railway station and to work independently of me and to meet me eventually at the train. He was to put in his time loafing around Krasnovodsk and learning all he could. In particular he was to wander round the sidings and the jetties and was to count approximately the bales of cotton and also the rolling stock and locomotives.

Gulab Hussein had picked up quite a useful smattering of the local Persian dialect by this time. He had even acquired a number of commonplace names and expressions in Russian and he never showed the least hesitation in wandering off on his own. He must have been a bit of a puzzle to the local natives, but his stock explanation was that he came from the south of Persia, from Fars, where the language was quite different. This invariably satisfied the curious and his relatively fair complexion never aroused the slightest suspicion that he really came from India.

I had little difficulty in locating Semov. He at once became very friendly and invited me round to his house where I was introduced to his family. Then, when the inevitable glass of tea and cigarettes had been produced, he took me into a private room and we got down to business.

He first of all asked me to tell him all about the situation in the Caucasus and then about the British in Persia and the course of the war in general. He made an excellent impression on me from the first and I felt that here was a man one could trust implicitly. I decided to put my cards on the table and told him the exact nature of my mission. 'Is it true', I asked, 'that the Germans are over here buying cotton?'

'I should just think they are. They are working it direct from Moscow. It has nothing to do with us here, but Astrakhan have sent down a whole lot of ships specially for cotton. We are chock-a-block with cotton here and we have instructions to load up the ships and push them off to Astrakhan as quickly as we can.'

'Have they gone yet?' I asked anxiously.

'No, not yet. Three ships are actually loading at the present moment. You must have seen them when you came in this morning. Two more are standing by and we expect several more to arrive within the next few days. The German mission in Askhabad has been arranging for train loads to be sent down here, until we haven't got a single available siding left.'

'Look here,' I said, 'whatever happens we have got to stop them sending it away.'

Semov scratched his head, 'I'm afraid that's not going to be easy,' he said. 'The ships are already here. Two of them, perhaps even three of them, ought to finish loading some time tonight. Their orders are to push off immediately they are finished. They should be away before midnight at the latest.'

'But think carefully,' I said. 'Surely we can do something?' If only we could delay this cotton — even for a few days, well, anything might happen in those few days. I thought of Dunsterville held up in Enzeli, only just across the water, and of our Indian detachments strung out along the road to Meshed.

'Semov,' I said, 'we have *got* to do something. Believe me, the British are not going to allow the Turks to get across the Caspian. I swear we will not. We have a force in Enzeli; they will be across in Baku any day now and we have any number of troops just over the border in Meshed. If the Turks show any signs of getting across, we shall march our troops in straightaway and you can take it from me

64

that we have more than enough men to hold up many more Turks and Germans than there are in the Caucasus.'

My words were obviously having effect and I continued to plead with all the earnestness that I really felt.

'The only chance is to stop the loading,' he murmured. 'If only we could find some reason for holding up the work!' He was obviously thinking hard and I watched his face anxiously. 'Even if we managed to stop the loading. . . . I could perhaps find a way of doing that. . . . it would soon become known. They would know at Astrakhan, and at Askhabad. They would want to know the reason why. We should have to find a reason. . . .' He was muttering to himself and I hung on every syllable. A light came into his eyes.

'I have an idea,' he said, after a pause. 'It is only an idea . . . but it might work. Only I shall have to get help. Do you mind if I bring another man into this?' I shook my head. I did not mind what he did, so long as something could be arranged to upset this cotton business.

'Have you any money available?' he asked. 'We may not want much, but we shall probably require some. We may have to do a bit of bribery and we ought to have the money handy.'

I still had a fair sum in Russian Imperial notes. Of this I should require enough for the road and the rest he could have.

'*Otlichno*, splendid,' he said and then he proceeded to tell me what was at the back of his mind. He had a friend whom he could trust in the Krasnovodsk wireless station. This friend was not actually in charge — the Reds had put their own people in control — but as a technical expert they had kept him on and if anything went wrong with the apparatus, he was the only person in Krasnovodsk who knew sufficient about the job to put things right. The Reds had cleared out all the remaining staff with the exception of one or two junior operators, but they dared not dismiss their only *Spets*, as they call their technical people. Here as it turned out was our great opportunity.

Then followed a brief discussion as to what might be done. 'Better not count too much on it,' said Semov, 'until we have an opportunity of discussing this with D. He may have some better suggestions to offer. I'll send my wife to get a message to him through his wife and ask him to call round here as soon as possible. He drops round here most days, so there will be no difficulty about that.'

About an hour later, during which time I had drunk several glasses of weak tea sweetened with *kishmish*, D. arrived. He was a young man, about 30, well-educated and spoke a little English. Semov introduced us and told me I could speak with complete frankness and safety.

We thereupon got down to the business. For my part I just listened while Semov unfolded his scheme. Briefly it was this. The loading of the ships must be stopped and stopped without any delay. More than that, the stoppage must be carried out in an official manner, or at any rate it must have the appearance of being official. The Bolshevik authorities in Astrakhan had sent the ships and Astrakhan was the destination of the cotton when loaded. Hence, any orders of cancellation must emanate from Astrakhan. The only way such orders would come would be by wireless, for the Krasnovodsk radio station was in direct communication with Astrakhan.

Latterly, it appeared, the communications had not been too good, and the Krasnovodsk station had several times broken down. Certain spares and tools were required and a report to this effect had already been made on more than one occasion to the local Soviet committee in Krasnovodsk. The scheme, therefore, was for the Krasnovodsk radio station to receive wirelessed instructions from Aṣtrakhan, cancelling the loading of the ships, and for the station then to go out of action. D. could easily put it out of action and with the help of a little *bakshish* [payment] he did not anticipate much difficulty in getting the necessary message received and delivered to the local authorities in the proper manner.

Actually, of course, the message would be concocted by us and written out in the Krasnovodsk station by one of the signallers whom D. felt confident he could buy over. Then, as far as the breakdown of the station was concerned, D. accepted all responsibility.

'As a matter of fact,' he said cheerfully, 'it is much easier to arrange for it to break down than it is to keep it going, the way things are being run at present.'

'Remember,' I said, 'there is no time to be lost. Those ships may possibly finish loading earlier than you expect and it would be heartbreaking to lose them.'

'No they won't,' replied Semov. 'Now we have this matter

settled, I am not afraid of that happening. Furthermore,' he added, with a chuckle, 'once the wireless station is out of action, we can do almost anything we like. We'll not only cancel the shipment of the cotton, but we'll send the ships away so that they will not be available in case the wireless unexpectedly begins to function again.'

'What we have to do,' broke in D., 'is to put together a really plausible message from Astrakhan. I know how to word it; I have seen so many of them coming through lately. The Krasnovodsk Executive Committee will be ordered to cease the loading of all cotton immediately, as all available shipping is to be kept in readiness for the transport of petrol and heavy oil to Astrakhan.'

'And what about the three ships already loading?' I asked.

'. . . and all ships already loaded to be unloaded and sent to Petrovsk?' continued D.

'Splendid,' chuckled Semov. 'That ought to do the trick, but it will make the Petrovsk people scratch their heads when the three ships arrive there.'

'It should work all right,' said D., 'but goodness knows what will happen when they learn about it in Astrakhan.'

'If the worst came to the worst,' I said, 'you could run across into Persia and you could count on our people looking after you.'

'All right then,' said D., 'you can count on me doing my part of it. I'll go and get busy on it at once. But you might let me have a little money now, if you can,' he added, 'for I shall have to pay something to the operator I mentioned, perhaps even to both of them.'

'Certainly,' I said, 'lend me a knife!' Taking off my coat, I slit open the lining and counted out a little packet of Nikolaevsky ten-rouble notes. Then, with a shake of the hand and a brief '*Do svidania*' he was gone.

'He'll do it all right,' said Semov. 'I am sure you can rely on D. for that, and once those instructions have been delivered I will personally guarantee that not a bale of cotton leaves Krasnovodsk by sea. You can leave that part of the business to me. The cotton is as good as saved; the Germans have not got away with it and, *dai Bog*, they never will.'

And they never did.

D. acted with great promptness. Early that same afternoon the wireless station broke down, the last message to come through being a peremptorily worded order to the Soviet Executive Committee to cease loading cotton and to off-load any that had already been put on board the ships.

The message caused much grumbling and not a little argument as to the reason for the sudden change. Rumours got about that all ships would be required for the evacuation of Baku. Others had it they were required for the carriage of large supplies of petrol from Baku before the place went up in flames. Other reports again suggested that the ships were required for the transport of British troops from Enzeli.

All that mattered was that not a bale of the cotton left Krasnovodsk. Our little conspiracy had saved it for the immediate present and Fate played directly into our hands. Before the sabotage in the wireless station could be rectified and before the Astrakhan Reds could demand an explanation or even suspected what had happened, events, as we shall see, moved with lightning speed.

As for the cotton, it came in most useful. Someone obligingly fomented a scare that the Yomuts were planning an attack on Krasnovodsk. Defences were rapidly constructed and bales of cotton were largely used for the purpose. The hydraulically compressed bales were bullet proof and afforded excellent protection. The example of Krasnovodsk was followed on many of the smaller railway stations along the line. Quite a lot of bales found their way back to Askhabad and the accumulation in Krasnovodsk was finally accounted for.

The story would not be complete without some mention of the armoured train. Subsequently, when military operations resolved themselves into a 'railway war' large numbers of bales came in useful as protection for trucks. There was a shortage of steel sheeting and the only sheet metal the railway workshops could produce was soft iron, which, of course, was not bullet resisting.

One day a Russian railway engineer came to me with a scheme for using cotton as a protective lining for closed-in trucks and rendering them bullet proof and suitable for armoured trains.

The idea seemed feasible enough and the finished specimen truck looked very imposing with its outer covering of sheet-iron, sinister looking loop-holes, and double walls, with a thick layer of cotton in between.

I was invited to inspect this latest product of the Kizil Arvat

68

railway workshops and a practical demonstration was arranged. It was suggested that the engineer and myself should shut ourselves inside the truck, whereupon fire would be opened on us from two machine-guns.

The engineer seemed quite willing to undergo the ordeal, but I suggested that the machine-guns should first fire at the truck while it was empty. They did so. We then went up and inspected and found that every bullet had gone clean through the truck. The cotton lining had only been pressed by hand!

We took the 2 p.m. train from Krasnovodsk. This time I knew *13.7.18* the ropes better and had taken with me a supply of bread and a bottle of milk. I resolved that whatever happened I would not miss the bridge this time. I accordingly took up my seat by the railway carriage window and marked down every culvert as we passed it. Night came on and it grew dark. Resolved not to be beaten, as I could no longer see out of the window, I went out on to the platform at the end of the Pullman and stood there. The attendant appeared to be rather suspicious of my being out there alone and would not let me remain there. Now travelling in the train was a girl of not unattractive features aged not more than nineteen. She had made decidedly glad eyes at me on several occasions, so I asked her to come out on to the platform and chat. She did so and we stayed out there and flirted most of the night. What the attendant thought I cannot say. Anyway he left me out there and said nothing. I kept one eye on the line the whole time, but saw not a sign of any bridge. There were only a number of culverts and these, if destroyed, could easily have been made passable for trains in a few hours.

We reached Askhabad shortly after midday and found the town *14.7.18* in a turmoil. A coup d'état had taken place on the evening of the 12th. The local anti-Bolsheviks, who comprised practically the entire population, including the Turkmans, under the leadership of the local railway workers had seized a store of arms, distributed them indiscriminately to anyone who asked for them and made a sudden attack upon the Bolshevik authorities. A number of the latter were shot and nine Commissars who had been tyrannising the people were hanged.

The train did not stop long and by 4.30 we reached Kaahka. There was now not a moment to be lost. I had wired from Krasnovodsk for some mules to be got ready for me, but on arrival found that no telegram had been received and there were of course no mules. Gulab Hussein and I went round to the *sarais* and after half an hour's search discovered a muleteer who would be prepared to go to Meshed at once if I paid him sufficiently well. He named an outrageous sum, whereupon we began to bargain and I eventually got him down to something more reasonable. Then the fun began. I stipulated that we should start immediately. The muleteer thereupon had to go off to his home and take leave of his family. Then he had to go and purchase some green stuff for the animals, until with one thing and another it was already sunset before we actually got started.

We clattered along the dusty road out of Kaahka across the plain towards the Persian hills. How long the distance seemed to those hills, behind which the sun was then just sinking, a tremendous ball of fire. I was afraid that if we arrived at the frontier too late, we might have trouble with the Russian guards. We hurried our animals on as fast as we could and the muleteer laughed when I told him that I wished to do the journey to Meshed in two days. He thought I was joking.

We reached the Russian frontier post in the dark and were very savagely attacked by some large dogs. I was afraid the men might open fire on us, as it was a wild spot, and honest folk did not generally arrive there after dark. We eventually reached the building. One of the men recognised me and called his officer. The latter came out and I explained that I had been through to Baku and was racing home with a report. I described the situation in Baku and the officer, for he was one of the officials of the old regime, said that things looked very bad and very kindly offered me a glass of tea.

I left again a quarter of an hour later, and after another fifteen minutes we reached the Persian post. I was for going on, but the muleteer absolutely refused, saying that the road to Khakistar was dangerous and that we should do better by resting here and going on very early in the morning. This seemed sensible, so I gave way. The Persian frontier official was inclined to be obstreperous and wished to insist on our sleeping inside a sort of wired-in enclosure round his post. I refused very definitely and said I would sleep exactly where I liked. I was not in a mood for argument and Gulab Hussein was ready to knife anyone who would have opposed us. We both regarded this trek as a great race against time and were resolved that nothing should be allowed to delay us.

We were up before dawn, the mules were packed and off we went. *15.7.18* We reached Khakistar an hour later and then a most disastrous thing took place. On coming up to the customs post I was stopped by a couple of *tufangchis* and told that I was in quarantine and that I would not be allowed to proceed for five days. I immediately laughed and began to bluster, but it was no good, the men had had distinct orders and all they could do was to refer me to the doctor. The latter had meanwhile heard our voices raised in discussion and now came out.

I spoke to him very politely, reminded him of our last meeting and said that I relied on him to give me every assistance to proceed with my journey without delay. To my intense disappointment, however, the wretched little man began to stand on his dignity and told me that he regretted very much, but that I must stop there for five days. I then saw that I must use bluff. I asked him if he realised that he was holding up a most important official of His Majesty's Government and that if I were materially delayed there would be the very devil to pay when I got to Meshed and the whole blame would lie on his head. He then replied blandly that if it were like that, he advised me to wire to Meshed asking for orders to him to permit me to pass. I cheerfully agreed to do this, but five minutes later an underling came up and informed us that the telegraph line between there and Meshed was down and there was no knowing when communication would be re-established. I turned to the doctor and said, 'Very well, now you have no alternative but to let me pass.' The little devil stuck to his guns, however, and definitely refused, so I decided to have breakfast and think everything over.

While I ate the food which Gulab Hussein had procured for me, I instructed Gulab Hussein to work back quietly down the river bed, climb up the mountainside, and see if there was a possible way over the ridge down into the gorge the other side. I determined that if only there was a goat track I could get across, I would leave the mules and Gulab Hussein and would set off on my own on foot. An hour later Gulab Hussein returned saying that there was not a single track or way down on either side. The mountains fell away in sheer precipices and no one could get down. I was afraid that this would be the case and I knew that Gulab Hussein, a hill man himself, would make no mistake about it. I would back him against a Kurd any day in the hills.

Seeing that I was absolutely up against it, I resolved to have one more try to get round the doctor, failing which, I would creep past the sentries under cover of darkness. I asked for the doctor once more. He came up and in the most serious and deliberate voice I could muster I told him that there was nothing further to be discussed. He knew as well as I did who I was. I was not a chance wayfarer, but was an important official courier, travelling with despatches of a most urgent nature. Furthermore, I was a British officer and we were in a state of war with the Turks. If I failed to get through with my message it would be a shooting case for someone. I would not hesitate to lay the blame on the doctor and he would assuredly pay the penalty, as the Governor-General was a staunch friend of the British and a word from the Consulate and . . . (I drew my finger across my throat in as suggestive manner as I could). I then went on. 'As regards myself, it is my duty as a British officer to allow nothing to prevent me in the execution of my duty. You, doctor, have admittedly done your duty in trying to prevent me and you have failed. That is not your fault and I shall see that you do not get into trouble for it!' I pulled out my watch. 'It is already half past twelve. I am going now to order my mules to be loaded up. I shall remain here on this rock until one o'clock exactly. At one o'clock I shall start off with my mules for Meshed. You will order your men to prevent me. I shall nevertheless force my way past them. They will fire and I may be killed. *My blood will be on your head!*'

I repeated this last sentence in as impressive a manner as I could and to my delight it had effect. The little man wavered and finally said, 'Well if you are determined to go, I suppose you must, but will you give me a statement in writing stating that I did my best to prevent you and also that you have been inoculated against cholera during the last two months?' I would have written out a will leaving him all my property and bequeathing him the moon if he had asked me. I had a paper written out immediately, shook hands with him warmly and then told him he had better warn his *tufangchis* and get them out of the way.

To reach Meshed the following night appeared ridiculous now, but I nevertheless did not abandon all hope. I set the pace and I made the others keep to it. At sunset we were at the bottom of the main range itself. Here we met a Persian road guard. He said it was sheer madness to try and get over the hills in the dark. There was no place to camp, we should be frozen, even if we did not fall over some precipice. Our own muleteer was speechless at the idea, but I soon dealt with him. I drove him with the mules.

On the upper slopes we dismounted and Gulab Hussein and I marched on foot to spare the animals all we could. We reached the crest of the range in bitter cold and with a piercing wind. My hands and feet were freezing and my face was cut into open cracks. We climbed laboriously down the long steep descent into the valley, and once out of the biting wind, we began to get warm again. Still leading our beasts, we pushed on ahead without a pause and, under growing protests from the muleteer, who had long since concluded that we were raving madmen, we began wearily to ascend the slopes of the next range. We groped our way through the darkness, and very tired and hungry reached the summit at one o'clock in the morning.

We turned the animals loose to graze in the dark and also gave them some of the green fodder from Kaahka. We ourselves lay down by the side of the path and went right off to sleep.

At 5 a.m. we were up and off again, getting some milk in a village, *16.7.18* the village of the thousand skeletons. The path now led downhill all the way. I started off walking and walked as fast as I could, practically without a stop, till well into the afternoon. I then rode a little and by 3 p.m. we had come to the last village on the road to Meshed. I now realised that we should actually get to Meshed that night, for it was only twenty-one miles away. We unloaded the mules, the muleteer protesting that it was rank madness to try and make the animals go any further that day. I gave him one hour for a rest, but he took two, then took the mules off to water them. I told Gulab Hussein not to let them go out of his sight.

At 5.30 we started off once more. I ached in every limb and I am sure the wretched mule did. I had changed animals now and taken a young mule that had been so far lightly loaded. I set the pace, leaving Gulab Hussein to bring up the rear. This was the last lap and I did not care what happened so long as I got into Meshed before midnight.

I will not dwell on the last twenty miles of the trip. The mule was at the point of collapse and so was I. I tried walking every now and then, but as soon as I dismounted I found I had the whole weight of the

73

mule to drag behind me and it was more than I could manage. The animal had to be kicked and pushed at every step. Poor little brute, I am afraid I was very cruel to it, but I was very nearly done up myself, and could not afford to think of the animal. Mile after mile we laboriously put behind us, until we finally saw the lights of Meshed. Gulab Hussein and the muleteer were by this time several miles behind.

I sighted the lights of Meshed when I was still nine miles away from the town and never had nine miles seemed so long as these. Our rate of progress was not more than four miles an hour, for the mule stopped dead every now and then and I had to get down and drag it. I was so stiff and tired myself, that small as the animal was — it was no larger than an ordinary donkey — I had great difficulty in getting my leg over its back again.

Finally we reached the city wall. Never will I forget its black jagged silhouette against the starlit sky. There was no entrance to the city at this point and I was faced with the question as to which direction to take. I decided I ought to follow the wall in a clockwise direction. I did so. It was already 11 p.m. and I ran a considerable risk of being fired at by a *tufangchi*. Someone might well have mistaken me for a thief lifting someone else's donkey. I *was* in fact practically carrying the beast at this stage.

After going some way round the wall, it seemed a mile at least, and finding no entrance, I discovered a place where the wall had broken down and I decided to try and effect an entrance that way. It had now become a point of honour with me to get home before midnight. I dragged the wretched mule down a slippery bank into the wide ditch which might have been dug for a moat around the wall, but it was now the main depository for the city garbage and carrion. The stench left little doubt of that.

I picked my way across the bottom of the ditch, stepping into all kinds of filth in the blackness and with much pulling, pushing and tugging eventually hauled the animal across the ruined wall. The next moment all the dogs of Meshed came out on the housetops and howled, and at the same moment I realised that I was not only inside the town but also in someone's back garden. I thought that this time I would certainly be shot and for a moment thought seriously of abandoning the mule and making a bolt for it. Again it seemed a point of honour to arrive at the finishing point complete with mule, so I frantically broke down several more feet of wall and the two of us rolled amid a cloud of dust back down to the bottom of the ditch.

The mule was so impressed with the seriousness of the situation, or else he was so frightened of the dogs, that he actually started to trot. This was too good to miss, so I ran by his side encouraging him and thus we trotted along the bottom of the foul and stinking city drain. Fortunately the dogs did not venture down to chase us — no Persian dog would — and a little further on we were able to clamber out of the moat onto the road. As we did so we nearly frightened to death a slumbering Persian who uttered a wild yell and bolted into the darkness.

Fortunately one of the city gates was not far off and with a great feeling of relief we turned in.

We had hardly entered when we were rushed upon by half a dozen armed men, who seized us and apparently started to congratulate themselves on having made a good haul. My temper was rather short, but I was too tired to quarrel and fortunately they were open to reason. I told one of them I would give him a good reward to conduct me to the British Consulate. He agreed and set off forthwith. It was as much as the wretched mule could do to keep up with him. The Consulate was right across the other side of the town and it took us half an hour to reach it. I went in the back way and stopped at the Attaché's house. I nearly collapsed as I rolled from the mule. Feeling rather like Phileas Fogg, I looked at my watch and saw to my surprise that it was only 11.30.

I found Redl, Jarvis and Bingham sitting sleepily round a table, and the next moment I was drinking a neat whisky, while Din Muhammed, overwhelmed with joy at seeing me back again, promptly went off to cook me some dinner. I sat up for a couple of hours giving a brief description of the state of affairs in Trans-Caspia. 'What about getting a report off to India?' I asked.

'No, that's all right,' said Redl. 'I forgot to mention, we have a General here now, just out from India. General Malleson has taken over the Mission. He's already gone to bed and I don't think he'd like to be disturbed. But he'll certainly want to see you in the morning!'

A General! Gone to bed! Not to be disturbed! I looked at Redl, resplendent in his red tabs, and at the signs of comfort surrounding me. Half an hour before, I had been straining every nerve in my body

75

and dragging an exhausted mule through the stench and filth of city drains in an attempt to beat the clock. Now it seemed as though I were suddenly in another world where time was of no account.

I thought of all that was happening in the Caucasus, of the advancing enemy force, of the thousands of men, women and children whose lives were at stake, fated to be brutally murdered in cold blood. I thought too, of the maddening frustration at the Persian quarantine post and I recalled also the Chief in Simla with his urgent demand for news with all possible speed.

And now this was Meshed — or was it Shangri-La? The General was in bed! He must not be disturbed! Tomorrow. . . . !

The Malleson Mission

◆

I had heard much about Malleson, but breakfast was the first opportunity I had had of meeting him personally. I cannot say I was very much struck with him, though he seemed practical enough, took down the gist of what I told him and sent it off in the form of a telegraphic despatch.

Redl was present at my interview with the G.O.C. and after I had made my report asked if I knew anything about a certain General Junkovsky in Trans-Caspia. I replied that I did not, whereupon Redl, with the consent of the G.O.C., proceeded to explain that this Junkovsky had come down from Trans-Caspia and had introduced himself to Redl as the head of a political organisation in Turkistan known as the Turkistan Union. The objects of this organisation were to fight the Bolsheviks and to run a widespread system of propaganda in Turkistan directed against the Bolsheviks and the Turks. Both Redl and the G.O.C. had been so impressed by Junkovsky that they agreed to his request for financial assistance (how often we were to hear this term 'financial assistance' in the future!) and actually gave him bills on London or Calcutta for the sum of something like £25,000.

When I heard this I was amazed and at once foresaw considerable trouble. By letting a number of British bills loose in the country we were giving the Bolsheviks and other hostile elements an excellent handle against us. I pointed out to the G.O.C. that if money had to be paid it must be given out in the local paper currency or in Russian gold or Persian silver, but in no case in English bills or money. Fortunately Malleson saw the force of this, but said that the damage was already done, as the money had actually been paid to General Junkovsky. I thereupon said that I felt so strongly about it that I would run the risk of offending the man and would go and get the bills back from him. This I did.

I was very nice to General Junkovsky and he smiled with rather a sickly smile when I pointed out that it was useless his taking English bills as he would never be able to realise on them in Turkistan; it would be much better to have the money in something else. He therefore surrendered the bills and the situation was saved. We then discussed the whole question anew and it was decided to give him the sum of £500 in Persian Tumans. The old man was far from satisfied, but I told him it was more than most people would give for a venture of which they knew nothing. Junkovsky then departed.

I never have understood how Redl and the G.O.C. came to be so impressed with the man. Time and experience showed them that the money might have been much better expended in other ways, but we were all fated to learn much by experience during the next few months. I may say at once that time taught me to place no reliance whatever on Redl's sense of judgement or discretion and still less on General Malleson's, whose main quality lay in his cleverness in picking other people's brains and turning to his own advantage the work of others. This had been his reputation before and it was certainly substantiated during his command in Meshed and Trans-Caspia.

In spite of the fact that I had just come from Trans-Caspia, I was able to give only a very obscure description of the actual situation in Askhabad. All I knew was that a coup d'état was reputed to have occurred there on the 12th July. One fact seemed definite: the Bolsheviks were no longer in power.

Feeling that we must get in touch with whatever was going on, I volunteered to go on another trip into Trans-Caspia. The G.O.C. agreed and I made arrangements to leave Meshed on the 21st July. I must say I was rather sorry to leave again so soon. Jarvis and Bingham had made a large number of friends among the Russian colony and were obviously having a very good time. I would rather have liked to have stopped and had a rest. On the other hand the idea of the journey enthralled me and I was really eager to be off again.

Ward was still in Meshed and much to his disgust had been roped into the 'cipher section' which kept all busily occupied at all hours of the day and night coping with Malleson's long-winded telegrams to India. It became notorious that any statement by any casual agent or

Nielsen
Queensgate Press Division

3731 Eastern Hills Lane
Cincinnati, OH 45209
513/321-5200
800-543-1913
FAX 513-321-5315

Kayla
Hughbanks
4mos.

Performance That Earns Confidence

camel driver in the bazaar would be made the subject of a long foolscap wire. Needless to say the G.O.C. was most unpopular in the eyes of the 'cipher section'. Ward was chafing at his enforced inactivity and begged me to take him with me on my forthcoming trip. I mentioned it to the G.O.C. and as the G.O.C. did not appear to want him particularly in Meshed, it was agreed that Ward should accompany me.

Still feeling that there must have been a bridge somewhere, or else Ward would never have been sent out all round the world to blow it up, I broached the subject to Redl very cautiously, but said quite boldly that I did not believe that there was any bridge between Askhabad and the Caspian. Redl consulted the Military Report, and of course there was no bridge worthy the name with the exception of the Charjui bridge over the Oxus several hundred miles to the East and a small bridge at Tejend, also east of Kaahka. It was therefore apparent that Ward's mission had from the first been an absolute farce. Ward himself had travelled round the world at government expense in circumstances of extreme secrecy in order to blow up a bridge which had never existed! If anyone wanted to annoy Ward, they henceforth only had to mention the word 'Bridge', while Redl also did not go out of his way to encourage discussion on the subject.

There were very few preparations to be made, surprisingly few in *21.7.18* view of the length of our journey. Mules were ordered and started off in charge of Din Muhammed early in the afternoon. Ward and I borrowed horses from the Cavalry and in the afternoon went down to the bazaar to make a few last purchases. These included two loaves of Persian sugar which were intended one for the Arkannikov family and one for anyone else who might prove helpful on the road. I also took two large pots of newly made apricot jam. This would have been a godsend to anyone in Trans-Caspia, but they were doomed never to arrive, for both were broken by Ward, one the second day out, and the other just over the Russian frontier.

Both in nondescript trader's clothes, we left Meshed about 5 p.m. accompanied by two *sowars*. Ward for some reason was very uncompanionable on this occasion. I fancy he was still chafing about the bridge, and the last few weeks in Meshed had certainly not improved his temper. He assured me that now he was at last free from Malleson he would go straight through to the Caucasus and nothing on earth would induce him to return to Meshed. Poor devil, he was doomed never to leave Russian soil again.

The journey was uneventful. We did not rush things and nighted at the usual stages, save that to make sure of catching the morning train, our last halt was in the foot-hills some nine miles from Kaahka.

25.7.18 We were up soon after daybreak and Din Muhammed set off back on the return journey to Meshed. Ward and I then started off with our four mules and a muleteer. Ward and I were each riding on one, two were carrying baggage and the muleteer was mounted on a very slow donkey. We started off at a brisk pace with the result that he and his donkey were left behind.

We kept the baggage mules moving along at a respectful rate and so long as we were on the narrow stony path leading down the ravine from Khakistar we were masters of the situation. Once, however, we reached the open foot-hills, the two baggage mules with one accord left the track and moved rapidly up the hillside. I tried to head them off, but no sooner did my mule quicken his pace than they quickened theirs. Unable to make my mule go fast enough to catch up the baggage animals I dismounted and yelling to Ward to look after it, started running along the hillside to try to head off the runaways. The latter seemed to become suddenly imbued with new life. One of them cantered over the top of the hill while the other began to buck-jump and to divest itself of its load. By this time the sun was up and it was getting appreciably warm. I was perspiring freely and according to Ward my language was perfectly disgraceful. The second mule, having got rid of its burden, proceeded to put a range of hills in between us and itself.

'We shall never see Kaahka today,' I thought as I started off in pursuit. A couple of villagers appeared on the hillside and joined in the chase. Between us we eventually succeeded in rounding up the runaway, meanwhile the muleteer had come up on his donkey and had managed to catch the second animal which was quietly grazing the other side of the hill, while Ward was having a chase all on his own after my own animal, which had ambled playfully out of reach the moment I had dismounted. The little divertissement lasted for about an hour and an half and took us a considerable distance out of our road. We had no time to lose if we wished to catch the train, so placing the muleteer and his donkey ahead of me, I drove him forward at the same rate as the mules. The latter must have regretted their escape, for Ward and I kept them mercilessly on the run all the way into Kaahka, where we arrived fortunately in time.

The train was crowded with people and in the general rush of securing places Ward and I were unnoticed. During the journey, however, our conversation in English attracted a certain amount of attention and one or two fellow passengers envinced an interest in our doings. One of them eventually turned to me and quite politely introduced himself as 'Rotmeister Krasnovsky' of the Frontier Guards. He asked if we were Englishmen, and when I said that we were both of us officers the whole of the occupants of the carriage became at once very attentive and commenced to overwhelm us with questions. Had we come from Meshed? Was it true that the British had an entire army in Meshed and were they coming up to Trans-Caspia? Would they come and assist the Trans-Caspians against the Bolsheviks? Did I think that the Turks would take Baku or would the British prevent them?

Captain Krasnovsky was convinced that in us he had made a very valuable discovery, and at the first wayside station sent a telegram to Askhabad. He presumably reported our presence in the train, for we stopped nearly half an hour at the station and after we had started again Krasnovsky asked whether I would object to interviewing the Commander-in-Chief at Askhabad station. I said I would be very pleased to do so and the conversation carried on. Ward, who of course did not understand a single word, spent his time in passing very uncomplimentary remarks about our fellow passengers.

We reached Askhabad only at dusk. Krasnovsky immediately took me in tow and the next moment I found myself being introduced to a group of very shady looking individuals. These were the Commander-in-Chief and his staff, or to be more exact, as I ascertained afterwards, they were Comrades Dokhov, Funtikov, Kurilev and Company, the prime movers in the recent coup d'état, who having kicked out the Bolsheviks and murdered the chief commissars, were now in fear of their lives and dreading what must inevitably happen to them when the Soviet forces would arrive from Tashkent.

It was now quite dark. We had moved into one of the station waiting rooms and were seated at a plain wooden table, the only light being a tallow candle stuck into a bottle. I introduced myself as a

British officer, member of the staff in Meshed, proceeding urgently to the Caucasus. Comrade Dokhov and Co., who were very typical railway subordinates of the semi-educated type, looked significantly at each other when I said I belonged to the staff in Meshed and after a number of questions concerning our presence and strength in Persia, asked whether I thought the British would agree to send troops up to Askhabad to help the Mensheviks (as they called themselves) against a possible return of the Bolsheviks.

I replied very cautiously that I was not in a position to discuss a question like that without conferring with my Chief in Meshed. However, I said, I could give them an idea of what the British attitude towards the general situation was. For three whole years Britain and her Allies had been fighting the war on many fronts against the Germans and Turks. Russia had been our ally and had fought valiantly side by side with us against the common enemy. Then had come the Revolution and the Bolsheviks had suddenly ceased fighting and had made terms with the enemy. The powerful Russian Army of the Caucasus which had been fighting the Turks in close co-operation with the British had thrown open the front.

Now the Turks, already defeated in Mesopotamia, had built up a new army and were preparing a fresh offensive eastwards. Their leaders made no secret of their intentions. They planned to occupy both the Caucasus and Persia. They would seize the Baku oil-fields and then continue their advance through Trans-Caspia to join with Afghanistan in a direct threat to India. The threat was a serious one and it was to prevent this eastward Turkish thrust that we had sent troops into Persia. Britain had no interest whatsoever in occupying foreign territory, either Persian or Russian. We had been hoping that the Russians themselves would take steps to prevent the Turks advancing through Trans-Caucasia into Trans-Caspia and we had been greatly concerned that no measures had been taken to do so. On the contrary, the Bolsheviks declared that the war was now over and ever since the signing of the Treaty of Brest-Litovsk they had refused to fight the Turk and had collaborated with the Germans in sending them supplies of oil and cotton to enable them to continue fighting the war.

What the Trans-Caspians were now asking had nothing to do with opposing the Turks. Indeed, they had made no mention of either Germans or Turks. Instead, they were asking the British to send up troops to help them fight their own Bolsheviks, with whom Britain had no quarrel. However, if the Trans-Caspian authorities were seriously contemplating taking such a step as inviting British troops into their country, I was sure that our military authorities in Meshed would be willing to give the matter serious consideration. Meanwhile, in lieu of any assistance we might give the Trans-Caspians, we should expect the latter to expel any enemy agents from Trans-Caspia and prevent the Germans getting any cotton away. Dokhov expressed their willingness to do this.

I also explained that it was imperative that I should hurry on to Baku, but said that if the Askhabad authorities would give me permission to send a cipher telegram to Meshed from Krasnovodsk, I would acquaint Meshed of the situation. Whereupon Dokhov consulted with his companions and wrote me a 'recommendation' requesting everyone to give me all facilities.

Neither Dokhov nor his companions were in the least impressive. Dokhov, who acted as spokesman for his comrades, was lean and slovenly in appearance, with a hungry look about him and a shifty glint in his eye. Funtikov was thick-set and flabby, with a heavy moustache and red veins in his nose and cheeks. His breath smelled strongly of alcohol. Kurilev was of medium height and build and had the sharp thin features and quick movements of a weasel. They looked exactly what they were, typical railway workers, dirty and unshaven and obviously very frightened.

Fate and circumstances had driven these men to lead a revolution. The tyranny of the Bolshevik regime had driven them to desperation. They had risen and overthrown their late tyrants, and now they were just beginning to realise that they alone were quite incapable of maintaining the situation which they had created. They were, in fact, in a state of mortal fear as regards the immediate future. From them I obtained a brief but complete story of the recent events in Trans-Caspia.

During the early part of the year the Bolshevik authorities in Trans-Caspia had made themselves very unpopular by their tyrannous and licentious methods. Their intolerant and brutal regime had called forth passive resistance on the part of the workers on the Central Asian Railway, always a powerful element in Trans-Caspia. Some passages of arms between the railwaymen and the authorities had been the natural result. The central Soviet authorities in Tashkent were disturbed by the constant reports of the lawlessness of the Trans-Caspian population and decided to settle matters once and for all. They accordingly sent down an 'Extraordinary Commissar' in the person of one Fralov.

Fralov, by nationality a Lett, was one of the lowest types of criminal set free by the Revolution. He arrived in Askhabad heralded by a past reputation which overawed the population with terror and accompanied by a bodyguard consisting of one hundred armed Austrians and Magyars. No sooner had he arrived than Fralov began to live up to his reputation. Murders and executions became the order of the day. Fralov would 'dispense justice' by day and carouse by night. His carousals took the form of drunken orgies and Fralov would frequently end up the evening by dashing round the town in a motor car with a party of drunken women, firing his revolver at any lighted windows.

One day Fralov sent a small party of his bodyguard down to Kizil Arvat to arrest certain railway workers on some charge or other. The party arrived to find the birds flown, and the population showed such a hostile attitude that the Bolsheviks returned to Askhabad and reported the circumstances to Fralov. The latter flew into a passion, summoned his entire bodyguard, ordered a special train and proceeded in person to Kizil Arvat to settle the matter. Arrived at Kizil Arvat, the Extraordinary Commissar was met at the station by the leading representatives of the railway workers, who apologised for their comrades' action in shielding the offenders. They had no time to say more, for drawing his revolver Fralov shot three of the representatives dead and his followers opened fire on the crowd, which naturally fled.

News of the crime was immediately telegraphed up to Askhabad and the local railwaymen, profiting by the absence of the tyrant, hurriedly called a meeting and decided to take immediate action. In this affair they appear to have acted with considerable promptness and thoroughness. They first of all cut the telegraph wires to Kizil Arvat, then proclaimed a revolution in Askhabad. The Austrian bodyguard was down the line with Fralov and there were practically no armed Bolsheviks left in the town. The local town militia declared themselves on the side of the rebels, who surrounded the Soviet and arrested all the members before they had time to escape. Nine of the commissars were summarily executed. The military stores were broken open and some six thousand rifles were distributed to the population. This distribution of arms was made quite indiscriminately with the result that some five thousand Turkmans, who had never handled a rifle in their lives, now suddenly found themselves possessed of both a rifle and ammunition.

Without wasting a moment, a detachment of two hundred men with six machine-guns was hurried into a train and started off in the direction of Kizil Arvat. Many of them had never fired a rifle in their lives and therefore the train was held up at various places on the line, while impromptu musketry practice was carried out. The machine-guns were mounted in covered-in trucks, two in the foremost part of the train, two in the centre and two at the end. Thus prepared, the train made its way to Kizil Arvat and arrived there about ten o'clock on July 12th.

Fate was kind to the rebels, for Fralov and his merry men had taken possession of the station and had been engaged in a drinking bout the night before. They were now all lolling about the platform, many of them asleep in small groups. Fralov himself was sitting in an armchair when the train came in. The train appeared to be an ordinary goods train and caused no undue attention. Having moved right into the station it stopped, the doors of the goods vans were suddenly opened and a concentrated fire from rifles and machine-guns was immediately opened on the doomed Bolsheviks. Fralov was killed, as was also his wife, and not one of his party was left alive. The news spread through the town and was wired on to Krasnovodsk. In the latter place the local Bolsheviks immediately surrendered and the regime changed hands without any bloodshed.

By this prompt action Trans-Caspia freed itself from Soviet control, much of this excitement taking place during those few days when I was hastening back from Krasnovodsk and during my last few days' stay in Meshed.

My interview with the Askhabad leaders lasted over an hour and a half, and it was late when I rejoined the train. I now regarded our journey in quite a different light. In one point I had already succeeded. I had established touch with the Trans-Caspian authorities and no longer would there be any need for me to conceal my identity. I began to know the sort of people with whom I was dealing and, although I was pestered by curious fellow travellers, I refused to say anything and maintained an air of silent importance, calculated to impress any local officials or other individuals who might be inclined to be obstructive. Thus we reached Krasnovodsk again late at night and Ward and I dossed down and slept among the crowded stinking mass of travellers who covered the floor of the waiting room on the station.

26.7.18   The next morning I resolved to get into touch with Meshed as soon as possible. I decided that my meeting with the Askhabad leaders was of such great importance that I must delay my further journey to Baku until I could get negotiations started with Meshed. I wrote out a long cipher report on the situation and handed it in to the telegraph office in Krasnovodsk. Meanwhile I decided to send Ward across to Baku in my place. He was to go across, acquaint himself with the situation and then return to report.

I next called on Nikolai Nikolaevich Semov. He was delighted to see me again and told me at once that his scheme for holding up the cotton had been successful. The entire stocks were still in Krasnovodsk and he added, 'Now that the Bolsheviks are out of power, here they will stay'.

Semov insisted on my staying at his house and I was very pleased to be able to present his wife with one of the two sugar loaves I had brought from Meshed. No one in Trans-Caspia had tasted sugar for a very long time and the Arkannikovs were no less pleased with the loaf I gave them.

I stayed a couple of days with Semov and was very pleased to have a brief rest from travelling. There is the most wonderful bathing at Krasnovodsk and the Semovs had their own bathing place very near the pier and never have I enjoyed bathing so much. The water was wonderfully clear and one could see every little pebble and all the crayfish crawling about on the bottom at a depth of sixteen to eighteen feet.

Semov took me round to the so-called *Statchkom* [Strike Committee] and introduced me to the members, in particular the President Vassili Kuhn, a big burly man with a pleasant face and a rough outspoken manner. Up to the present he had been an engineer on the railway; henceforth he was destined to play the role of Dictator of Krasnovodsk. We had a brief talk, and from Kuhn I learned that the Askhabad Committee, as they now called themselves, had sent a telegram to General Malleson in Meshed, asking that a meeting be arranged to discuss the question of mutual assistance.

On the night of the 29th after a series of bathes in the afternoon *29.7.18* and a boating party to the wireless station in the evening, I went round to the Semovs for a late meal and was surprised to find there General Junkovsky and his secretary, a young but masterly young lady named Lubov Mikhailovna. They had apparently just come in from Askhabad and were full of news regarding the situation there and the growing feeling that the British would accept the invitation of the Askhabad Committee to move their troops into Trans-Caspia. News had just come through of the murder of the Tsar and Imperial Family and Junkovsky, who was evidently a fervent Monarchist, appeared to be very upset at the news. Junkovsky was very friendly towards me, and appeared to have quite forgotten how I had handicapped him in the matter of the money.

At lunch the next day, I met a student named Constantine *30.7.18* Ivanovich Freimann, who like myself was bound for Baku that afternoon. We both had our tickets and remained at the Semovs until a warning signal told us it was time to go down to the steamer. This was the *Arkhangelsk*. We went aboard and were seen off by the Semov family.

There were not many passengers on board, but among them was rather an attractive little Russian girl, Miss Valya Alexeeva, who it appeared was an acquaintance of Freimann. We chatted together the whole day. She was going across to stay with her uncle in Baku. The uncle was employed in Nobel's works in Cherny Gorod, the oilfield suburb of Baku, and the family lived at Ufra just outside Krasnovodsk.

We arrived at Baku about nine o'clock the following morning *31.7.18* after a very pleasant trip. As I was in no immediate hurry I accompanied Miss Alexeeva as far as her uncle's house in Cherny Gorod and then made for the Hotel Europe. There appeared to be a lot of excitement about the town.

At the hotel I found Ward. From him I gathered that the Turks were just outside the town and were expected to enter that evening. MacDonnell was away, having gone down to Enzeli to see General Dunsterville. The various Baku governments were in a state of panic, as also was the Armenian portion of the population, thousands of whom were rushing for the steamers and trying to get away. Realising that the situation was extremely critical I told Ward to try and get me a map of the harbour and coastal defences of Baku, while I went round to interview people and incidentally get my visa to leave the town.

On my way to the passport office, I bumped into an American who was employed in one of the oil companies. He advised me strongly to get back to Krasnovodsk while there was yet time and urged me not to worry about a visa, as I would almost certainly be arrested if I appeared at the Passport Control.

It did not take much examination to see that the town was indeed on the point of collapse. I rushed back to the hotel where I found that Ward had obtained a map. It was a large blueprint about five feet by four, and he had obtained it through one of the consular agents from whom I had ordered it during my previous visit to Baku. My idea was that, supposing we had to give up Baku, we might still be able to thwart the Turks by mining the harbour. I had mentioned this idea at Meshed and Malleson had impressed on me the necessity of obtaining a large scale map of Baku harbour defences.

I had now obtained the map, but the question arose as to how I was going to get it safely out of Baku. (Ward had decided to remain there.) I knew that everyone leaving the port was subjected to a strict search and I knew quite well that a suspicious individual like myself, for I was still in a nondescript trader's dress, found with an important military map in his possession would be shot immediately. I had with me a small zinc trunk containing a few odds and ends, but it would have been quite impossible to conceal the map inside the trunk. Also I knew that both the trunk and myself would certainly be searched. For a moment I did not know what to do. Then an idea struck me. I purchased a newspaper and folding the map up inside it, so as not to show, I put the paper under my arm, and carrying the trunk made my way down to the quay.

I found the whole of the landing place packed with a seething crowd of refugees, mainly Armenians, largely women and children, though with a fair admixture of men, all of them seeking escape from the wrath to come. I thought of little Valya Alexeeva and wished I had had time to go and warn her. This would have been impossible, as it would have taken me at least two hours to have gone to Cherny Gorod and back, and I had the precious map to get away. I dared not risk losing the last steamer.

After much pushing and jostling I got as far as the customs, where I was stopped and made to open my box and turn out my pockets. I put on as bold a mien as I could. As often happens on suchlike occasions, one man was perfectly satisfied, the other was suspicious and seemed inclined to demand a more thorough search. Fortunately at this moment there was a rush from the crowd without, and the officials and gendarmes standing inside the barrier turned round to the barricade. I melted into the throng of bystanders and, with my precious newspaper safe, made my way unobtrusively on board.

I went straight down to the saloon, which was fortunately empty, and I was just trying to decide what I should do with the map, when a hoarse voice outside shouted, 'All men off the ship, line up for examination.'

I just had time to slip the map and its covering newspaper under one of the red plush cushions in the saloon, when a Red soldier with rifle and fixed bayonet entered the saloon and tackled me. 'Now then *Tovarishch*,' he said, 'what are you doing here? How old are you?' I was rather taken aback at this question, but replied civilly enough that I was 29. 'Then you must come back on shore and join the detachments for the front at once.'

Here was a nice kettle of fish. I realised at once that this was the most critical moment I had yet faced, so I immediately produced a big bundle of notes from the lining of my coat and thrust them into his hands, begging him to take them and let me go. The fact that we were alone doubtless saved the situation. He looked hurriedly round, nodded hastily, thrust the notes into his pocket and left the saloon. He bumped into somebody just outside, but evidently satisfied him that there was no one in the saloon and I was left alone.

I lay down on one of the berths and made myself as inconspicuous as I could and did not venture on deck until I gathered from the sounds that we were preparing to weigh anchor. I then came on deck, after putting the precious map into the zinc trunk. It was about three o'clock in the afternoon when we pushed off from the quay. It was crowded with refugees, who were thronging into several other steamers which lay alongside the landing stage. The decks of our own ship were equally packed with women and children, most of them bewailing their menfolk who had been pulled off the ship at the last moment.

The ship was the *Arkhangelsk*, the same vessel in which I had arrived that very morning. The weather was beautiful and the crossing most enjoyable. My pleasure was marred by the thought of Baku being a doomed city. The Turks were possibly already entering and the local Tatars had also perhaps already commenced their terrible and gruesome work of massacre. For the Armenian population there was no hope once the town fell into the hands of the Turk. For weeks past the local Tatars had been sharpening their knives and gloating over the prospects of the vengeance and bloodshed they were shortly to enjoy. One shuddered to think of it, and miserable and forlorn as were the wretched refugees crowded together on the decks, theirs was a happy lot compared with the majority of their relatives left behind to perish like cattle at the hands of butchers.

I thought of little Valya Alexeeva and wondered whether she would be in danger. Her people lived on the outskirts of the town in the oil-field area and this would be one of the first places to be raided by the bloodthirsty Tatars. I felt very sad at the thought that only the previous night she had sat and chatted with me on the deck of this same ship and I wondered whether it would ever be my lot to meet her again.

1.8.18   We arrived at Krasnovodsk about the middle of the next morning. I was met by the Semovs who seemed to be expecting me, as news had got across the Caspian that Baku was on the point of falling. I went home and had a meal with them. They told me that a British Colonel had arrived from Enzeli and was staying at the hotel and also informed me that there was no fresh news from Askhabad, but that rumour had it that the Bolsheviks in Tashkent were arranging to send fresh troops down to Trans-Caspia.

After lunch I went up to the hotel and saw Colonel Battine, Indian Cavalry. I introduced myself and we had a chat. I took rather a dislike to Battine, who appeared to me to be a snob, whose chief anxiety was to impress the local natives with his own superiority. I introduced him to Semov, who took us round to the Committee and I introduced him to Kuhn and all the members.

2.8.18   I spent the following morning in walking out to Ufra, a small bay some three or four miles out of Krasnovodsk down the line. It was here that the main oil companies had their reservoirs and I wished to ascertain what stocks they had in hand and what the possibilities of obtaining more fuel would be if Baku were cut off. I called on Vladimir Nikolaevich Alexeev, the father of the girl I had met on the boat and he gave me all the particulars I wanted. I ventured to advise him to write to his daughter and get her back again as soon as possible, as Baku was not going to be a healthy place for young girls.

That afternoon I took the afternoon train for Askhabad, arriving at 2 p.m. the following day. I was met on the station by Miss Lubov Mikhailovna, Junkovsky's secretary. She conducted me to the house of a Count Dorrer. The Count was away at the front, but I met the Countess and General Junkovsky. We had an excellent lunch and I was persuaded to stay the night. I decided to stay in Askhabad until I could get some definite news on the situation in Baku. *3.8.18*

Late that night Jarvis arrived from Meshed, having been sent by General Malleson to interview the Committee in reply to their application to the British for military assistance. The next morning, we went down to the Committee together. The place of assembly was the railway board office which comprised also the main telegraph office and was situated in convenient proximity to the station. We found the entire Committee assembled at a long table: 'President' Funtikov and his assistant Kurilev, Lev Alexandrovich Zimin, late schoolmaster from Merv, and a number of others whose names will figure from time to time in this story.

Various speeches were made describing the critical situation in Trans-Caspia, the imminent danger of a Bolshevik attack in force and the inability of the Trans-Caspians to defend themselves against such attack. The question of British assistance was then raised and having ascertained from Jarvis that under certain conditions the British military authorities in Meshed might be prepared to render assistance, a resolution was passed providing for the forming of a special tribunal to work out in detail the question of applying to the British for military assistance. Jarvis then left by a special train.

As the meeting broke up I had talks with a number of the members and discussed ways and means. I insisted particularly on the necessity for declaring Trans-Caspia a zone of military operations and for the interning of all enemy aliens without delay. I knew that there were a number of German and Austrian agents in

Askhabad and it was obvious that once they saw the way things were going, they would endeavour to leave the country. I had already taken necessary steps with Semov and Kuhn to prevent any of them leaving Krasnovodsk and it now lay with the Askhabad authorities to rope them all in. I was particularly keen on action being taken at once. I had compiled a pretty accurate list of the people we wanted from information furnished by Junkovsky's secretary, who had apparently been doing a little spying on her own.

5.8.18 The President and one or two members of the Committee came round to Dorrer's house and discussed with me the question of interning enemy aliens. I insisted that they should take immediate action, as I had seen the entire group of German and Austrian agents at dinner the night before in a public garden. Moreover, one of the Germans was wearing what appeared to be a counterfeit British uniform. It was agreed to arrest the whole party that evening.

A wire was received from General Bicherakov in Baku stating that the town had been saved at the last moment and calling on Trans-Caspia for assistance in defending the town against the Turks and Germans. The wire added that the British had also been asked to send assistance. The last referred of course to General Dunsterville and his mission who had been hung up all this time in Enzeli. I left by a special train that night for Krasnovodsk. Before I left I heard to my great satisfaction that five of the Germans and Austrians had already been arrested and that the remainder would be rounded up that night.

6.8.18 Arrived in Krasnovodsk, I heard that an advanced party of 'Dunsterforce' was already in Baku and I decided to go across at once. I therefore took the afternoon steamer.

Battle for Baku

◆

I reached Baku by midday and immediately went to my old rendezvous at the Europe Hotel. I found everything astir. One of the first persons I met was Colonel Stokes, G.S.O.1, and Colonel Keyworth, who was in command of the advanced detachment. I had my first interview with Stokes sitting on the top of the main staircase in the hotel. *7.8.18*

It appeared that the town had been saved in a most miraculous fashion on the evening of the day I had so hurriedly left it. The Turks had felt so certain of their victory that they did not hurry to occupy the town, nor did they trouble to shell it, but they decided to walk in casually that same afternoon.

Meanwhile, there was of course, tremendous confusion in the town. General Bicherakov decided that all was lost and made arrangements to evacuate his forces to Petrovsk, while one of the Bolshevik leaders, Petrov, had collected as many of the guns and ammunition he could with a view to removing them to one of the ships and getting them away to Astrakhan. He had got half-a-dozen field guns lined up in the Church square prior to embarking them, when someone pointed out the Turks strolling leisurely down the slope towards the outskirts of the town. Petrov was known to be a moody individual, with the temperament of a prima donna, and totally unpredictable in behaviour. Instead of embarking the guns he now trained them on the Turks and opened fire.

The enemy were entirely taken by surprise and beat a hurried retreat. A sally from the town sent them flying back to their positions and the town was saved for the time being. Bicherakov decided to make a stand and appealed for help to the British, which resulted in the arrival on the scene of the first party of Dunsterforce.

One of the first questions Colonel Stokes asked me was whether I was responsible for the presence in Baku of one Ward. I replied that I was responsible for his presence there, but that he would now have to return to Trans-Caspia and report. 'Thank God,' said Stokes. 'We will get him off tomorrow.' I learned that, on the day of the first arrival of British troops, a steamer had come down from Astrakhan with a number of German staff officers on board. They sailed boldly into the port and on dropping anchor sent ashore to enquire where Turkish Headquarters was. So very German. They had been told that the Turks would occupy the town on such and such a day and arrived quite expecting to find the Turkish flag waving over the town. They were sorely disillusioned.

Ward got to know about these Germans and seizing his revolver got a boat and went out to the ship. He boarded and proceeded to arrest the Germans, whereupon a Russian boat came alongside and took them prisoners. The Russians, however, felt that their internal affairs were being interfered with and complained to Stokes. Hence his desire to get rid of Ward, whom he regarded as a dangerous individual. So Ward returned to Trans-Caspia.

That afternoon I walked out to Cherny Gorod and met Miss Alexeeva. They had spent an exciting time on the 30th and 31st July, as the Tatars had actually begun to come into the town. I do not think any of them had felt very happy about it, as the part they lived in was one of the Armenian centres, and the Tatars could not always be relied upon to discriminate whom they were massacring.

In the evening I accompanied Stokes to a reception given by the Combined Powers that Be. There were the usual speeches and Stokes asked me to get up and say something on behalf of the British. I also interpreted a speech for Colonel Keyworth.

To gain a clear understanding of the political situation in Baku, it is necessary to turn back for a moment to the early part of July. The Bolsheviks were then in power in Baku, but although they were in touch with Moscow through Astrakhan, they were daily losing power, owing mainly to their lack of policy and indecision as regards the Turks. The Social Revolutionary Party was rapidly growing in strength, but was afraid to attempt any overt act, as the forces in Baku were entirely dependent on Astrakhan for both food and ammunition.

Bicherakov, the Cossack leader, who had been co-operating with General Dunsterville, sailed for Alyat during the first days of July with the object of organising the forces opposing the Turks. In addition to his own Cossacks he took with him four of our armoured cars. It was agreed between him and General Dunsterville that so long as the Bolsheviks were in power in Baku, he should throw in his lot with them. In a letter written on July 13th, Dunsterville wrote: 'None but myself, Russian or English, believes in him [Bicherakov], but I do so sincerely. In any case I should have to believe in him, as he is literally our only hope at the present moment. He is all for Russia and the plans he intends to carry out are in the interests of Russia in general and the North Caucasus in particular, but they entirely coincide with our interests.'

In the same letter it is interesting to note the following: 'The Krasnovodsk situation from our point of view has not developed. I am sending on a small body of officers and men to see how they are received. *If the cotton there can be saved from the Germans it will be a great thing, at present it is being shipped up the Volga via Astrakhan for their use.*' General Dunsterville, unlike General Malleson, fully appreciated the importance of the cotton question, but he need not have worried about it, for the day before he wrote this letter I was in Krasnovodsk and had arranged with Semov to hold up the entire cotton shipment, and thanks to this the Germans got none. Colonel Battine and his mission did not arrive in Krasnovodsk until some time afterwards.

After disembarking at Alyat on July 5th, Bicherakov had advanced hurriedly and assumed command of the Baku Red Army operating astride of the Tiflis railway towards the bridge of Yevlakh over the Kura River. The bridge, however, had already been captured by the Turks owing to the cowardly behaviour of the defending troops and Bicherakov realised that in the circumstances there was nothing to be done but to fall back on Baku, fighting a rearguard action the whole way and delaying the enemy sufficiently to enable the Baku people to prepare a proper line of defence covering the town. As a matter of fact the military authorities in Baku were far too occupied with politics to think of defending the town, with the result that no defence works worth mentioning were ever constructed.

The brunt of the fighting fell always on the Cossacks, and the relations between the latter and the Red troops rapidly became so strained that Bicherakov severed his connection with the Bolsheviks, preferring to continue the struggle on his own. Henceforth the Bolsheviks regarded the Cossack leader as a dangerous man and did everything in their power to thwart him.

Meanwhile, the Bolsheviks had become so discredited as the result of their failure to hold up the Turks that on July 26th in the middle of fighting which brought the Turks right up to the town, a coup d'état took place in Baku, the Bolsheviks were deposed and their place was taken by a new body calling themselves the 'Centro-Caspia'.

Despite Petrov firing so effectively on the Turks on July 31st, the two Bolshevik leaders Petrov and Shaumian determined to leave the town with their followers. With as much as they could steal of the military supplies and guns, they decided to take ship to Astrakhan which was now the sole port on the Caspian Sea remaining in the hands of the Bolsheviks. They accordingly seized thirteen ships, in which they embarked the greater part of the Red Army and also loaded them up with the entire contents of the arsenal and everything else on which they could lay their hands. Had they succeeded in getting away with all these ships it would have been impossible to continue the defence of Baku for a single day, but luckily the Caspian Navy was opposed to Petrov's venture. The gun-boats pursued the runaways and the whole convoy was brought back into harbour while the usual interminable discussions took place.

As soon as the coup d'état had been brought off they sent messengers to Enzeli asking Dunsterforce to send them assistance. General Dunsterville decided to accept the invitation and although he had no troops available at the moment, except in the form of very small detachments, he sent Colonel Stokes across with a small party. These arrived in Baku on August 4th. Meanwhile Dunsterforce succeeded in obtaining possession of several steamers in Enzeli including the *President Kruger*, which General Dunsterville eventually occupied with his staff. The *Kursk* and *Abo* were also obtained in Baku, the idea being to have a number of ships up our sleeve in case we had to evacuate our troops in a hurry.

As one of the very few officers with a knowledge of Russian, and liable to be called upon at any moment of the night to answer the telephone, interview Russian or Armenian staff officers, or act as interpreter to Colonel Keyworth, I found myself at a grave disadvantage as regards dress. I could not possibly accompany other staff officers smartly dressed in uniform when I was wearing a ragged trader's costume. I managed to raise a pair of puttees and turned a pair of khaki slacks into breeches. Someone presented me with a field service cap he had had made up in the bazaar in Kazvin, and from another I borrowed a very ancient khaki tunic. A very home-made Sam Browne completed the kit, save for the boots which were the most difficult item of all. I eventually found a very heavy pair of soldier's boots, with tremendously thick soles and tipped with heavy pieces of iron. In these I used to tramp across the wooden floors making a disgusting noise as I went.

The following are a few diary notes I wrote at this particular period.

I began the day feeling that I had had no sleep at all. From 8.30 to *13.8.18* 10 a.m. I was busy interviewing many people who came to offer their services etc. I also had to go out into the street and address a crowd of hungry women who had come with baskets on the assumption that the British Mission was making a distribution of bread to the starving. As a matter of fact this was nothing more than a cunning piece of provocation on the part of the enemy, who spread abroad the rumour that the British Mission were giving away bread to all who came for it. The result was a queue of starving Bakintsi clamouring for food, and we had to turn them empty away.

At 10 a.m. I set out with Colonel Keyworth in a motor to inspect the front.

The enemy positions were on a ridge nearly a mile to the west. We had a hot walk to the 'Mud Volcano' whence we were pointed out one of the enemy's pickets not more than a thousand yards away. Fortunately it turned out to be one of our own pickets. While motoring past one row of trenches some idiot fired a shot at us. Although only two hundred yards away, the bullet missed us and hit the ground in front of the car.

Late that night the Russian Commander-in-Chief sent an officer round to say that the men of No. 11 Battery had deserted their guns and had come quietly into town and joined Petrov. He coolly asked us to supply men for the guns thus abandoned. I expressed amazement that such a thing could be, but we managed to patch up an arrangement to man a couple of the guns.

14.8.18 Chief interest centres in the Petrov question, which becomes more complicated every hour. Yesterday three of Petrov's ships succeeded in moving out to sea, but were pursued by the gun-boat *Astarabad*, who fired a shot at them and brought them all back. They were put into the naval port, but again managed to slip their moorings and got away during the night. In the course of the day some others also got away, until there were no less than thirteen of them on the loose.

At 8 p.m. we heard that the gun-boat *Geok Tepe*, a paddle steamer, had run them down and rounded them up near Zhiloi Island. Three steamers and two barges were sent into Baku; the remainder refused to move. The *Ardagan* has decided to move out after them tomorrow morning. The gun-boat *Kars* held a meeting in the course of the morning and came to the conclusion that they were neutral. Some eighteen of the crew who sympathised with Petrov subsequently packed up and went off to one of the latter's steamers. Their example was followed by a number from the *Krasnovodsk*.

In the absence of Petrov & Co. the town is experiencing a feeling of relief it had not enjoyed for a long time. The question is by no means solved, however. Let Petrov go by all means, but with him are all the guns and ammunition without which Baku must fall. We must recover Petrov's ships at all cost. The last thing we heard tonight was that the *Astarabad*, the only really loyal ship of the lot, was hunting in the dark and had rounded up several ships.

15.8.18 The fleet question has become more complicated than ever. The Dictators of the Centro-Caspia held a special meeting and decided that action must be taken. Orders were wired to the effect that Petrov was to return or else the fleet were to sink him and his ships. Those who do not know the Caspian fleet may have expected some action here. But no. At 8 p.m. a message was received to the effect that the number of ships now at Zhiloi Island was sixteen. Petrov still refused to return and the fleet had so far refused to fire on him.

The position was thus stalemate, but could not remain such for long. The problem was really solved by the small armed steamer *Astarabad* who gave Petrov an ultimatum and getting no reply fired a shell and actually hit. The moment this happened the entire convoy of ships up-anchored and turned obediently for Baku.

On arrival they were all brought up alongside the arsenal pier in turn and the contents of the hold removed and stacked on the wharf. The ships had been loaded anyhow and the contents of the hold varied from guns and ammunition to gramophones, clothing and stores of every kind, from which it appeared obvious that the statement of the Bolsheviks as to the necessity of removing a certain amount of ammunition for purely military purposes was only a cloak to cover a general looting of the town. The process of disarmament lasted several days, at the end of which thirteen of the ships were permitted to proceed to Astrakhan with their disarmed troops, a free gift to the Bolsheviks. Shaumian and Petrov were imprisoned in the town jail.

General Dunsterville reached Baku in the *Kruger*. He had *17.8.18* transferred his H.Q. on board already on August 10th in Enzeli, on which occasion he had hauled down the Red Flag and substituted the old Russian tricolour. He had no sooner changed the flag than he was boarded by a deputation from the local Bolshevik committee asking for explanations and enquiring whether he was counter-revolutionary. The General replied that he was not, but that he was also not revolutionary and objected absolutely to flying the Red Flag. A compromise was effected permitting the Russian flag to be flown on condition that it was flown upside down with the red band above the white. This was agreed to, and the *Kruger* thereafter sailed the Caspian Sea under the Serbian flag, the Russian revolutionaries not being aware that the Russian tricolour flown upside-down constitutes the flag of Serbia.

The situation thus obtained was really ludicrous and is best described in General Dunsterville's own words: 'A British General on the Caspian, the only sea unploughed before by British keels, on board a ship named after a South African President and whilom enemy, sailing from a Persian port, under the Serbian flag, to relieve from the Turks a body of Armenians in a revolutionary Russian town.'

By this time I had added to my usual duties those of intelligence officer at Staff Headquarters. In this capacity I was personally responsible for obtaining all intelligence and for this purpose enrolled a number of agents. I had been working at intelligence for about ten days, when Colonel Stokes told me that Malleson had been 'raising Cain' about my not having returned to Trans-Caspia. He had received several wires from Meshed demanding my immediate return, but had replied regretting his inability to allow me to go. Malleson thereupon wired to Simla, who in turn wired Dunsterville. The latter replied protesting, but Malleson retorted quoting the very serious situation in Trans-Caspia and insisted that my presence was most urgently required in Askhabad.

It appeared that the Bolsheviks had invaded Trans-Caspia from Charjui. The Trans-Caspians had endeavoured to stem the attack, but had been beaten. Meshed had thrown a machine-gun section of the 19th Punjabis under Captain Pigott over the border and the detachment had done heroic work at Bairam Ali, but had been compelled to withdraw as far as Merv. The situation was indeed critical and unless we could send assistance from Meshed, the chances were that the whole of Askhabad would once more fall into the hands of the Reds.

Nevertheless General Dunsterville sat tight and refused to release me and it was only when he was abruptly called upon by Simla to give his explanation why he refused to obey orders, that he agreed to let me go.

24.8.18   I had breakfast with him in the *Kruger* and I left that same afternoon, thoroughly disgusted with my fate that tore me away at such a critical moment.

While it had frequently assumed the appearance of a comedy, the drama of Baku had never for a moment been free from the atmosphere of tragedy. The more casual among us playing actual roles in the drama were at times inclined to laugh at some of its grotesque and fantastic phases, yet we were nevertheless constantly weighed down with the presentiment of impending disaster.

The disaster was to come on September 14th when the Turks broke through the Baku battalion holding the strongest portion of the whole line. The problem for Dunsterville was now simply how to save a rout and to hold up the enemy long enough to enable an orderly evacuation of our troops to be completed.

The total casualties of his small force during that last fight were 180 killed, wounded and missing of all ranks, or about 20 per cent of the numbers engaged, but the result of the day's battle was that the Turks were fought to a standstill and the extrication of our troops was successfully accomplished.

The Turks and Tatars then entered the helpless town and worked their savage will on the wretched Armenian population. Reports differ as to numbers, but the fact appears substantiated that the attackers slaughtered in cold blood between fifteen and twenty thousand Armenians, sparing neither man, woman, nor child.

That the Dunsterforce venture ended militarily in failure in no way reflects discredit on its leader, General Dunsterville. However feasible the original objective of the operation may have appeared, namely to train and equip the large numbers of anti-Muslim and anti-Turk racial elements in Trans-Caucasia, in practice the venture was doomed to failure because of two main factors (among many others): the force was too small for the task assigned to it, and it arrived much too late.

For neither of these two factors could General Dunsterville be blamed. He had been faced with an impossible problem, for, apart from the overwhelming superiority in numbers of the Turks, he was baulked and threatened by cowardice and treachery in his rear. And, as if that were not enough, the situation with which he had to deal was rendered even more chaotic by a vacillating policy at home.

It stands to Dunsterville's very great credit and to the credit of the small but valiant body of men serving under him that, while greatly outnumbered, he was able to hold the enemy in check as long as he did, and that he finally succeeded in extricating his embattled force, together with their sick and wounded, and in bringing them back safely to Enzeli.

To anyone who knew the complexity of the local situation and could appreciate the magnitude of the odds against our troops, the Dunsterforce venture was a magnificent effort, and I, for one, am proud to have had the honour of serving with General Dunsterville and his gallant force.

From the Frying Pan into the Fire

◆

No sooner had the curtain begun to drop on the Baku tragedy, than it was rung up afresh on a new drama, of which the scene was centred in Trans-Caspia.

During my sojourn in Baku, relations between the Askhabad Committee and the British Mission in Meshed, relations which had commenced with my rencontre with Comrades Dokhov and Co. on the Askhabad railway station, had developed with great rapidity. The imminent fear of a fresh Bolshevik incursion on the one hand, and of the fall of Baku on the other, showed clearly to the Askhabad and British authorities alike that there was no time to be wasted if they were to co-operate against the common enemy.

An agreement was drawn up, approved by the Government of India and signed by the Askhabad Committee and General Malleson. On the one hand the Askhabad authorities undertook to place all their resources at our disposal, including the free use of the railway, on the other the British undertook to send up such troops and military stores to the Bolshevik front as could be brought up the Meshed line, and further undertook to supply financial assistance and generally help the Trans-Caspians in their struggle against the Bolsheviks until the latter would be cleared out of the province. While I have unfortunately preserved no copy of the famous agreement, I do remember my impression at the time, that we had promised to a very great deal, much more than I really felt was in our power to carry out.

Meanwhile the Bolsheviks in Tashkent had become thoroughly alarmed at the reported presence in Meshed of almost an army corps of British troops. Their alarm turned to despondency when they heard from survivors that the British had already sent reinforcements to the Trans-Caspian front and that as a result of these reinforcements, the Red troops on the Bairam Ali front had suffered a severe reverse. As a matter of fact the reinforcements consisted in the very gallant machine-gun section of the 19th Punjabis, under Captain Pigott, numbering thirty-nine men in all.

The Bolsheviks, who were quite unused to meeting an enemy that stood up and fought at close range with deadly accurate machine-guns, were very badly shaken and took back with them most fantastic stories to Tashkent. Meanwhile the Trans-Caspians wisely withdrew to stronger positions in the vicinity of Merv, but finding themselves still very inferior in numbers to the Reds, retired still further along the railway to Kaahka.

It was at this stage of the proceedings that I arrived back in Trans-Caspia. I reached Krasnovodsk on August 25th. My orders had been to proceed to Askhabad, but when I heard that fighting was going on at Kaahka I decided to give Askhabad a miss and go straight to the front. If the situation at the front were as serious as it appeared to be, then there would be urgent need of every man and certainly every officer we could get. *25.8.18*

I left by the afternoon train. That evening at Jebel we were overtaken by a special troop train, which was taking a battery of 3″ field guns to the front. I therefore transferred from the passenger train to the troop train, where for the first time I found myself travelling on active service with Russian troops. We were all jumbled up anyhow in the ordinary *teplushki* [closed luggage vans], there being no distinction between officers and men. They were a good lot of fellows and, although very badly off for clothes and very short of food, were very cheery and continued singing songs right through the night.

We reached Askhabad at midday on the following day. We found crowds on the station and a band playing popular airs. Someone caught sight of me at the carriage window in my home-made Baku uniform and immediately the bank struck up 'God Save the King'. I believe this was the first time such a thing had ever happened in the history of Trans-Caspia. Everybody appeared very cheery and there was any amount of enthusiasm, particularly on the part of the onlookers. A fresh detachment of *Dobrovoltsi* [volunteers] boarded the train, and from them I gathered that there had been serious fighting at Kaahka on the previous day, that the Bolsheviks had *26.8.18* launched an attack, but had been beaten off with loss. There were also rumours of the arrival of British (Indian) troops from Meshed via Muhammedabad. We were delayed about four hours at Askhabad, as it was found necessary to clean and oil the guns, which were in a very rusty condition. We started off again at four o'clock.

I stood long at the carriage window, pondering over the situation, relieved that no telegram from Meshed had kept me in Askhabad. The sun was still high above the horizon, but was sinking into a bank of haze or dust, such as one sees so frequently at the close of a hot weather day in the Punjab. We passed by the ancient and deserted city of Annau, its crumbling mosque still standing erect above the remaining ruins of the town. An occasional Turkman plodded along the dusty track on horseback, or with a camel laden with saxaul made his weary way towards the neighbouring *aul* [village]. I wondered what lay ahead of us and whether this was really going to be war, or merely another false alarm. I trusted the former, for I was still disgusted at having been dragged away from Baku at the height of the excitement.

The train drew up at Artik and here I saw the welcome sight of a detachment of the 19th Punjabis and a few *sowars* of the 28th Lancers entraining at the siding. They had only just arrived by road from Muhammedabad and were pushing on to the front without delay.

At 9 p.m. we reached Kaahka, and I found the station full of rolling stock, most of which appeared to be inhabited. It was quite dark by this time, but after stumbling over numerous sleepers and clambering over endless trucks in order to pass from one line to another, I eventually found the train containing the H.Q. staff.

Having explained my identity to the sentry I was ushered into a Pullman car, where I found a council of war in progress. Here I recognised Major Bingham and Lt Col Knollys of the 19th Punjabis. After exchanging greetings I was introduced to the Russian staff and to the Commander-in-Chief, a fine looking old Turkman named Oraz Sardar.

I was insufficiently au fait with the situation to understand the proceedings which were just finishing, but Bingham afterwards explained briefly that with the detachment of Punjabis I had passed at Artik, due to arrive that night, we should have about 500

Indian troops, with just a handful of cavalry, and that we should want every man jack of them before many days had passed. The Bolsheviks outnumbered us at least three to one and had a preponderance in artillery, not to mention one aeroplane. They had launched a determined attack the previous day, which had only just been beaten off with difficulty. They had a large proportion of Austrians, mainly Magyars, who were excellent fighters and had shown no hesitation in coming up to close quarters.

Knowing Bingham's temperament I allowed for a good deal of exaggeration, yet the situation certainly appeared serious. Still I felt a great difficulty in persuading myself that this was really war and that we might at very short notice find ourselves fighting for our lives. Someone very kindly lent me an army blanket, and rolling myself in it I was soon fast asleep.

We were awakened the following morning by the droning of an _27.8.18_ enemy aeroplane circling above us. Some of the *sepoys* [Indian troops] opened fire on it and soon every man in the garden was letting off his rifle. The sound of rifle fire seemed to satisfy the plane, which hovered round for a few minutes and then flew back to the Bolshevik positions. This at any rate looked like war.

The first thing I did was to borrow a solar topi from the M.O., Captain Sinton, V.C. It was very battered, but quite serviceable and I was fortunate in finding one, for it is extremely unusual for anyone to carry a spare topi about with him, particularly on a harum scarum show like this. I now met Ward again. He had been put in charge of explosives and gun ammunition and was busily engaged in checking the stores which had come up from Muhammedabad.

After breakfast we went for a staff ride over the positions. Our party consisted of the Russian Chief of Staff and one or two other Russian staff officers, Colonel Knollys, Bingham and myself. The positions were not much to look at. In fact they were nothing but a small dry stream bed which ran roughly north and south at right angles to the railway, the latter crossing the stream by a bridge some 1½ to 2 miles east of Kaahka station and village. From here the land gradually sloped up in an easterly direction, and the Bolsheviks were in force just behind the ridge in which this slope culminated.

105

The only advantage in this position from a military point of view was that the enemy would have to attack over one mile of open country under heavy fire from our machine-guns. It was this exposed slope which had broken him on the last occasion he attacked. If he could only survive our rifle and machine-gun fire, there was nothing else to stop him wiping us out. He had a number of heavy guns in position just behind the ridge and, with the aeroplane to direct his fire, he was in a position to make things desperately uncomfortable for us.

As for us, we were in no position at all. We had no wire, save a few hundred yards which had been hastily thrown up at one of the more isolated points of the line. The obvious thing appeared to be to fix our line, get supplies of wire and then dig and wire ourselves in. Providing the wire would be forthcoming in sufficient quantities and providing always that the enemy would give us time in which to do it, we had hopes that we might make ourselves sufficiently strong to keep the enemy back until we received further reinforcement.

That afternoon we spent in allocating our different units to the various points. As far as our own troops were concerned, this presented little difficulty; there were so few that it was soon done. The chief difficulty arose in knowing the other elements which were available to co-operate with us. None of us had at that time any clear understanding as to how many Russians and how many Turkmans were at the front. We were told that altogether the Trans-Caspian forces numbered about 700, and I think that this figure was about correct. This included all those combatants who were in attendance on the Staff in Kaahka itself, so that the total number of troops on the front was scarcely a thousand.

Both Russians and Turkmans were a very uncertain quantity. With the exception of a small percentage of regular soldiers who had seen actual fighting during the war, the remainder had never had a rifle in their hands until they were given one in Askhabad on the occasion of the recent coup d'état. Very few indeed among the Turkmans had ever fired their weapons and as subsequent events proved they were a positive danger to their own side in action. Our artillery was not strong in guns, but the personnel was excellent. The artillery commander was Colonel Mesdrikov, who had gained considerable distinction in the heavy fighting at Sarykamish. The battery comprised two Russian 3" Q.F. field guns and two old-fashioned 3" guns. The total gun ammunition was only about 2,000 rounds and consequently had to be used most sparingly.

That evening we had just finished our dinner when a report was brought in that the enemy were contemplating a night attack. This was no joke. At night we should lose all the advantage of an open field of fire, and our men, knowing nothing of their particular sectors which they had scarcely seen in the daylight, would be at a loss to know where to fire.

In the absence of Bingham who was acting as liaison officer with Oraz Sardar in Kaahka station, I was the only British officer with a knowledge of Russian. I therefore had to keep in close touch with Colonel Knollys and at the same time had to watch the Russians. What worried me more than anything was the fact that the *sepoys* had not the slightest idea what the enemy looked like. It was impossible to describe him to them, for neither the Russian Bolsheviks nor their Austrian and Magyar mercenaries had any definite uniform. Also the *sepoys* were very much at a loss over the Turkmans, as many of the Bolsheviks were also wearing goat-skin hats.

Fortunately the night passed quietly without a single alarm. I had no overcoat or blanket and to my surprise the night was very cold. The only covering I could find was a heavy tarpaulin from a cart and I shivered away until the early hours of the morning under this. I shall never forget how relieved I was — in fact we all were — that the enemy had not attacked during the night.

The morning broke clear and bright and not a sign of any enemy *28.8.18* could be seen. We stayed in our positions for an hour until the sun was well up and then began to discuss returning some of the men to Kaahka for breakfast. We would have a heavy day before us, for we dare not risk another night in the open without any cover, or defences of any sort.

Then a burst of machine-gun fire on the left flank made us jump to our feet. Our *sepoys* appeared to be firing at some moving mounted figures. The thought occurred to us that the mounted men could be nothing else than a Turkman patrol which had been sent out during the night, and was now returning. This was just one of the things I was afraid might happen, so jumping on to a horse I galloped across to the left flank. It was as we supposed. The

Turkmans were very startled, but by making a wide detour came in behind without any casualties. I explained the mistake to the Russians and then made my way back to the bridge.

At this moment one of those excellent institutions, a Russian field kitchen, was brought up and we were invited to have some hot tea. We gladly accepted and seating ourselves on the brickwork of the bridge parapet were chatting pleasantly together when a Russian officer who had been scouring the countryside through his glasses suddenly said, 'Look out, the enemy,' and pointed into the far distance beyond our left flank. 'They are trying to outflank us.'

I cursed the fact that I had no glasses and it was only with the greatest difficulty that I could pick out the moving dots which represented line after line of mounted men and wheeled transport advancing in open order with the obvious intention of moving unperceived round behind our flank and attacking Kaahka village and railway station in our rear.

Our 3″ battery opened fire, but only succeeded in holding up some transport. The infantry disappeared from view behind an old fort and almost immediately afterwards the sound of heavy machine-gun and rifle fire was heard from that direction. The enemy artillery now opened fire, the shots going wide over. No effort was made to correct their aim and the shells fell frequently but harmlessly in the open. Meanwhile news reached us that the 400-odd Turkmans in Kaahka who had been sent out to meet the enemy and prevent his entering the town had been forced to retire. The enemy had occupied the fort, an old ruined structure, and also the gardens immediately surrounding the town, and would soon reach the railway station. Our reserve detachment was ordered to proceed direct to the railway station.

By this time a hot fusillade was in progress in the gardens surrounding the railway station. The latter was practically deserted save for a cluster of Russians and Turkmans firing wildly into the air. Sending Subedar Fazl Khan through the station to work on the extreme left, I collected the Russians and some of the Turkmans and began to beat through the gardens. The firing in front of us grew less and, though bullets continued to come through the bushes, the enemy was obviously retiring.

We beat through a number of gardens and re-established touch with Subedar Fazl Khan's party on the left. We collected straggling

Turkmans from the various gardens as we progressed. Their heart was obviously not in the fighting, and they lagged behind whenever opportunity offered. This beating-up of the gardens took till about midday. We found one machine-gun abandoned in a garden from which the enemy had only just retired. Rifle fire now opened afresh from the side of the fort and we turned in that direction. By this time I had a following of about eighty Turkmans and forty Russians.

By the time we had reached open ground, the firing had ceased. I noticed a number of people standing on the walls of the fort and a number more along a wall extending towards our right flank. They were enemy who, adopting a common form of Bolshevik tactic, had put down their arms and made a show of wanting to come to terms. They also sent a couple of emissaries across to us and for the moment it was thought the enemy wished to surrender. The emissaries, however, demanded our surrender, calling on the Russians not to fight against their brothers etc.

The position was a ticklish one. Our troops were all out in the open and the enemy, though ostensibly standing still, were nevertheless quietly moving up along the low wall commanding our flank. All men were warned to keep under cover. One emissary returned without any reply to his own people, the other was led away protesting to the Russian Staff. Three minutes later fire was opened by both sides. Ours soon ceased, but the enemy kept up a hot machine-gun fire for about ten minutes. The eighty-odd Turkmans and the majority of the Russians I had succeeded in collecting had faded away to the rear the moment the firing began, and there were practically none but our own troops up in the front on the left. Being in the open we were much annoyed by Turkmans in our rear firing just above our heads. In my own case three times in succession I raised my head to look round and a bullet promptly whistled past within an inch or two, coming obviously from these Turkmans. Finally it became so bad that I had to send a Russian to the rear to stop it.

The enemy fire now slackened and I decided to advance. While rising to do so, I was hit by a machine-gun bullet high up in the left thigh, which knocked me over and made me unable to follow further developments.

The general feeling was that a disaster was most narrowly averted, that such disaster was in any case unnecessary and that the Russian Staff showed an appalling lack of competence and initiative. The behaviour of the Turkmans also was the subject of much comment, and doubts were openly expressed as to the firing from the rear being either accident or mere carelessness. The suggestion of treachery is strengthened by a definitely established case of a Russian officer having been shot from the rear by a Turkman in one of the previous engagements up the line.

After I myself had been wounded, I came across Ward lying wounded in the open. I crawled towards him and found him in great pain. He told me that he was sure that he had been shot from behind. He apparently attributed it to gross carelessness. The bullet had passed through his abdomen and he was obviously in a very bad way.

Ward and I were thus once more thrown together. Some bearers came along and picked us up and carried us back to Kaahka station, which had so narrowly missed being captured by the Bolsheviks. We found a hospital train drawn up in one of the sidings and Captain Sinton in charge. He shook his head at Ward's wound, but said that provided there was no blood-poisoning mine was all right. Bingham had also been wounded very slightly in the neck. Some forty other ranks were picked up wounded and loaded into the train, which then left for Askhabad.

There were some pretty bad cases among the *sepoys* but one I shall never forget. He was a down-country follower. How he got wounded I do not know, but it was only a slight wound in the hand. He made a great fuss about it, and I cursed him soundly before all the rest.

We reached Askhabad some three hours later, having been held up at a bridge which the Bolsheviks had apparently tried to blow up, but had not succeeded. There were crowds waiting to receive us on the platform at Askhabad and a great fuss was made of us. We were carried to the railway hospital, where we were all put into one large ward.

They placed Ward in the next cot to me so that I could interpret for him. It was Fate that had brought us so much together and now at the last decreed that I should continue to interpret and look after him until the end, for poor old Ward only lived a couple of days and then went out of this world in as brave a manner as anyone could wish for. I was delirious for want of sleep and from the pain from the wound, so do not remember Ward's last moments. He died early in the morning of the 30th August.

That same day I had a visit from Count Dorrer and Miss Lubov Mikhailovna. The former insisted on my going and staying at his house and the latter appointed herself my nurse and looked after me most assiduously, and I may add even jealously, until I was well enough to walk about again. *30.8.18*

Lubov Mikhailovna had a mania for 'running things'. She used to issue all sorts of orders in my name, even to the extent of holding up trains, requisitioning carriages etc. She was not a bad girl, but I eventually had to restrain her political activities as they were becoming extremely embarrassing. She used to carry an innocent little handbag in which were a Colt .32 automatic and a small notebook containing a list of suspected persons. To do Lubov Mikhailovna justice, she did some excellent work in rounding up Germans and Austrians in Askhabad, but she required a lot of looking after, and I was greatly relieved when she eventually packed up and went to Baku.

From now onwards I assumed all responsibility as Political Representative in Trans-Caspia, but owing to internal bleeding I remained confined to a couch for about ten days, after which I was allowed to walk about on crutches. One of the first things I did was to despatch all the party of German and other enemy agents down to Meshed. I did not envy them their trip, for owing to the small number of the *sepoys* forming the convoy, I decided it would be necessary to handcuff the prisoners. We therefore chained them together in batches of six, eleven batches in all, placed them in carts, with a couple of *sowars* of the 28th Lancers with each cart, and thus started them off on their four days' journey to Meshed. I was sorry for them in a way, but after all it was war, and they were our active enemies.

As Political Representative I was solely responsible for all direct relations and negotiations between the Askhabad Committee and General Malleson in Meshed. He was given the use of the direct telegraph line twice daily for two periods of an hour each. I was given an expert telegraphist named Sgt Duckworth, an excellent fellow and a first-class signaller.

Gulab Hussein and old Din Muhammed arrived about a fortnight later. Both had been very anxious about my wound and

Gulab Hussein in particular was in despair at the thought that after travelling about so much with me, he had not been with me in action. Both of them soon settled down in their new surroundings. Din Muhammed used to delight the Dorrers with all sorts of sweet dishes and puddings, while Gulab Hussein turned himself into an A.D.C., and used to sit by the side of the coachman when I went out driving and chatter with him in broken Persian and Russian.

The Committee and the Commissars

◆

With the arrival of the British and the opening of a fresh front, little Trans-Caspia began to hold its head up. Infected with the prevalent but dangerous disease, 'Self-determination of small nations', it began to feel that it was really playing a big role in the world. This being the case, it was considered as *infra dig* to refer to the local authorities as the Executive Committee, and they now expressed the desire to be referred to and treated as the 'Government'. I entered into the spirit of the game and gained much amusement from watching events which might have been of world-wide importance had there not been a big war still in progress.

The Government certainly merits some description. At first it merely consisted of the original committee which had formed itself on the expulsion of the Bolsheviks and which was a very mixed affair. Later on it reorganised itself so as to comprise two separate bodies, the principle being that of an upper and a lower chamber as existing in all the best civilised forms of parliament. In this case the upper chamber was called the Board of Directors — when we wished to be very official we referred to it as the Council of Ministers — and the lower chamber was the Executive Committee.

The President of the Committee — somehow we could never bring ourselves to call him Prime Minister — was Comrade Funtikov. Before the coup d'état in July suddenly called him to play the role of village Hampden, Funtikov had never risen to anything higher than engine driver on the Central Asian Railway. In his proper sphere of life he had no doubt been a very worthy fellow and when sober probably a very good engine driver, but he was no earthly use as a Prime Minister. He was very crude in his manners, extremely illiterate, but like so many of his kidney, painfully verbose and pretended to a certain skill in cheap rhetoric, so dear to all revolutionaries, particularly in Russia. His greatest weakness was drink, and although vodka and other strong beverages were supposed to be taboo, nevertheless, Funtikov — F-F-Funtikov as we generally called him, and he not infrequently called himself — was very rarely properly sober. I fancy he used to reason that drink helped his rhetoric. In point of fact, he rarely opened his mouth without making an ass of himself.

I had very little to do with Funtikov at first, as the Committee, realising how thoroughly unversed they were in diplomatic usage, very wisely selected for liaison work with myself one of the few individuals among them who had any pretensions to being presentable in society. This was the 'Foreign Minister', Lev Alexandrovich Zimin, a man of scholarly training and by profession a schoolmaster from Merv. Zimin was quite well read, especially on eastern and Islamic subjects, but he was nevertheless extremely narrow-minded. In fact, he was a typical minor schoolmaster of the type so common in Russia, and like his colleagues would have been well advised to have left politics alone. Of weak health and nervous temperament, Zimin frequently allowed his better judgement to be warped by petty spite or personal irritation. Nevertheless he was straightforward and strictly honourable and as such stands out from among his fellows, to the great majority of whom these qualities can by no means be ascribed.

President Funtikov had as his Deputy, Kurilev, another railway employee, a fairly bright lad, much less ponderous than F-Funtikov and with a well-developed sense of humour. Kurilev revelled in the importance of his position. It gave him considerable prominence in the eyes of the population at large and of his railway comrades in particular. Furthermore it gave him the right to carry about with him a gigantic revolver, which he held cocked on his knee when sitting on a chair, or when driving about in his carriage. In addition to the revolver he carried about a large leather *porte-feuille* filled with numerous 'resolutions', 'proposals', 'schemes', 'estimates', and other documents. When in conversation he wished to refer to one or other of them he would turn out on the table all the contents of the portfolio, but somehow never succeed in finding what he was looking for. Kurilev liked to play the role of a strong silent man, but unfortunately he was neither strong nor silent and — I must add — was by no means brave. Though always employing such terms as 'stern action', 'repressive measures', and 'drastic punishment', I am positive he would not hurt a fly if he could help it and would certainly prefer to run away rather than face any personal danger.

Count Dorrer I have already mentioned, a man of very different stamp. His brother, the elder Count Dorrer, had been an outstanding figure in the Social Revolutionary Party and as such had fallen an early victim to the Bolshevik repression. He died a terrible death by torture in Tashkent in the autumn of 1917. Count Alexei Iosephovich Dorrer was an inferior personality to his deceased brother and, though also a member of the Social Revolutionary Party, was not regarded as carrying much weight in that party. Of weak character, he was easily influenced, and towards the end of 1918 became discredited in the eyes of the Social Revolutionaries, who accused him of reactionary tendencies. Personally he was a charming man, and was always extremely kind to myself and other British officers. He had a charming wife, the Countess Victoria Vladimirovna, to whom I can never be sufficiently grateful for the hospitality and kindness shown to me while I was wounded.

Comrade Dokhov, whom I first interviewed on the railway station at Askhabad, was nominated the Government Representative in Meshed, and remained there most of the time. He was a typical Social Revolutionary, all theory and no practical ability. He was a bigamist. I believe in fact he had committed bigamy several times over. This of course did not disqualify him from the Government, but it is apt to cramp one's political style when one has a number of women one has illegally married coming round clamouring for one's blood. It is not unlikely that the presence of the women accusers in Askhabad had something to do with his remarkable keenness to stay in Meshed.

There was also one further name, which stands out above all others as meriting individual record. This was Simion Lvovich Drushkin. A Jew by birth, a lawyer by profession, and a Social Revolutionary by politics, Drushkin presented a personality as interesting as it was enigmatic. To most of us he was in the beginning, and remained until the end, a mystery. He arrived in Krasnovodsk on September 10th from Astrakhan, then came straight through to Askhabad.

I first met and was introduced to Drushkin at the Dorrers' house. I happened to be lunching there when Drushkin was brought in and joined us. Nobody seemed to know him, but he claimed to have been in Tashkent with Count Dorrer's brother and stated that his own brother had been tortured to death at the same time as the deceased Count Dorrer. This statement, which was subsequently found to be correct, satisfied the company present that Drushkin was a bona fide Social Revolutionary. His description of the life he had been living in Astrakhan, where for months he had been slaving under appalling conditions of enforced labour and had been mainly employed in cleaning out public latrines, was so convincing, and was so clearly substantiated by the papers and certificates that he had brought away with him, that he was accepted without more ado by the Trans-Caspian authorities as a most reliable supporter of their cause.

Drushkin insisted that among the passengers who had travelled down from Krasnovodsk with him were a party of Bolshevik agents from Astrakhan whose object was to spread propaganda among the troops at the Front. He offered to point out the individuals whom he regarded as suspect. His offer was accepted and that night he took a posse of police round to a number of hotels and lodgings and arrested practically all the individuals concerned.

By this initial demonstration of goodwill Drushkin thoroughly ingratiated himself with the Government, particularly with those members who happened to belong to the Social Revolutionary Party, and it was only about a fortnight after this, his first appearance, that I heard he had been appointed chief of the C.I.D. in Askhabad. I remember expressing surprise that a complete stranger should have been placed in charge of such an important post. Dorrer agreed with me that he considered the action of the Government to have been most hasty and added that it was typical of the Social Revolutionaries who, whatever their other faults, and they were legion, never failed to help or favour another member of their own party. However, his great energy and his assiduity in routing out and taking drastic action against any persons suspected of Bolshevik sympathies soon caused Drushkin to be regarded as one of the mainstays of the Government.

As Political Officer in Askhabad every moment of my time was devoted to supervising the activities of the Government and to dealing with the internal political situation of Trans-Caspia. Needless to say, if I never obtained any rest, I cannot complain that there was any monotony. During the next five months I was destined to have to face one crisis after another embracing practically all the troubles, economic and political, that can possibly threaten an unfortunate country. However, I was no longer in direct touch with the Fronts and was dependent for my information on such telegraphic or other reports as came in from the troops down the line.

On the eastern Front, the attack on Kaahka, in which I was wounded, was followed by a brief lull, the Bolsheviks having apparently received more than they cared for. We spent every available minute strengthening our position and with the arrival of some reinforcement, both infantry and cavalry, from Meshed felt that we should soon be in a position to assume the offensive. Meanwhile the Bolsheviks had also received reinforcements from Tashkent and orders for them to retake Trans-Caspia at all costs.

On the Caspian side, Enzeli was in British hands and Norperforce (the British command in Northern Persia) were busily reorganising their forces in view of possible further action against the Turk. Astrakhan was still in Bolshevik hands, while Petrovsk was held by Bicherakov, who had with him the bulk of the Caspian shipping and the great majority of the Baku refugees.

The Turks were in Baku and for the time being were concentrating their attention on fighting Bicherakov. For the present they were making no open preparations to continue their advance eastwards of the Caspian, but that they had not wholly abandoned their hopes of ultimately coming across was evidenced by the continued activities of the numerous Turkish agents, particularly south-east of the Caspian.

Trans-Caspia was thus almost entirely cut off from the outside world and in consequence was unable to obtain the supplies of food and fuel which in normal times had always been imported from without. Normally the country relied for its grain supply on stocks regularly imported from Siberia or else from Northern Persia. Communication with the former country was out of the question now and importation from Persia was extremely difficult, in fact practically impossible, owing to the lack of money wherewith to pay for the goods. We were thus faced at once with the question of a food scarcity.

The lack of fuel also presented grave difficulties. The railway in Trans-Caspia ordinarily used oil fuel. Owing to lack of foresight, and also owing to a certain extent to circumstances over which the Trans-Caspian authorities had little or no control, they had omitted to provide themselves with the maximum quantity before the fall of Baku and were now consequently faced with the danger of an early shortage. Wood fuel was equally scarce. The saxaul plant, which is widely used throughout Turkistan for engine fuel, is abundant in the bed of the Oxus, but it is very scarce in Trans-Caspia, there being none this side of Charjui. The outlook for the winter was therefore not a promising one.

Finance too caused me real anxiety. When the Mensheviks overthrew the Soviet administration in July, they succeeded in capturing the entire Bolshevik treasury, which contained the very useful sum of Rbls 17,000,000, the rate of the rouble being then forty to the Pound Sterling. Owing to maladministration of the finances in the beginning, this sum was soon expended, and the Government were unable to pay out the wages of the railway workers. The sums due to the workers in arrears increased month by month and it was not long before their demands for payment became more and more insistent and we were called upon to face the possibility of a railway strike.

While these were the salient economic problems of the moment, there were constant political difficulties arising, none of which concerned me, but all of which were referred to me for settlement, until without any exaggeration I found the onus of government gradually shifting on to my shoulders. The Trans-Caspians would have been only too pleased to have placed the entire responsibility for the government on me personally and I was therefore in the awkward position of having to keep the reins of control in my own hands, enforce my own line of action, often in the face of considerable opposition, and at the same time avoid any direct attitude which would give rise to the idea that I was really controlling the internal administration or interfering in any way.

Quite apart from all the administrative troubles and problems of the State, I was faced with the necessity of looking after our own interests in the country. Thus in the very early stages of my relations with the Government, I was called upon to organise a hospital for the treatment of our sick and wounded who were arriving almost daily from the Front.

There was no other Britisher in Askhabad with a knowledge of Russian, and our casualties comprised both British and Indians. Apart from the difficulties of language, the Russian medical staff had never before had anything to do with Indians, did not understand a word of their language and were totally ignorant of their habits and customs. I found it most difficult and wearying in those early days, when, still suffering from my wound and hobbling about on crutches, against doctor's orders, I had to go the round of the hospital several times a day in order to interpret to Sepoy Hira Singh of Ludhiana, Jan Muhammed of Jhelum or Fazl Gul of Swabi that he was not to keep taking his bandage off and that he was not to get out of bed, or that he would be all right and was not going to have his arm amputated. On the other hand it was most difficult explaining to the Russian staff the difference between Sikh and Mussulman and the necessity of obtaining their meat from the Tekke bazaar.

There were thousands of other questions such as the enlistment of recruits and raising of reinforcements for the Front, the organisation of intelligence and measures for internal security, which were constantly demanding very early action. These will be dealt with in their proper course, but the first incident worthy of note was the arrival in Krasnovodsk of Messrs Petrov and Shaumian of Baku fame, accompanied by a large party of Bolshevik commissars and armed followers.

When Baku fell, Petrov, Shaumian and party were released by their friends and hurried on board a ship, whose captain was told to make for Astrakhan. While out at sea, someone informed the captain that he had a large party of armed Bolsheviks on board, whereupon he was much taken aback and decided to make for Krasnovodsk. The Bolsheviks noticed the change in course and immediately threatened the skipper, demanding to be taken to Astrakhan. The captain was compelled to assent, but during the night secretly changed his course again and made for Krasnovodsk. He timed himself so as to arrive off Krasnovodsk at daybreak.

On approaching the harbour he started sounding the siren and *14.9.18* thereby attracted the attention of the guardship. The latter came alongside, immediately grasped the situation and ordered the steamer to make for Ufra and come up alongside the pier there. The guardship proceeded to escort her thither, and in the meantime sent a boat into Krasnovodsk, explaining the situation. Kuhn immediately sent an armed guard down to Ufra, who covered the incoming steamer with their machine-guns. Petrov and party had come hurriedly on deck at the first sound of the siren, but the guardship was dangerously near and would have sunk them at the first sign of hostilities. The whole party put down their arms and walked sullenly ashore, where they were promptly arrested and marched off to the local jail.

The capture naturally caused a great sensation in Krasnovodsk and the news was immediately wired through to Askhabad. Kuhn and the Krasnovodsk Committee expressed anxiety to get rid of the prisoners as soon as possible as their prison was full up and the presence of such important Bolsheviks as Petrov and Shaumian would most certainly have a disquieting effect on the local Bolshevik elements, who might quite well instigate a rising and attempt to storm the prison. The Askhabad Committee were not at all anxious to take over the prisoners and came and asked my advice. They also sent a wire to their Representative in Meshed, Dokhov, with instruction to try and persuade General Malleson to take over the prisoners and deport them to India. In reply Malleson explained that it was very difficult to find the necessary guards to send them down to India and suggested that the Trans-Caspian authorities should find some other way of disposing of them. He said that he had given Dokhov his answer and asked me to inform him what action the Government eventually decided on.

18.9.18   That afternoon a meeting was summoned at Dorrer's house to discuss the matter. I attended. I have rather a hazy recollection of what was actually said, but I remember that Funtikov, Kurilev, Zimin, and Dorrer were present.

The question to be discussed was what was to be done with the prisoners. Kuhn had said that they could not keep them in Krasnovodsk. The Askhabad jail was full and could not hold any more. General Malleson was not keen on taking them over. There remained only the question of shooting them. There appeared a little hesitation to decide on this course. Funtikov proposed it and he was supported by Kurilev. Zimin expressed the opinion that if

120

possible some other measures should be taken, but could not suggest any. The same attitude was adopted by Dorrer. I remained strictly neutral and took no active part in the discussion, except to repeat Malleson's message. The discussion went on for some time and eventually I left the meeting.

It was not until the next evening that, after questioning, *19.9.18* Funtikov informed me in confidence that it had been decided finally to shoot the prisoners and that he, Funtikov, had despatched a man to Krasnovodsk on the previous night to make the necessary arrangements. On hearing this I immediately wired General Malleson accordingly. It was not until three days later that I was able to elicit any definite information from Funtikov, but upon obtaining his statement 'that the majority of the prisoners had been quietly shot', I immediately wired General Malleson in these terms.

This is the entire story so far as I am concerned. I ascertained some time afterwards that Kurilev and Kuhn had organised the execution themselves. The prisoners, twenty-six in number, had been put in a train, had been taken out and shot at a lonely spot by the wayside.

For a long time nothing more was heard about the episode and in the course of a few weeks we had forgotten all about it. The Bolsheviks did not forget, however, nor did the relatives of the dead commissars. In particular the wife of Shaumian assumed a most vindictive attitude and stirred up very considerable trouble in Moscow. The next that was heard of it was in the spring of 1919 when a certain Chaikin made a special trip to Askhabad, which was on the eve of being evacuated by the British, and interviewed Funtikov on the subject of the missing commissars.

Funtikov had at that time fallen into disfavour and was himself languishing in the Askhabad jail. Knowing that the British were about to leave Trans-Caspia and realising that the Bolsheviks would sooner or later return there, the late President was in a terrible state of anxiety. To save his skin he decided to throw the entire blame on the British in general and on myself in particular. In short, Funtikov asserted that the execution of the commissars had been insisted on by myself and that I had planned out the details of the actual execution. With this material Chaikin returned gleefully to the Caucasus and by publishing a most exaggerated version of the story, instituted an active press campaign against the British in the Caucasus. The campaign was taken up by the Moscow press and the matter has been resuscitated at odd intervals ever since. The last effort was a book on the subject recently published by Chaikin and also an article written by Trotsky.

Such is the tragedy of the twenty-six commissars. Peace be upon their souls. The Bolsheviks proclaimed that they would put to death all those who had taken any part in the execution, one individual for each of the victims. Twenty-five had already been shot and it was understood that the twenty-sixth place was being reserved for myself, but this number has now been exceeded, the total number of persons executed by way of reprisal being over forty. Whether the Bolsheviks are yet satisfied remains to be seen, but if I may make a prophecy, I feel that before the tale is quite complete, Chaikin will himself have joined the number.

H.M. Representative in Askhabad

$\blacklozenge$

From the middle of October I kept records of most of the daily incidents at Askhabad and it will perhaps be clearer if I reproduce them in the sequence in which they actually occurred. The different questions will have to be treated in little bits, but this is unavoidable since almost every day saw some fresh development in one or other of these questions. It can readily be imagined how very varied and at times trying, not to mention anxious, my work was at this time.

Received a telegram from Malleson which gave me serious *13.10.18* ground for thought. 'How is it,' the telegram ran, 'that Minorski, a notorious enemy of Great Britain, should have obtained a complete copy of my telegram No. . . . . . Not only has he obtained a complete copy but he has wired it to the Russian Minister at Tehran. Please find out how this has happened.'

Hereby hangs a tale. Minorski was a prominent member of the Russian Corps Diplomatique and previous to the War had been in Tehran. He was known to have very strong anti-British views and had been associated with some deep intrigue against us and our influence in Persia. I personally knew nothing of Minorski beyond the fact that a person of that name had arrived in Askhabad a few days previously and had put up with the Dorrers.

Now comes the story of the telegram. Some little time previously we had intercepted a message from the Russian Legation in Tehran to the Askhabad Government, the contents of which suggested that the Legation were arranging or trying to arrange, apparently with some success, for the Askhabad Government to remit to them for their maintenance a portion of any money which the Trans-Caspians might ultimately succeed in screwing out of the British.

General Malleson was naturally very wrath at the idea of the Trans-Caspian Government, who were actually bankrupt, promising to remit a portion of our subsidy, should we eventually pay them one, to the Russian delegation in Tehran. The latter still comprised all the old Tsarist diplomatic officials and their attitude towards the British in Persia at this period was by no means too friendly. With their own position rendered hopeless by the Revolution, these haughty representatives of what had once been Imperial Russia, were now compelled to see their hereditary rivals, the British, predominant in the very centre of the former Russian sphere of influence. Their natural feelings of jealousy were further aggravated by their own helplessness; being unable to take any action, they confined themselves to intrigue.

There was a certain fine irony in the thought that they, extreme Monarchists as they were, should persuade the Socialist Revolutionary government of Trans-Caspia to give them financial support, and their satisfaction was further increased by the thought that the money would really emanate from the coffers of the British Government.

General Malleson sent me a telegram instructing me to convey to the Government 'his amazement that they could possibly contemplate giving any assistance to the Russian Mission in Tehran, since it was notorious that the Mission, as also the Russian Consulates throughout Persia, were nothing but so many counter-revolutionaries . . .'

On receiving this telegram, which was sent en clair and was not even marked 'confidential', I sent for Zimin and conveyed to him the literal text of the message. He protested that there must be a misunderstanding, but I could see that he was much perturbed. He asked me to give him the text of Malleson's message, as he wished to show it to the other ministers. I saw no harm in this and let him have it.

Somehow or other Minorski obtained possession of a copy of it. In its somewhat caustic and undiplomatic wording his intriguing brain saw a possible handle against the British. He immediately wired the whole text of the message to the Russian Minister in Tehran and emphasised the fact that Malleson had called them all counter-revolutionaries. The Russian Minister lost no time in lodging a formal protest with his British colleagues, who felt compelled to pass it on to the Foreign Office. The latter referred it to the War Office, who wired to India, who wired to Malleson asking him for an explanation. Malleson had no very satisfactory explanation and wired me for one. I could only say that it was a regrettable breach of faith on the part of Zimin, but that as the telegram had been sent to me en clair and not even marked 'confidential', at a time when Malleson was daily sending me cipher messages, I had seen no objection in handing over the text of the message in confidence to Zimin.

I heard afterwards that Malleson had been thoroughly alarmed at the incident and finally wired to India laying the blame on my shoulders: 'the indiscretion, to a certain extent excusable, of a young and very over-worked Political Officer'. Had I known of this at the time I should have protested most strongly at the very unfair shelving of the responsibility. However, experience subsequently taught me that this was unfortunately very characteristic of Malleson. Thus the matter ended, save that Malleson asked me to emphasise in all my subsequent telegrams conveying requests for assistance by the Askhabad authorities the fact that they, the Trans-Caspian Government, were compelled to appeal for assistance to the British since their own Russian Mission and Consulates were not in a position to afford that assistance!

The Government asked me if I could suggest any method of *14.10.18* utilising some of the surplus prisoners for whom there was no room in the local prison. The latter was already overcrowded and the question had been complicated by the arrival of 300 Bolsheviks recently captured on the Front. The Government were very keen on our taking over a number of the prisoners and deporting them to India. I declined to take over the prisoners, but suggested that it might be found possible to organise them into gangs for construction work on the road between Meshed and Askhabad.

Meshed wired to approve the formation of a Special Detachment *14.10.18* to be recruited entirely from among the Russian officer class and to be equipped and trained in Meshed. Numerous Russian military elements were knocking about with nothing to do in Askhabad who had not found it compatible with their dignity to go and fight at the Front under a Turkman Commander. (It must be remembered that the Commander-in-Chief was Oraz Sardar, a Turkman, who had nevertheless held the rank of General in the Russian

Army.) I proposed to utilise a small mounted detachment of thirty men, which had been kept on the frontier at Muhammedabad, and started by getting these men in to Askhabad. On inspection they proved quite a useful little party, though their mounts and equipment left much to be desired. I proposed to keep them as a mounted detachment and in addition to raise another thirty men and form of them a machine-gun detachment. All that now remained was to get them sent off to Meshed.

14.10.18   Two prisoners arrived from Meshed under convoy and were handed over to me. They had been arrested in Meshed on suspicion of being Turk–Bolshevik agents, I fancy on information supplied to Redl. I interrogated them, but they seemed harmless enough. They were Caucasians and apparently had numerous relatives and connections among Muhammedan circles in Askhabad. I learned that a strong Muhammedan deputation was preparing to come and appeal to me for the release of these two men and therefore welcomed a fortuitous proposal of the Government to take them over pending an enquiry into their case. The deputation duly came. I received them attentively. We spoke Persian. I told them that as far as we were concerned, there was nothing serious against the two prisoners, but that the Russians had taken them over and proposed to enquire into the charges against them. The matter was out of my hands, but at the request of the deputation, I promised to see that the matter was taken up without delay. I was already aware that Muhammedan feeling in Askhabad was veering round in our favour and the deputation which contained a number of prominent Mullahs confirmed this. I seized the opportunity to impress on them the good intentions of the British Government vis à vis the Moslem world and we parted on excellent terms.

15.10.18   I had a visit from Zimin and from the agitated way he was stroking his beard, I knew at once he had unpleasant news. He proceeded to communicate to me a number of disjointed reports that had come in by wire during the night. It appeared that the Trans-Caspian and Indian troops had last night launched a combined attack on Dushak. They took the Bolsheviks by surprise and forced them to retire in disorder, leaving horses, ammunition and other material behind them. The Trans-Caspian troops then got out of hand, commenced looting and scattered. The Bolsheviks must then have counter-attacked and the Trans-Caspians had to fall back on Arman Sagat. Casualties were said to be very heavy. Zimin guardedly said that no British officers had been killed, but a large proportion had been wounded. I immediately passed this news on to Meshed for what it was worth and went down to the Railway administrative offices where the Government was wont to assemble and where we had direct telegraphic communication with the Front. I found a number of the Government collected round the telegraph instruments, with very long faces.

I stayed at the instrument most of the day trying to get some definite appreciation of the situation, but it was not till 6.30 that we received a somewhat vaguely worded official despatch from the Russian staff. From this I gathered total Trans-Caspian casualties were 40 killed and 170 wounded, the great majority of whom were Indian troops, both cavalry and infantry. Bolshevik losses were much heavier. They were supposed to have had 200 killed in the actual fighting, plus 500 cut to pieces by Indian cavalry.

It was clear that what might have been a brilliant victory for our troops was turned into a disastrous defeat owing to the undisciplined behaviour and subsequent desertion of the less reliable elements among the Trans-Caspian forces. That the Bolsheviks had been dealt a very severe blow cannot, however, be denied. As a matter of fact, subsequent investigation showed that their losses had been even heavier than was at first supposed. Thus in the initial attack one of our shells made a direct hit on a truck containing gun ammunition. The explosion that ensued worked indescribable havoc and wrecked not only the bulk of the rolling stock in Dushak, but the entire station buildings as well. The behaviour of our Indian troops was throughout splendid. From the beginning the brunt of the fighting fell on their shoulders and this was evidenced by the very heavy casualties.

The unsatisfactory feature of the whole operation, saving of course the heavy casualties among our own Indian troops, was the treacherous and undisciplined behaviour of the Turkmans. In addition to the detachment belonging to Kara-Sirdar who looted Dushak, another detachment was operating under Aziz Khan, a Turkman headman of Tejen. The latter had been instructed to harry the Bolsheviks in their rear. They did nothing active, save barter information to both sides, until the Bolsheviks evacuated Tejen. They then entered Tejen and under a cut-throat named

Allahyar raided all the houses, murdered all the men and carried off the women and children into the steppe, where they brutally violated them. The incident caused a very painful impression in Askhabad and made us realise the undesirability of employing these guerrilla Turkman detachments, whose one idea was loot and rapine.

While the Bolshevik troops were so badly shaken that they retired all the way to Merv and thence to Bairam Ali, the Trans-Caspians were in no better plight. They decided that serious fighting was not in their line and after falling back on Nauroz Chashme, they rested a while and then without either orders or warning, they packed up and withdrew themselves to Kaahka. Nor was the sorry tale yet completed. Some 152 Bolsheviks were taken prisoner and it was understood that they were being sent into Askhabad. I was looking forward to their arrival, as I hoped to elicit some information from them regarding the position in Tashkent. I now received information from the staff that they regretted very much that of the 152 prisoners all but 32 had been murdered on the way.

The crime was subsequently placed at the door of the Turkmans. The latter were at this time showing signs of getting out of hand. This was quite understandable when one considered that their civilisation was after all only two generations old. The Turkman is by nature not a warrior, but he makes a very good freebooter. Two generations of the Pax Russica had turned them into very decent steppe dwellers, but the events of the last twelve months had shaken more stable elements than the Tekke Turkman and the dog was already showing every symptom of turning into the wolf. The question of controlling and limiting their power now began to appear to my mind as a serious problem.

On this occasion the murderers, whoever they were, were never punished and though Malleson addressed a strongly worded telegram of remonstrance to the Askhabad authorities, the latter could only agree with every word of it, but could themselves do nothing, poor things.

I was very interested in finding out what had happened to fifteen machine-guns which had been carried off and hidden by our Turkman detachments when they entered Dushak. It was subsequently admitted that all these M.G.s had found their way into the

Turkman *auls* where they were being hidden for future use. I did not like this either, and did my best to raise trouble over the question. On my suggestion Malleson in Meshed put in a claim for these weapons, as they had been virtually captured by our troops, and we really needed them to equip the Russian detachments we proposed to train in Meshed. Though the Russian staff were themselves only too eager to get the machine-guns, they failed to do so and we never saw them again.

With the advent of nearly 150 casualties from among our own troops, the hospital question again became acute. The number of cases of pneumonia was deplorable. The *sepoys* seemed to crumple up at once under this dire disease. They lost all their stamina and I had to agree with the Russian hospital staff that they made very bad patients.

We were assisted by the very opportune arrival from Krasnov-odsk of the complete staff of an Armenian hospital which had been evacuated from Baku. The senior surgeon offered to place his entire staff at our disposal if we would find him accommodation. After much discussion, in which I pointed out the difficulties attending the care of the Indians and their caste and other prejudices, we decided that it would be better for the Armenian Hospital to take up the care of the Russian sick and wounded, and such cases of Indians as would be unable to find accommodation in the Railway Hospital. I got the Committee to requisition a large building for the Armenians and in an incredibly short time the latter had installed themselves, and had rigged up an excellent hospital.

With this increased number of our men in Askhabad, the question of feeding them became a very serious problem. I arranged with Meshed to send up a regular ration convoy and from the Russians I took over the local cavalry lines. We turned the lines into a regular depot, but the question of transport was a difficult one. Camels were apparently scarce in Meshed, all available animals having been taken for work on the main lines of communication. The local form of transport consisted in the Russian country carts known as *fourgons* drawn by three and sometimes four horses abreast. At the request of Meshed I began collecting these *fourgons* and in a short while I succeeded in hiring over a hundred through a local contractor, who sent his men out into the district and produced *fourgons* from all over the countryside. I had a large number of convalescents and these I now managed to despatch to Meshed in *fourgons*. At the same time I also sent off the detachment of 60 men for training.

21.10.18   Among the numerous economic questions which were constantly arising were firstly the despatch of petrol from Trans-Caspia to Meshed and secondly the exporting of grain from Persia to Trans-Caspia. The petrol question soon became a very sore one. I had instructions to get as much of this commodity sent to Meshed as possible and promptly began to collect every available tin. Unfortunately it was found impracticable to send these tins by *fourgon*, as they invariably got broken on the road and I therefore had to depend on camel transport. The grain question was complicated by the lack of money wherewith to pay. Large supplies of grain had been collected in Persia, but the Persian trading agents would not part with it until they had received payment either in money or in kind. Arrangements were finally made whereby payment was made in kerosene, but much telegraphic and other correspondence took place before the deals were actually put through.

The respective questions of wheat and petrol soon came to be regarded as permanent items on the agenda for my daily interviews with Zimin. Our people in Meshed needed the petrol, the Trans-Caspians required the grain. If the latter would really bestir themselves and send us petrol, we promised to take measures to induce the Persian traders to expedite the grain.

The difficulties I experienced in making any progress in this very ordinary matter can be seen by the following, which is the gist of telegrams I sent to Meshed.

'The Russian Staff originally informed me by telephone that they had placed 50 puds of petrol at my disposal. I reported to Meshed accordingly the same evening and I have since been trying unsuccessfully to locate these 50 puds. The Staff declare that they have been handed over to Zimin. The latter denies this and he is obviously speaking the truth. The Staff also declare that the 50 puds have been sent to Meshed, a statement which is also false. Zimin and the Staff are now fighting it out. I have spent the whole morning in different departments each one of which now violently accuses the other of interference resulting in the miscarrying of the petrol. As a final result I have extracted a promise that all available petrol in Askhabad, amounting to 56 puds, will be handed over to me today, while 20 puds will be handed over tomorrow. I will despatch half of this to Kuchan immediately.

'Regarding petrol at Krasnovodsk, the Staff informed me this morning that they had just received definite information that stocks there consisted in 1,000 puds first-class and an unknown quantity second-class petrol. I immediately put in a demand for 800 puds to begin with and more on arrival here. After considerable hesitation as to whether they could undertake the responsibility of giving me a definite answer, they gave me a promise of 800 puds and undertook to wire for it immediately. Half an hour later Staff regretted to inform me that the quantity had been wrongly reported as 1,000 puds and was really only 100 puds. I have since heard from the so-called "technical department" that there is no petrol in Krasnovodsk at all and I am inclined to believe this.'

Krasnovodsk had indeed become a source of anxiety, though the fear of an actual invasion from without was lessened by the fact that we now had a British garrison there. This garrison consisted of detachments of the Royal Warwicks and the Hampshires with some artillery. It was under the command of Lt Col Fleming, a most able officer, who was called upon to deal with a series of critical situations as varied as they were serious.

While the economic situation in Askhabad was such as to cause considerable anxiety for the future, the state of affairs in Krasnovodsk was scarcely less precarious. However, the original *Stachkom* which had been hurriedly organised on the 12th July had remained in power, and under the leadership — one might almost say the dictatorship — of Kuhn, had given us practically no trouble. Kuhn had the sense to appreciate the advantages of the presence of a British garrison and throughout played up to us in a most loyal manner. Semov became at this time Port Commandant, and as such made himself invaluable to the British Command.

Following on the fall of Baku, the British Naval authorities who had come up through Persia, but had been unable to reach the Caspian in time to save Baku, now commenced a systematic arming of steamers, with a view to forming an armed British flotilla on the Caspian. Their actual base was at Enzeli but the port of Krasnovodsk was naturally of considerable importance to them and it soon became necessary to exercise control over the movements of shipping to and from that port. This was rendered all the more necessary by the fact that Bicherakov, who was still fighting the Turks in Daghestan, regarded Krasnovodsk as his dumping ground for the thousands of refugees and other superfluous mouths, which were causing him considerable embarrassment.

The refugee question was a very difficult one. In the general exodus from Baku many shiploads of these wretched fugitives had gone down to Enzeli, where the British troops did their best for them, to the extent of sharing their bedding and their rations with the crowds of starving women and children. The main bulk of the refugees, however, had moved up to Petrovsk and had thrown themselves on the mercy of the town, already crowded to overflowing with the influx of fugitives from the North Caucasus and in a semi-starving condition. A general rally of political elements took place in Petrovsk, with the result that Bicherakov was elected Commander of the whole of the Navy on the Caspian and of all the non-Bolshevik Russian troops in the Caspian area. This was an obvious counter-move to the British, whose deliberate seizure of Russian shipping, and the creation therewith of an armed flotilla under the British flag, had aroused feelings of vague suspicion and jealousy on the part of the Russians, who feared the loss of their so-called sovereign rights and national prestige.

This feeling existed among both the local governments of Askhabad and Krasnovodsk and there is no doubt that although British troops were at that moment alone holding back the Bolsheviks, the weak-kneed Trans-Caspians deplored the fact of our increasing influence and the non-working classes at any rate would have welcomed the appearance on the scene of any outside elements representing a Russian government.

Nevertheless Bicherakov was not such a fool as to place himself in deliberate opposition to the British, from whom he still hoped for assistance, and in fact on this same day the Petrovsk authorities decided to approach the British in Enzeli for pecuniary assistance. Bicherakov was naturally also anxious to keep on good terms with the Trans-Caspians and accordingly proposed to send down some shiploads of supplies to alleviate the food shortage there.

Both in Krasnovodsk and Askhabad the belief was popularly entertained that Bicherakov would also send armed reinforcements to the Trans-Caspian Front, or if he were compelled to evacuate

Petrovsk, he would transfer his entire forces to Trans-Caspia. The British Naval authorities in Enzeli, quite awake to the possibility of Bicherakov's supporters endeavouring to seize Krasnovodsk, decided to anticipate them by taking prior action. A Naval officer was sent to Krasnovodsk and promptly demanded that the entire control of the port be vested in him. This move was regarded in anything but a friendly light by the Krasnovodsk Committee, who lost no time in telegraphing Askhabad and protesting against the British action.

The Askhabad Government in the person of Zimin came round to see me in a very perturbed state of mind. He pointed out that according to the Meshed Agreement, there had been no stipulation that the British should interfere in the control of the port and shipping of Krasnovodsk, and that this was a matter for the Russians alone. Furthermore he added that whereas reinforcements for the Front were urgently needed, we had not the troops available, while Bicherakov on the other hand had expressed the desire and readiness to send troops to the assistance of Trans-Caspia.

I pointed out in reply that we doubted very much Bicherakov's ability to send troops when he himself was fighting for his existence around Petrovsk and that what Bicherakov was really after was a place to which he could evacuate his surplus population of refugees. As regards Bicherakov's offer to send food, I referred to the arrival some few days previously of two ships from Bicherakov with supplies. The ships had been so crowded with refugees that they had consumed most of the supplies, so that the advantages which might have been obtained were completely neutralised. In short, with one explanation and another, I overcame Zimin's objections and he left, though in a far from satisfied state of mind, to inform the Government. The latter in turn could do nothing and were obliged to inform the Krasnovodsk Committee that they were helpless in the matter.

As a matter of fact I afterwards satisfied Zimin that the presence of Bicherakov's troops would be a very mixed blessing for Trans-Caspia. If Bicherakov himself came over he would immediately assume complete control and where then would be the democratic Askhabad Government? If the Daghestani troops came across without Bicherakov, I could foresee endless trouble with them both at the Front and in the rear. They would doubtless find Askhabad a good place to live in, and things were difficult enough to manage without having a number of lawless Daghestani brigands on the rampage. As a matter of fact my words were truer than even I imagined. When later some Daghestanis did come across they found Askhabad so much pleasanter than Petrovsk that nothing on earth would persuade them to go to the Front. Their presence in the town was the cause of endless trouble and the local authorities lived to rue the day they had allowed them to come to Trans-Caspia.

Meanwhile Colonel Fleming in Krasnovodsk was called upon to face the question on the spot and make the best of a very awkward situation. Fortunately he was loyally supported by Kuhn, whose influence, however, had become somewhat weakened owing to the somewhat tactless attitude of the British Naval Commander. The latter had only recently arrived in Krasnovodsk, knew nothing about the local political situation and had proceeded to take possession of the shipping and move ships about without any reference to Kuhn. This naturally damaged the latter's prestige and his enemies were not slow to take advantage of it and used this fact to show that the British were taking everything into their own hands, including Kuhn and the Committee.

The situation became very ticklish for Colonel Fleming, who like myself had been kept in complete ignorance as to what our policy on the Caspian was to be. This was only one of the many instances in which we, the British Representatives on the spot, were kept in ignorance of facts of first-class importance, being constantly called upon to give explanations for actions of the real motive of which we ourselves were totally ignorant. Thus in the present instance, the Askhabad Government failed entirely to understand what possible objection we could have to reinforcements coming from Bicherakov to help the Trans-Caspians on our Front.

I have myself never understood why we made such a fuss about it. We naturally did not want Bicherakov to seize Krasnovodsk and, as I have said before, we did not want undisciplined Cossacks beating up the civil population of Askhabad. Fleming however was more than strong enough in Krasnovodsk to prevent any serious attempt to seize the place from without, while in Askhabad I felt confident that I could cope with any ordinary disturbance, as I proved later.

There is no doubt that much misunderstanding arose through General Malleson declining to venture over this side of the frontier. He may have had good reasons for not doing so, but the fact that he crossed into Trans-Caspia for the first time on the 17th November, and then only stayed a few days, made a very bad impression on the Russians. Sitting in Meshed the whole time, it was naturally impossible for Malleson to have a clear idea of the local situation. Though it may be argued that by remaining at a distance one is enabled to obtain a better idea of proportion, how could anyone sitting in an isolated spot like Meshed have a better idea of proportion than by living in the centre of things in Askhabad?

A great misfortune was the entire lack of co-operation between the different forces or missions working in Persia and Russia at this time. Thus for instance there was *Norperforce*, the successors to *Dunsterforce*, centred in Kazvin and Enzeli, who were responsible for Fleming's military detachment garrisoning Krasnovodsk. Fleming was working in the closest contact with the local Committee, who were really subordinate to the Government in Askhabad. At the same time the Naval authorities had assumed complete control over the port and shipping at Krasnovodsk and insisted on having direct relations with the Committee entirely independently of Fleming. Furthermore the Naval authorities were directly and only responsible to their own H.Q. which was in Bagdad.

Finally, although the Krasnovodsk Committee considered itself subordinate to the Askhabad Government, the political relations between the latter and the British were confined exclusively to myself as representing the Malleson Mission in Meshed, while the latter had nothing whatever to do with the situation in Krasnovodsk. Add the fact that there was every indication of no love being lost between the heads of the different forces, not one of which would go out of his way to assist the other with information, and the reader will appreciate how difficult was the situation for us wretched military and political officers actually on the spot. That the situation continued so smoothly in Krasnovodsk is due almost entirely to the tact and patience of Colonel Fleming and the loyal support of President Kuhn.

The Allies' armistice with Turkey of October 31st anyway changed the entire situation on the Caspian, and the pressure on Bicherakov was relieved. On November 16th arrangements were made by General Thomson at Enzeli with the local authorities at Baku for the evacuation of the Turks, the withdrawal of the local forces and the occupation of the town by a combined force of British and Russians. Bicherakov agreed to co-operate, and on November 17th he and his force accompanied General Thomson with part of Norperforce and the British armed flotilla to Baku. The drama of the Caspian was over as far as we were concerned.

The Turkman Frankenstein

◆

As the month of October drew to its close, the problems which daily presented themselves for solution became not only more numerous, but more and more complex and difficult to handle.

Happily, Miss Valya Alexeeva, who had had a very narrow escape from destruction in Baku and who had been evacuated to Enzeli, came down to Askhabad and acted as typist and secretary to the Mission. Also I was joined by Captain Haines of the X Jats, a most able officer with a good practical knowledge of Russian. He remained in Askhabad as my assistant and proved invaluable. His presence made life much cheerier and we were together able to manage things much more satisfactorily.

Captain Haines took over the supervision of what may be called the domestic problems. These included anything from telling off *Sepoy* Hira Singh for spitting on the floor of the ward, to arranging barracks for an incoming convoy, or dealing tactfully with weeping Armenians who had lost their relatives in the Baku massacre.

Henceforth, I was able to concentrate my attention on the more pressing 'affairs of state'. Fortunately for Haines and myself, we were both of us blessed with a saving sense of humour, and though, as in so many similar situations, the whole course of events might well have been regarded as a comedy one could never free oneself from the feeling that in the end, things must inevitably lead to a tragedy.

For some weeks past I had been aware of growing difficulties in the relations between the Turkman and the Trans-Caspian authorities. While, strictly speaking, the matter was one which did not directly concern me, yet I gathered from frequent remarks made by Zimin that the question was causing the Government no little concern, and that my advice would be welcomed. There was, as yet, no question of my opinion being officially sought and had this happened I should at this stage have most certainly declined to give one on the plea that I could not interfere in matters affecting the internal administration of the country. In any case I had no desire to become entangled in vexed questions affecting the native population, whose language and customs I did not understand and with whom I had never had occasion to come into contact.

Turkmans represent 65% of the population of Trans-Caspia as compared with 12% Kirghiz and 8% Russians, the remaining balance being made up of Persians and other miscellaneous elements. They are thus in an overwhelming numerical majority.

Prior to 1881, when the Russians crushed the Turkman opposition at Geok Tepe, the Turkmans had lived a predatory tribal existence in which raiding over the Persian frontier and the sale of Persian slaves had formed the main basis of their livelihood. Russian statistics estimate the total number of slaves, chiefly women, brought over from Persia in the course of one hundred years, at no less than one million.

With the Russian occupation and the construction of the railway, the Turkmans gradually abandoned their predatory habits and settled down in their *auls* to the more peaceful pursuit of agriculture. In the course of one generation they turned into a law-abiding people, and prior to the Russian Revolution, most Turkmans in Trans-Caspia had kept to their *auls*. The Bolsheviks had treated them badly, however, and the constant seizures of horses and crops, accompanied not infrequently by excesses on the part of the Soviet authorities, had worked the Turkmans up into a state of frenzied hatred towards their Bolshevik masters. Thus, when the tyranny of Commissar Fralov drove the population of Askhabad into revolt, it was not surprising that the Turkmans came forward and offered to participate in the rebellion. The coup succeeded and the Askhabad 'Mensheviks', in the anxiety of the moment, issued over 5,000 rifles with ammunition to the Turkmans without discrimination.

Thus did the Tekke become an armed power in the country, with almost every Turkman carrying a rifle, the situation changed, and during the first two or three weeks following the revolt, the Turkmans were on the tiptoe of expectation. Emissaries from the

Caucasus told of the advancing victorious Turkish army and presaged the freeing of Trans-Caspia. Anti-Russian and of course anti-British propaganda was disseminated. Religious enthusiasm finds no place in the mind of the Tekke Turkman — tenets of the Faith and the name of the Prophet leave him quite cold — but the loot of Askhabad and the rape of Russian women were things more after his heart.

Then came the advent of the British and the Turkmans felt they had been cheated of their prey. There was a period of sulky suspicion and scarcely veiled hostility. I had been repeatedly fired at by Turkmans as I lay out in the plain at Kaahka and it is an open question whether Ward had not been killed by them. Then they saw our fighting qualities and were struck with admiration at the valour of our Indian troops, coloured people like themselves. The enthusiasm of our Indians infected the Turkmans and from hostility their feelings changed to admiration. The end of October saw their attitude changing radically in favour of ourselves, but deteriorating rapidly as regards the Russians.

The situation was a complex one. At the Front the Commander-in-Chief of the Trans-Caspian troops was Oraz Sardar. He had been a regular officer in the old Russian Army and had played an important part in the overthrow of the Bolsheviks in Askhabad. The Mensheviks had no senior military officers amongst them and turned naturally to Oraz Sardar, who rallied a number of Turkmans round him and formed an impromptu Front against the Bolsheviks. Thus we found him at Kaahka on our first arrival in the country and from that time onward he came to be regarded officially as Commander-in-Chief. He was never viewed in a favourable light by the Russians, who would naturally have preferred a Russian officer had they possessed one. Though subsequently a number of Russian senior officers turned up, the old Turkman was by that time too firmly rooted to be dislodged, had the British even wished it, which they did not.

Oraz Sardar enjoyed considerable prestige among the Turk-mans. He was none other than the son of the famous Tikma Sardar, who had led the Turkmans against the Russians in 1881. Oraz Sardar had held the rank of Colonel and had commanded the Turkman regiment on the Caucasus front. He was admittedly of weak character and at this time was considered to be very much under the influence of the Turkophile party among the Turkman. He had been in correspondence with the Emir of Afghanistan. He was also on good terms with the Emir of Bokhara. Politically, Oraz Sardar was of the opinion that the day of Russian power in Turkistan was past and that the fall of the Bolsheviks would be followed by the establishment of a number of independent Khanates.

Of the other prominent Turkmans who figure in this page of Trans-Caspian history, the next most deserving of mention was Haji Murat. He had been a Lt Colonel in the Turkistan Rifles. After the overthrow of the Soviet in Askhabad, he became Oraz Sardar's assistant, but being wounded in one of the first actions, he returned home and formed what he called the Turkman Central Executive Committee, whose headquarters were at the village of Bezmein, a few miles outside Askhabad. He was afterwards appointed a member of the Provisional Government of Trans-Caspia.

Being well educated gave Haji Murat a standing among the tribesmen to which he was not entitled by birth. He was ambitious, but level-headed. Prior to the Turkish collapse he had held decided pro-Turk views. While compelled to work for the time being hand-in-hand with the Russians, he, like Oraz Sardar, was convinced in his own mind that the Russians would not last and the Turkmans would come into their own again. He was, however, possessed of sufficient common sense to realise that more could be gained by waiting than by precipitating matters. In this respect he differed radically from his friend Ovezbaiev.

Ovezbaiev was a would-be 'young Turkman'. He had been Adjutant of the Turkman Regiment and towards the end of the Caucasus campaign had commanded a squadron. Following the disbandment of the troops, he returned to Trans-Caspia and acted for a time as secretary to the Trans-Caspian Mussulman Committee. After the latter had been dissolved by the Bolsheviks, he took refuge in his village and thence went to Khiva, only returning after the expulsion of the Bolsheviks in July 1918. He was an enthusiastic pro-Turk. He had no fundamental influence among his tribe, but had succeeded in collecting a body of men around him who were ready to fight or not to fight as he bade them.

The Askhabad Government made a great mistake at the beginning of August when they paid him the large sum of two million roubles with which to raise a regiment. He utilised the money in spreading his own influence. He raised about 1,000 men, who were of little military value and were not trusted by the Russians. He had naturally many enemies. In August he quarrelled with other Turkmans, being charged with embezzling money intended for military purposes. Ovezbaiev was a hot-headed young man and very anti-Russian. I prophesied and still prophesy that he will give serious trouble one day unless he comes to an untimely end.

Mahtum Quli Khan was an old Turkman of the old school. He was a staunch supporter of the old regime and was convinced that the Russians would once more make their power felt throughout Turkistan. When the Turkman Committee was first formed, he was offered the post of President. He refused to accept it on the plea that he did not want to act against the Russians. He had lost influence since Ovezbaiev came to the fore, but still commanded a greater following than either Ovezbaiev or Haji Murat. His followers were, however, without arms and he was therefore more or less at the mercy of the more progressive party.

There was now a growing feeling of independence and power on the part of the Turkman leaders, coupled with increasing symptoms of incipient anarchy throughout the Trans-Caspian province. This in itself was bad enough, but where I foresaw further serious difficulty was in our own attitude. At the Front, our military authorities were on the closest possible terms with Oraz Sardar. They were even more eager to keep on good terms with him than with the Russians, for the simple reason that without his holding the command, the Turkmans would have packed up and gone home to the last man. This was a factor to be taken into serious consideration, for bad fighters as the Turkmans undoubtedly were, they were no worse than the majority of the conscripted Russians and were infinitely more loyal and subordinate. Hence it can be readily understood that I viewed with considerable misgiving the deteriorating relations between the local Turkmans under the leadership of Haji Murat on the one hand and the Government on the other.

There is no doubt that the Turkmans were beginning to take advantage of the weakness of the Russian authorities. Complaints became more frequent of the trains being boarded by armed Turkmans, who searched the passengers and stole their luggage. Cases of equally high-handed action began to occur in the bazaar in

Askhabad itself. Then followed the tragic raid at Tejen when Aziz Khan attacked the town and the freebooter Allahyar massacred and abducted the Russian inhabitants. This last incident frightened the Government. They realised that things were going too far and they decided that the Tejen incident must not go unpunished. I quite agreed with them, for if the Tejen outrage were allowed to go unpunished, the last atom of prestige the Askhabad authorities had would have vanished and we should have found ourselves in an impossible position.

Beyond a very unreliable town militia, however, composed of very mixed elements, there was no garrison in Askhabad, and the only controlling influence which could be brought to bear on the Turkmans was Oraz Sardar, commanding the troops at the Front. He had promised to take stern measures to punish the offenders in the Tejen outrage. Some 167 of Allahyar's detachment had been rounded up. Oraz Sardar, however, had shown no great anxiety to take any action in the matter and had allowed all the delinquents to return to their unit. The Government thereupon sent an order to Oraz Sardar to send all the offenders into Askhabad for trial. Oraz Sardar declined to obey and the Government could do nothing.

The result was simply a further weakening of the Government's prestige. It was generally felt that Ovezbaiev was sheltering the Tejen culprits and the Askhabad authorities very unwisely issued orders demanding Ovezbaiev's presence in Askhabad. This was really childish, as in the first case the Government had nothing tangible against Ovezbaiev and secondly he was much less harmful in his place at the Front than kicking his heels about in Askhabad. However, Ovezbaiev did not come to Askhabad and feeling the ground somewhat shaky beneath their feet, the Government turned to me and for the first time officially asked me for my support.

Up to the present I had successfully avoided interfering in any question affecting the internal administration and I was particularly anxious not to get entangled in any such questions. I was impressed, however, with the potential dangers of this crisis between the Russians and Turkmans and accordingly on October 28th I paid a hasty visit to the Front, then at Tejen, to discuss the whole matter with the military authorities.

28.10.18   At the Front I found, as I had expected, that the tension between the Turkmans and the Government in Askhabad had made itself felt down there. Colonel Knollys was very concerned about the whole matter, particularly since the state of the Trans-Caspian troops and the military situation generally left very much to be desired. Knollys confirmed my previous opinion, namely that with the exception of the Artillery, which was exceedingly good, the Russian troops were practically useless. Knollys's relations with the Turkmans, however, were very good and their leaders were co-operating cordially with him. He emphasised how fatal it would be to the military situation at the Front if complications were allowed to arise between Russians and Turkmans at the present moment.

The Turkman element declared itself disgusted with the attitude of the Askhabad authorities, whose one aim was directed at curtailing the power of the Turkmans. They put forward the argument that it was they who were doing the fighting, not the Russians, and that therefore it was only right that they should have the power. I explained matters as clearly as I could and smoothed over a number of the misunderstandings that had been enlarged upon until they had assumed the character of grievous wrongs.

On my return home I was at once visited by Zimin who informed me that in my absence a further passage of arms had occurred between the Government and Haji Murat. It appeared that at a meeting of the Executive Committee of the Government which Haji Murat had attended, the latter had permitted himself to use 'unparliamentary' language. Thereupon one or two of the Russian members had retorted in similar manner and had told Haji Murat a number of home truths. Haji Murat had walked out of the Committee livid with rage and had declared that the Government could consider relations with the Turkmans severed.

At the same time evidence had come to light showing that the Turkman Committee had been organising a plot to overthrow the Askhabad Government by force and to kidnap a number of its members. This had not improved the temper of the Government and Haji Murat now openly declared his intention of going to the Front and causing a schism there.

I found Zimin very much perturbed and not without reason, for I could see that the situation really was very critical. The Government was definitely helpless to do anything. With things as they were, Haji Murat could quite easily carry out his threat of going to the Front. A word from him there and the Turkmans would pack up and come home. Then, with armed bands of them roaming about the districts, the situation in Askhabad would have been at their mercy. The situation was obviously coming so rapidly to a head and complications at the Front might at any moment lead to a critical situation for our troops, that I decided that I must act and act very promptly.

I had a horse brought round, and with a couple of *sowars* as escort, and without saying anything to Zimin, I rode round to the Askhabad residence of Haji Murat. The latter was very surprised to see me. I explained at once that this was purely a private visit and a friendly one. I told him I had just returned from the Front. I gave him my impressions of the situation and repeated to him Col Knollys's remarks regarding the value to us of Turkman co-operation, how necessary it was for all parties to pull together and that the slightest misunderstanding would be fatal to us all. I said nothing of having met Zimin and I eventually succeeded in drawing Haji Murat out.

He complained that the Committee was too autocratic in its attitude towards the Turkmans, and he took particular exception to the recent introduction of a new system of commissars in the more important district centres. He also objected strongly to the appointment to a public position of Mahtum Quli Khan. His criticism was that Mahtum Quli Khan had taken no part in the fighting and was therefore not entitled to the honour it was proposed to accord him.

I pointed out that questions of that nature were, of course, no affair of ours, but that, as an ally fighting side by side with the Russians and Turkmans, I felt it necessary to emphasise the importance of avoiding any misunderstandings. I eventually obtained from Haji Murat a promise that if the Government would agree to a compromise, he would see that affairs were not brought to a head. I managed to work in a brief description of the present situation of Turkey and our own aims etc. and we parted quite good friends.

I later saw Zimin, who informed me that since our conversation in the morning, the Committee had resolved to adopt a more conciliatory attitude. I subsequently learned that Zimin had so impressed his colleagues with the earnestness of the situation as I had described it, that even the more rabid members modified their tone considerably.

Thus, for the time being, was the Turkman problem shelved. I felt I could breathe again, but the respite was of short duration. A few days later found me faced with another 'situation' — the Financial Question.

Predlozheniya and Izlozheniya

◆

When the Menshevik Government overthrew the Soviet administration in July, none of the Menshevik authorities could boast of any previous experience in the administration of finances, and the natural result was that, through maladministration, the state funds dwindled at an alarming rate.

Now when General Malleson, on behalf of the Government of India, had drawn up and signed the famous Agreement with the Trans-Caspian Government, the latter had stipulated for some form of financial assistance. This was agreed upon in principle and, while the wording of the Agreement gave no explicit undertaking as regards any fixed amount, it certainly conveyed the impression that financial assistance would be forthcoming when it would be required.

In my daily interviews with Zimin, he had repeatedly mentioned the dwindling resources of the Government exchequer and had frequently hinted that a little financial assistance from our side would be very welcome. I replied by impressing upon Zimin the absolute necessity of going as slow as possible. We could hardly be expected to provide money to be wasted by the Trans-Caspian authorities. Zimin agreed and promised to draw up a detailed estimate for expenditure for the next three months. Meanwhile Zimin was having an uncomfortable time with his colleagues and begged me to send a wire to Meshed at their combined request. I therefore sent the following:

30.10.18   'The Government urge me to represent without delay the present desperate condition of their finances and appeal for a subsidy, with which to carry on until at least the end of the year. Their funds are now practically exhausted and it is proposed to float a loan in order to raise the sufficient money wherewith to pay the salaries of officials.

146

'The total expenditure from July 12th to October 1st amounts to 54 million roubles. The items are as follows:–

	RBLS
Maintenance of Army (including rations and equipment)	27,000,000
Salaries of officials	900,000
Medical department, maintenance and personal	500,000
Salaries of railway employees and workmen	10,000,000
Road construction and repairs	300,000
Public supplies	7,000,000
Advances to municipality and industrial enterprises	300,000
Interest payable on savings bank deposits ...	8,000,000

'The expenditure for the succeeding period will, of course, increase in proportion as the Front advances and more territory is included in the administrative area. In the case of the Front advancing up to Tashkent, which is unlikely for the present, the total expenditure would increase from 54 to 118 millions. The direct causes of such an increase would be the larger army, general rise in price of provisions, payment of salaries of government and railway employees at present in enemy territory, also the cost of repairing and reconstructing the railway and other property damaged by the enemy. . . .'

As a province of Turkistan Trans-Caspia had never been self-supporting, even under the Imperial regime. It had always been economically dependent on the rest of Turkistan on the one side and on European Russian on the other. In its present condition, cut off completely from the outside world, with its once staple industry — cotton culture — moribund and its once vital line of communication, the Central Asian Railway, collapsing for lack of working capital, the position was a parlous one.

One could scarcely blame the Powers-that-Be for hesitating to dip their hands into their official pockets in order to bolster up a government of amateurs and thereby prolong an artificial situation that was not of our creating, that no longer vitally concerned us and that must inevitably crash as soon as our support would be withdrawn. Yet there was another side to the question — that of moral obligation.

We British had thrust our way up into Central Asia because our vital strategic interests demanded it. The Trans-Caspian situation played into our hands and the Trans-Caspian anti-Bolsheviks were in a position, at a very critical moment of the war, to accord us valuable co-operation. We were very glad indeed to have this co-operation at the time and it was certainly not their fault that circumstances far remote from Trans-Caspia subsequently rendered their co-operation of less and less consequence to us, until, with the signing of the Armistice in November, our own troubles and interests in Trans-Caspia were to vanish. But there had been a mutual agreement and, though perhaps somewhat vaguely worded, that agreement had certainly provided for some reciprocal assistance of a financial nature to be accorded the Trans-Caspian authorities.

Where we laid ourselves open to criticism was not in failing to come up to scratch with the financial support when the Trans-Caspians first called for it, but in keeping the question so long in suspense and thereby allowing the situation to deteriorate until it became actually dangerous.

To myself on the spot, charged with the onerous and unpleasant duty of making an impossible situation 'carry on' from day to day, week to week, and month to month, the unsoundness and artificiality of the whole position was probably more evident than it would have been to the higher authorities at a distance with countless other problems of greater portent to distract their attention.

The Trans-Caspians were unbusinesslike, it is true, but what could be expected from a handful of amateurs of whom the majority were scarcely even educated? Would a small provincial town in England in similar circumstances have put up a better show? I doubt it.

We could have helped enormously if we ourselves had been more businesslike and more frank in our relations. We sent up troops: good. Then, having sent them up, we ought to have admitted our commitments and met our expenses as we incurred them. We ought never to have allowed the unbusinesslike Trans-Caspians — a schoolmaster and a few railway employees — to carry all our

148

expenses for weeks without even asking for an account or giving any indication of intending to pay.

As an Englishman, I confess I felt ashamed when, after we had had two hospitals occupied by our sick and wounded for some ten weeks, the Surgeon-in-charge came to me, cap in hand, and begged me to let him have enough money to cover that day's out-of-pocket expenses. They had not even enough money left to buy food for the patients. And I, the Representative of Britain on the spot, was with difficulty able to advance the sum required.

Day by day, and week by week, the financial situation steadily deteriorated. What else could it do with a civil war and foreign troops in the country and no possible source of revenue? Had the situation been suddenly sprung upon us, it would have been a different matter. But it was not sprung on us.

On November 11th I wired Meshed: *11.11.18*

'At present Government lack the means of continuing the payment of salaries of officials and railway employees. Failure to do this will lead to wholesale disorder and the collapse of the Government, accompanied almost inevitably with an attempt to reinstate the Bolsheviks. Discontent is increasing daily owing to the cold weather and almost complete lack of fuel, coupled with the rising price of bread due to the large number of refugees, running into thousands. If money is not forthcoming, and the present Government supported, feeling will inevitably turn against the British and the situation will become serious.'

I still did not know whether it was the intention of the Government of India to pay for anything at all. My policy throughout was to be perfectly frank and straightforward in my dealings with the Russians and as time went on they certainly seemed to place entire confidence in me. But the fact that I myself (and presumably also General Malleson) was most of the time in complete ignorance of what our ultimate plans would be, often must have given the impression that we were concealing ulterior motives. The Trans-Caspians could not believe it possible that we had pushed up troops all the way from India into the heart of Asia without any cut and dried plans or policy for the future.

It was not until the 24th November that General Malleson *24.11.18* reached Askhabad on his long deferred visit. He was accompanied by his three Staff Officers: Captains Ellis, Jarvis and Gordon.

149

Their arrival came as a particular relief to me, for the last two or three weeks had been one continual mental strain — meeting the daily requests, petitions and pleadings of Zimin and his confrères for money. Latterly Zimin no longer came alone on these visits, but either brought along Dmitrievsky, the 'Minister for Finance', or else some other member of the Government. I imagine his attitude was 'Well, gentlemen, (though a Social Revolutionary himself, I cannot imagine Zimin condescending to say 'Comrades'!) I have said everything I possibly can to the British Representative. If you don't believe me, come along and try to influence him yourselves!' The result was that practically every day and often several times a day, I received these unwelcome visitors and had to listen sympathetically to their exposition of the critical situation and tell them exactly nothing in as graceful a way as possible.

The most trying cases were those who came along with 'schemes' and 'propositions'. The Russians call them *Predlozheniya*, their exposition they term *Izlozheniya*, and their general purport was to demonstrate — on paper, of course — exactly how we might raise so many million roubles out of nothing in one week, etc., etc.

I could, of course, have simply locked myself up in my quarters and have put a notice up 'Not at Home', but to have done so would not have helped matters; so in the interests of the policy of 'Carry-On' I continued to lend a sympathetic but weary ear to all and sundry.

The last few days I had gained a brief respite, for the news that the Mission was on its way from Meshed had gone round the town and everybody, myself included, felt confident that its arrival would bring the solution to the problem we were all so anxiously awaiting.

Hardly had the General shaken the dust of Persia off his clothes, before the presence of Zimin and Dmitrievsky on the doorstep was announced. I could hardly repress a smile as I thought of all the 'Predlozheniya' and their 'Izlozheniya' which by this time were so familiar to me and which the Mission would now have the pleasure of hearing for the first time at first hand.

Attended by Captain Jarvis, the General received his two visitors. Zimin looked rather paler than usual and his thin fingers played nervously with his long beard. (Under less serious conditions he would certainly have been dubbed 'Beaver'.) He got quickly off the mark and, after a few courteous words of welcome to Trans-Caspia, he started on his arguments for an immediate subsidy.

But it soon became apparent that any hopes there might have been that General Malleson would open one of his trunks and produce therefrom a few millions of Pounds Sterling, or even roubles, were doomed to disappointment. Instead, the General merely pointed out that ready cash in any form was out of the question. We simply had not got it. The question was whether it could be raised in Trans-Caspia.

The next few days there followed meeting after meeting, but we did not make any progress. The General kept his lips tightly pursed as I translated 'Predlozheniya' and 'Izlozheniya' until I knew them all off by heart. But as the days went by, it became increasingly apparent that not only had the General no subsidy in his boxes, but he had no solution of the problem up his sleeve.

After a week of this sort of stalemate, during which time we had suggested, discussed, pulled to pieces and finally negatived every conceivable kind of combination, it was eventually decided to offer to issue drafts on Bombay or London in return for cash deposits paid into the Askhabad State Bank.

Zimin and Dmitrievsky agreed that this was a constructive suggestion, but doubted very much if there were still sufficient capital in private hands in Trans-Caspia to be worthwhile considering. Anyway, *faute de mieux*, it was decided to try out the scheme, and that night, assisted by Captain Jarvis, I spent several hours drawing up the necessary form of agreement so that we might reproduce it with an announcement in the local press.

The next day we found that Zimin had been before us and had published an explanatory article on the scheme, but had made in it certain statements calculated to give the impression that the British Government undertook to do more than was really the case.

When Zimin came round the next day, he was thoroughly hauled over the coals. The General was furious and his remarks were so caustic that I could not possibly communicate them literally in Russian. I therefore toned down the General's remarks to a fitting degree of pained regret, while Jarvis sat grinning at me with malicious delight, for he spoke Russian fluently.

As a matter of fact we might have spared ourselves the effort, for the result of the appeal in the press was a complete disappointment. Some 6,000 roubles were paid into the bank, whereas the minimum required was 5,000,000 roubles. Either there was no money in private hands, or else the scheme had failed to appeal.

Finally came the end of the month. Zimin had no further suggestion to make. Nor had the G.O.C. Zimin told me that his colleagues had decided to hang on to office as long as they could, possibly for a few days longer, because they were convinced that the only alternative would be a Bolshevik outbreak, unless, of course, the British decided to take charge. To this I shook my head. 'The railway workers will be in an ugly mood,' he said, 'when they learn that they are not to get their pay for the past month.' So should I be, I thought, and wondered what the General would do next.

The weather was getting much colder. Biting winds came howling down from the snow-covered Persian hills only a few miles distant across the plain. The shops were practically empty of merchandise. Trade was almost at a standstill. There was a scarcity of fuel and, with the fall in the rouble, the price of bread and other essential foodstuffs had risen. Sugar had been unobtainable for months past, and materials for warm clothing were becoming scarcer and more expensive every day. The poorer people pulled in their belts. The railway workers went about muttering and demanding their pay.

It was all quite understandable, but it did not show the British up in a very good light. Our men were well clothed and had plenty to eat, facts which gave the Red agitators an excellent handle against us. They did not fail to use them.

The situation, already one of complete stalemate, was rapidly threatening to become quite impossible, when the Government of India, with the approval of Whitehall, decided at the last moment to play the role of 'Deus ex Machina'. As there was no money available, we should create some.

In other words, it was decided that we should print our own currency in the form of promissory notes. We should issue notes of the face value of 500 roubles, and we were empowered to make a preliminary issue totalling, 5,000,000 roubles. This meant that we had to produce and issue exactly 10,000 notes. It was left to myself to put the scheme into practice.

The first step was, of course, to get the notes printed. No, I am wrong. The first step, as it turned out, was to find suitable paper on which to have them printed. I hardly hoped to find a supply of high grade bank-note paper in a little place like Askhabad, but I was disappointed when I failed to find any paper at all with a water-mark. I felt that the presence of a water-mark would have given the notes a certain *cachet*, apart from rendering them more difficult to counterfeit. However, it was not to be and the only paper we succeeded in finding was of very inferior quality, such as in India would have been classified in unofficial parlance as *Bumff*.

To design the notes was the simplest part of the programme. We were not aesthetically ambitious and favoured something quite plain and unpretentious. But whatever our tastes might have been, we were compelled to go for simplicity by the absence at the local printing establishment of anything but the most rudimentary forms of type. It was desirable to have the text printed in English, Russian and local vernacular and though we eventually succeeded in doing this, the getting together of the necessary type called for a good deal of patient activity.

Numerous dies were cut and scrapped before we finally secured one that seemed fairly presentable, and then we started the printing. Every precaution was taken to control the production of the notes and to prevent the turning out of surreptitious extra copies. While printing was in progress, an officer was always present, and kept an eagle eye on every sheet of printed paper while the die itself, when not in use, was kept under lock and key in my quarters.

At the same time I could not help feeling that it was like putting an expensive lock on a cheap box that could easily be prised open. For the design of the notes was so simple that to have counterfeited them would have been child's play. Fortunately for us, the local inhabitants were not sufficiently sophisticated for that, but it said a good deal for the prestige of the British that these flimsy bits of printed *bumff* were readily accepted by the local population as legal tender at face value.

For ourselves the issuing of these notes meant a very great deal of work, for every single note had to be signed in ink by myself or one of the other officers. All turned to with a will and we would take it in turns working hour after hour, late into the night, signing these flimsy bits of paper for which the whole country was by this time impatiently waiting, and without which the railway would soon have ceased to function.

Soon we would be busy buying them back again, redeeming them with silver coin sent up from India, for it would be dangerous to leave the notes in circulation too long. As it was, we found that some quick-brained Armenian had made all arrangements to have counterfeit notes printed in the Caucasus. Fortunately he was just too late to get away with it, but I actually came across one excellently produced counterfeit with my own signature photographically reproduced!

The reception by the public of our 'home-made' notes was so excellent that for once even Zimin began to look more hopeful. But the payment of the promissory notes could in no sense provide a solution to the problem. At the best it was merely a palliative, and because it had been administered far too late, its effect could only be of the most temporary nature.

However, so tensely were we living, that we were thankful for even a short breathing space. At any rate I was. The Mission was not so vitally affected, for it had only come up to Trans-Caspia on a short visit to satisfy its curiosity as to the local situation. This latter was, as we have seen, far from being a happy one and it was only natural that the thoughts of the Mission should turn longingly to its comfortable quarters and pleasant surroundings in Meshed. The General and his Staff packed up and left again in ample time to be back home for Christmas and New Year.

I regretted the departure of the Staff, in particular Ellis and Jarvis, for they were cheery and capable fellows and their presence acted on me like a tonic. Before their arrival I had become very stale and I was suffering from 'Blues Trans-Caspiana', otherwise a surfeit of 'Ziminitis'. I found myself taking life too seriously and I badly wanted a change, but with the arrival on the scene of these cheery lads my blues disappeared and I began to see the funny side of things again. Frankly, however, at this particular period, the funny side was becoming increasingly difficult to find.

To anyone with a sense of humour, the Mission itself was one big joke. I do not think the General himself had much sense of humour. I upset him badly one day at breakfast by remarking that I thought the tea was too weak. It transpired that the teapot I had picked up contained his own special brew of some super blend of pure Darjeeling which he kept exclusively to himself. The General growled and made some caustic remark about the inability of some people to discern a really good tea when they came across one.

Then there was the incident of the oranges. The Mission felt that it would like some oranges. Now oranges — like sugar — were unobtainable at any price in Askhabad, but they were plentiful across the Caspian in Enzeli, whence supplies used to find their way to Krasnovodsk. I therefore sent a wire to Colonel Fleming, in English in the following brief words: 'Kindly send fifty good oranges.'

In reply I received a message to the effect that the oranges would be sent along in due course.

Some ten days later a very smart N.C.O. of the Royal Warwicks came into my office, clicked his heels and with a magnificent salute reported: 'Please sir, I have brought the oranges.'

'Very good Sergeant. Where are they?'

'I left them on the station, Sir.'

'Well, you had better have them brought up here.'

'Very good, Sir, but what about transport, Sir?'

'Transport?'

'Yes Sir. I have got fifty big cases of them, Sir.'

I nearly fell off my chair. 'Fifty cases, Sergeant? Oh very well. I'll have to go into this.'

'Very good, Sir.'

I called for the telegraphist. 'Oh, Duckworth, you remember that message we sent to Krasnovodsk about some oranges? Did you send it off yourself?'

'No Sir. Our time on the wire was up, so I spelled out the message in capitals and the Russians transmitted it.'

The Russian transcript turned out to be all right, so I took the matter up with Krasnovodsk. The mistake proved to have been at their end. The Russians had transmitted the message correctly in Russian characters, but instead of writing 50 *good* oranges they had wired '50 *pood* oranges' (the Russian *g* being similar to a *p*). One pood is 40lbs.

What happened to the oranges? Well, the Mission took its quota and everybody sucked oranges for some days to come. The remainder were sent to the troops at the Front, where they were received and disposed of with great enthusiasm.

Alarms and Excursions

◆

With the departure of the Mission, I was left to carry on once more alone. 'Carry-on' just summarised everything. But how long could one 'carry on carrying-on'? That was the question.

We had paid over 5,000,000 roubles in promissory notes, but by the time we had paid them, another month's wages for the railwaymen were already due, not to mention the running costs of the public services, hospitals, and of the army in the field. In a very short time, counted in days, the effect of the palliative had worked off, and the condition of the patient was more critical than ever.

Meanwhile the railwaymen were being systematically 'got at' by professional agitators who had found their way into the country. At their meetings they were calling for action against the British whom they termed 'Capitalist Exploiters of the Toiling Millions of the World'. Allusions were not infrequently made to myself as the 'Accursed Representative of Bloody Imperialism'.

The railwaymen's leaders also began to demand that the Front should be opened and the Bolshevik troops invited in. (Although Merv had been occupied on November 1st by British and Trans-Caspian forces, the British troops had now been ordered to advance no further.) It was emphasised that the Reds were after all Russians, like themselves, and they had no quarrel with the railwaymen, but only with the Intelligentsia. They blamed the latter in general and the Askhabad authorities in particular, for the present penniless condition of the country, accusing now the Intelligentsia and now the British of having deliberately mis-appropriated the Government funds, to which they referred as the 'birth-right of the Trans-Caspian proletariat', and generally wound up by proclaiming their intention of cutting the throats of both Russians and British indiscriminately.

The Askhabad Government clung desperately to power in spite of the empty treasury, not from any love of official authority, but because they saw no alternative but massacre by the Bolsheviks. It was the instinctive fear of extermination that compelled the 'Intelligentsia minority' to hold together, however desperate the situation; meanwhile the more extreme members of the Government were showing a growing inclination to throw in their lot with the Reds.

At this juncture Drushkin, the mysterious and somewhat sinister Jew from Astrakhan, was coming daily more prominently to notice. He was nothing much to look at — a small slight figure, and swarthy. He was always dressed completely in black — black felt hat, black suit, black overcoat and a black leather *porte-feuille*. His energy and determination appealed to me very much at first; it made such a pleasant contrast to the lethargic and irresolute character of most of the Russians. Drushkin was a man of action. He got things done. He was invaluable in Askhabad at this particular stage.

To give a clear picture of the trend of events at the end of 1918 and in the first weeks of the New Year, I cannot do better than quote from my daily telegrams to Meshed.

20.12.18 'Colonel Urussov, Chief of Staff, has come here from the Front, and reports situation there to be very serious. Desertions are taking place wholesale among the Russians owing to loss of morale, due largely to British troops remaining in the rear, also to hard life under difficult conditions, such as lack of shelter and absence of warm clothing.

'Urussov maintains that action one way or another can be no longer delayed. Either an advance must be made and Charjui taken, or the troops must fall back on Bairam Ali. The ability to defend the latter place is doubted owing to the absence of long range artillery. Information from Charjui shows the Bolsheviks to be also demoralised and to dread attack.

'Urussov had come to appeal for reinforcements from Askhabad and for the co-operation of British troops. After a lengthy meeting it was decided to make one more appeal for permission for British troops to assist in the advance on Charjui.

158

'Askhabad can send no reinforcements at present. By removing all standing guards from public buildings such as the bank, Post Office, etc., 200 men might be raised, but this would only be possible on condition we could replace these guards with our men. Permission for this step is requested. It has been decided to declare forthwith a sweeping mobilisation of all between the ages of 21 and 26 and to send them to the Front forthwith.'

'Discontent among the railway employees at the non-payment of *26.12.18* wages is increasing, which discontent is of course being further fostered by agitators, and the cry "Are we going to work without pay?" is being raised.

'Kurilev, who enjoys popularity and has considerable influence among the Kizil Arvat railway workmen, says he does not like their tone at all and has again raised the question of the desirability of a British detachment being sent down there as a temporary measure.

'Government have promised to pay out the arrears of salary to the men by the 28th instant. This they cannot do. They think they may be able to put off payment until January 2nd, when the bank opens after the holiday, but longer than that they see no possibility of holding out.'

'Secret. The general mobilisation has proved a failure. The *28.12.18* public at large realise that the Government has no power and there is nothing left now but for the latter to resign. My personal opinion is that the present Government will not live longer than the first week in January, and if it goes, the only practical form its successor can take is that of a dictatorate. The difficulty, of course, would be the selection of the members of the dictatorate.'

'Secret. It appears that a number of carefully trained Bolshevik agents, after completing a course at the Soviet Academy at Moscow, have been sent down here and have established themselves as schoolmasters at Kizil Arvat. It is these who have been responsible for the great increase in the number of Bolshevik sympathisers in that town. There is definite evidence to show that the Bolshevik movement may come to a head there any day, so assured are its supporters of the inability of the Askhabad Government to take any measures against them.

'The town has now deliberately defied the Government in refusing to obey the order of mobilisation and has openly expressed its desire to make peace with the Bolsheviks and to open the Front.

159

The Kizil Arvat workers are said to be preparing for hostilities and are known to be making bombs in one of the railway workshops.

'Drushkin is confident that with the help of a small British detachment, say 30 men, and his own party of 19, he will be able to effect all necessary arrests, disarm civilians and search all houses and workshops he needs to search. This, in his opinion, will settle the Kizil Arvat question definitely. He thinks this will take two days and if he can obtain our assistance, wishes to commence action on Tuesday the 31st instant. . . .

'Kizil Arvat having been dealt with, similar measures will immediately be taken in Askhabad. Here, Drushkin estimates 120 of our troops would be necessary. The increased number is due to the larger area. No armed resistance is expected. Merv will be treated simultaneously with Askhabad. In the meantime Government wish to know definitely whether our troops will be permitted to co-operate in these anti-Bolshevik measures, including the sending of a party to Kizil Arvat for a day or two to assist Drushkin. . . .'

30.12.18 'The Board of Directors met last night and after a heated controversy, decided to postpone definite resignation until January 1st or 2nd. Resignation, however, is inevitable.

'I foresee two alternatives, viz. either a dictatorate of three or five, or else an Extremist, i.e. Bolshevist, committee. Certain influential members are for the former. The majority of Directors, on the other hand, have no definite policy and will go with the working classes. The latter are definitely inclined to Bolshevism and openly declare themselves in favour of abandoning the Front and inviting the Bolsheviks in.

'Thus Dokhov, at last night's sitting, openly declared they should sever relations with the British and join the Bolsheviks. This shows the extreme change of feeling.

'There is ample evidence to show that if the pro-Bolshevik party gets the upper hand, we shall be drawn into open conflict. The only possible way to avoid this is for the dictatorial party to get into power first. This can only be done by a secret and sudden coup, consisting in a proclamation of the dictatorial power immediately after the official resignation of the present Government, followed without delay by the arrest of all the leading opponents, and also by energetic measures to disarm the civil population.

'These measures will devolve largely on our troops, as no Russian troops can be trusted. The question is quite clear: Are we to undertake these measures or not? If not, and if we are not given full authority to carry them out thoroughly and immediately the moment demands, we must in honour bound warn those concerned and be prepared for disorders on a large scale.

'Bearing in mind our policy of strict non-interference in politics, we shall nevertheless be drawn into most undesirable complications unless we do support the proposed dictatorial government. The latter, on the other hand, stand not the slightest chance without our determined support.'

'A large meeting of about one thousand railway and other *31.12.18* workmen was held this evening and is not yet over. The tone of the meeting is actively Bolshevik and very strongly anti-British.'

This meeting was of particular importance in that it marked a turning point in my personal relations with the Trans-Caspians.

Events were moving so fast that with the slow process of informing Meshed, who in turn informed India and Whitehall, who for thousands of reasons were unable to arrive at any immediate decision, the situation was deteriorating before our eyes. Very prompt action was essential and it was becoming hourly more evident that it would have to be taken before the old year went out at midnight.

Up to the present I had done everything possible to avoid commitments and to keep out of entanglements. Now the Government was in a state of flux and so was the general situation. Plot and counter-plot were in the air. Each side were making their plans. It was a question as to who would move first. Many things might happen before midnight.

I did not necessarily expect any serious disorder to occur at the meeting, but I had taken the precaution of having my own reliable observers present on the spot, with arrangements to keep me informed by telephone at frequent intervals how things were going. I knew that at least three workmen members of the Executive Committee would attend the meeting, namely Funtikov, Byelov and another and I was interested to know what their attitude would be. Funtikov was generally half, if not wholly, intoxicated, but — *in vino veritas* — one never knew what home-truths he might blurt out.

161

I hoped against hope that the meeting would end peacefully without any immediate consequences. Whatever happened, I wanted no violent disturbances in the next few hours, before the present Government dissolved on January 2nd. If anything were to happen in the meantime, the Reds might act suddenly, the others might be caught at a disadvantage and the fat would be in the fire.

For every reason, therefore, I prayed for a peaceful termination of the old year, but with a subconscious feeling that something was about to happen and that I would be taking action before the night was out.

I was not kept very long in doubt, for about an hour after the meeting started, my informant at the Railway Institute rang up to say that the tone of the gathering had now become emphatically pro-Bolshevik. It was the usual story. For some time past, as we very well knew, trained agitators had been drifting into Trans-Caspia from Soviet territory, some of them straight from Moscow, others from Astrakhan and Tashkent. It was they who had organised this meeting and they saw to it from the first that only they themselves and a few selected individuals would be allowed to speak. Among the silent ones were Funtikov and his two companions. Funtikov had evidently reverted to type. He had probably decided in his blurred mind that Red was the winning colour and he therefore staked on Red. He could not foresee that though Red would finally win, he would still lose.

Further details came over the phone from the meeting. Wild speeches were being made. The British were coming in for a lot of abuse, but this was scarcely surprising. The slogans 'Long live the Soviets' and 'Down with the English' were by this time almost synonymous terms. The one was invariably followed by the other. But these people were now going further than that. One unknown but particularly fiery speaker called for action. '*Throw open the Front, Comrades!* That's what we have got to do. Then we'll show these – – – – English etc., etc.' Prolonged cheers. Yes, the meeting was certainly turning against *us*.

Mere rhetorical abuse was one thing, but to agitate for direct action was quite another. A threat to the troops at the Front was no longer an internal question. It was impossible for me to remain out of this any longer. The aim of the agitators was obviously to work up a mass demonstration there and then. A little more of this wild incitement and the crowd would begin smashing things. . . . We must act immediately.

I got O.C. troops on the phone. He had already been warned of the possibility of trouble and was prepared for action. I arranged with him to turn out a couple of patrols of the 28th Cavalry, with instructions to keep moving round the centre of the town, with one patrol in the immediate vicinity of the Railway Institute. Orders were also given for a couple of pickets with machine-guns to be posted so as to command the front of the building.

I then got my typist to type out in Russian a number of copies of a 'warning'. The text briefly reminded the workers that, whatever their grievances, the authorities could not tolerate any disorder and that since any public disturbance might endanger the safety of our troops at the Front, I, as British Representative, was determined to take all measures necessary to preserve order and would put down any attempts at violence by force.

By the time a number of these 'warnings' had been typed and I had signed them, O.C. troops phoned up to say that the patrols were out and the pickets in position. I handed the notices to one of Drushkin's men, with instructions to paste them on the doors of the Institute and also to have some copies handed to various individuals — preferably the agitators themselves inside the building.

Drushkin, I knew, had a number of his informers mingled with the crowd, and it was one of these who was responsible for keeping me informed. His latest report, which had just come in, stated that the meeting had almost unanimously declared itself in favour of throwing open the Front, and inviting the Bolsheviks in. A resolution was also passed to send deputations to the workers' centres at Krasnovodsk, Kizil Arvat and Kazanjik, inviting them to join the movement.

I could do nothing more now but wait and see what sort of reaction my warning notices would produce. Meanwhile the following wire came in from Colonel Fleming in Krasnovodsk:

'Position here very serious, as Bolsheviks and railway workers mean attacking Government tonight. Have taken all steps with means available. We mean to disarm everybody in Krasnovodsk tomorrow. After that I presume I shall have enough men to disarm Kizil Arvat if it is done quickly. Kuhn had a very narrow escape this afternoon.'

This news from Fleming was rather disquieting, for it made me wonder whether the Reds had perhaps already made plans for immediate and simultaneous action in Krasnovodsk and Askhabad and possibly also the Front.

It was the question of the Front that caused me most anxiety. The Askhabad situation we could deal with. I had no doubt whatever about that. But the real danger was that any open disturbance involving a conflict with the British authorities would be certain to produce a serious repercussion at the Front. How could we know that these agitators were not deliberately trying to create a conflict in order to distract our attention while the Red troops launched a surprise attack on our position? Knollys and his men were having a very difficult time, surrounded as they were by treacherous elements. All the more reason why this Askhabad business must be nipped in the bud.

As the clock ticked on and no further reports came in, the suspense began to make me really anxious. I felt very tempted to go down to the Institute myself. Anything rather than this inaction — sitting in ignorance of what was happening only half a mile away.

The telephone rang. It was Drushkin. 'Everything gone off well. The meeting has broken up and they are all going quietly home. I will be round in half an hour.'

'*Slava Bogoo*! Thank goodness!' I wanted to ask him more questions, but he had rung off.

I went and got myself a drink.

It was nearly an hour later when Drushkin put in an appearance and for the first time I felt really happy at the sight of his sinister dark figure and inevitable *porte-feuille*.

If anyone carried his life in his hands in those critical days, it was Drushkin and yet I believe that he never went armed. His weapon was his *porte-feuille* and the tell-tale dossiers it contained. But he always had a bodyguard well armed in the near vicinity. Today he was accompanied by his lieutenant, a cynical looking Georgian dressed from head to foot in black leather, the butt of a Nagan pistol protruding from its holster and a bandolier belt full of cartridges round his waist.

I had the *samovar* brought in; tea was poured out and Drushkin proceeded to tell me what had happened.

My warning notices were affixed to the doors of the building without anyone observing them. The remaining copies were then taken inside and thrust into the hands of various individuals. One of these was the particularly fiery individual who had been most loquacious throughout the proceedings. His reaction was immediate. He mounted the platform and at once began a fresh tirade against the British.

'*Smotreetye Tovarishchi*. What did I tell you? The English are here to take over the country. Down with the cursed English *Bourzhooi*, Capitalists and Counter-Revolutionaries. Throw open the Front!'

At this moment someone threw open the front door and in a loud voice shouted: '*Ostorozhno*! Be careful, Comrades, the place is surrounded!'

It was one of Drushkin's men. Simultaneously several others entered and shouted to the same effect. For a moment or two they were not heard. There followed a brief pause as the meaning of the shouts gradually sank in and then a scramble for the exit.

The fiery one continued his fulminations on the platform. More of Drushkin's militiamen, fully armed, appeared in the doorways and pushed their way inside. They shouted for silence. Even the fiery one paused.

Then Alanya, the Chief of the Militia, a Georgian — strong and thick set as a bull and with a voice like a fog-horn — started addressing the crowd. He reassured them that everything was all right and that nothing would happen to them provided they broke up quietly and went straight home. But there was to be no loitering and no going about in groups.

The crowd started leaving. The militiamen stepped aside and let them pass out. The fiery gentleman, shouting louder than ever, made an effort to hold them back and accused them of being cowards and slaves of the British, but he had lost his chance. The crowd was moving and as they came into the open air they heard and saw the cavalry patrols and glimpsed the machine-guns just across the road. In the bitter cold their spirits fell. They made for home without another word.

Inside the building the burly Alanya and his merry men were trussing up the fiery gentleman, together with two or three of his companions.

'The others will be roped in tomorrow,' said Drushkin. 'We know where to find them.'

'What will you do with them?' I asked, somewhat incautiously.

'That,' said Drushkin grimly, as he emptied his glass of tea, 'is a domestic matter which does not concern the British authorities.'

Then, excusing himself on the plea that it was very late and that he still had many things to attend to before the morning, he picked up his *porte-feuille* and made a polite bow, wished me a happy New Year and, followed by his leather-clad henchman, departed into the night.

A happy New Year! I rang up O.C. troops, thanked him for his co-operation and for the assistance of his men and told him that everything was now all right and that they could all go back to barracks. I did not think we should have any more trouble now and suggested that he should come round and have a drink. But he, stout fellow, declined, as he still had a lot to do. How busy we all were, in spite of the war being over!

On my table lay a telegram from Meshed. It had been received just at midnight and Sergeant Duckworth had irreverently scribbled on the cover: *New Year Message from the Mission*. It read as follows: 'Warn all ranks to beware of treachery and attempts at assassination! No officers or others to go about singly and all should carry arms.'

Thus began the year of grace 1919.

Scraping the Barrel

◆

The New Year opened on a note of renewed optimism.

Our little *tour de force* had proved even more successful than I had dared to hope. Orders had come through from India authorising the use of our British and Indian units to assist the Askhabad authorities in disarming the population and effecting arrests of undesirable elements. This gave a great impetus to the forces of law and order.

In particular the energy of Drushkin knew no bounds. I do not believe he ever slept. He lived entirely on his nerves. His *porte-feuille* contained long lists of suspected persons and he and his men proceeded to round them all up one after another, until the prison was filled to overflowing.

The Askhabad Government's interpretation of our attitude was that we would scarcely begin to give active support to the Askhabad authorities unless we had also decided to furnish the financial wherewithal to enable them to carry on, and they were now determined to get a Committee of Public Safety into the saddle with as little delay as possible.

The same spirit of hopefulness had also communicated itself to the population as a whole, and in a remarkable degree also to the railway workers. The fact that the British were now taking an active hand put new life and hopes into them. To the ordinary citizen it meant an assurance of safety. To the workers it meant that their chances of getting their pay would be much brighter. They now turned a deaf ear to their agitators and dropped the idea of a strike. The majority of them were not Bolshevik at heart, but merely wanted to work and earn their livelihood like any other mortals.

In a night, the situation had changed miraculously, as it were, for the better. But I was full of misgivings. Here were all these people — officials, workers and private citizens — all of them pinning their faith to the assistance of the British. They had been given a small sign that we would not permit disorder, and they assumed, rather naturally, though perhaps too naively, that we would therefore remove the cause of disorder by giving the government our support and means to carry on. But was this our intention?

So far I had not been given the slightest indication by Meshed that there had been any change in our Government's attitude towards the financial question. I had seen no symptoms that the matter was even under consideration, though I felt that with all my reports the Powers-that-Be must have realised that we could not possibly maintain our present position unless we did give some assistance.

During the first two days of January, the Askhabad Government were fully occupied resigning and reconstructing themselves and the financial question was not mentioned. But they were careful to consult me in every step they took; in fact they were at pains to show that the whole situation was in our hands, as my telegrams made clear.

1.1.19 'The Board of Directors officially resigned this afternoon, whereby they passed a resolution to the following effect. The resolution begins: "After consideration of the existing situation and realising that the fight against Bolshevism can only be successful when the Government consists of a few members and enjoys the complete confidence of the Allies and of the general public, the Board of Directors has decided . . . to appoint a Committee of Public Safety, having the approval of the Presidium of the Executive Committee and of the British Military Mission. Such Committee to consist of five members under the following conditions:

(a) The majority must be Russians.
(b) The policy of the Committee must be directed to the preservation of Trans-Caspia for Russia and the guarding of the interests of the working classes.
(c) The British Government will wholeheartedly support the new Government with a view to solving those problems

168

which were acknowledged when the Allied troops first entered Russia.'''

The next few days I was to experience the difficulties encountered by prime ministers in getting together a cabinet during a time of crisis. With a view to pacifying the Turkmans and keeping them friendly, it was decided straight away to give them two places. In making this decision, consideration was given to the fact of there being two distinct parties among the Turkmans, viz. the 'progressive' anti-Russian party, with Haji Murat at its head, and the older conservative school, whose acknowledged leader was Mahtum Quli Khan. This arrangement seemed reasonable to the Russians, but it remained to be seen what the Turkmans themselves would have to say about it. As things turned out, they were going to have a great deal to say.

There were now three places left to be filled. One of these ought to go to a representative of the working classes. There must also be a capable and strong personality to carry on the campaign against Bolshevism and there ought also to be somebody capable of maintaining liaison with the British.

'The selection of a Committee of Public Safety is proving a 3.1.19 much more complicated affair than I anticipated. The Committee want to leave it entirely to me. I have declined to accept the responsibility, but in view of the danger of a deadlock, I have decided to propose that I nominate one member.'

Difficulty arose over the Army, which also wished to have a representative in the Committee. The only acceptable candidate was General Kruten, an elderly man of very decided political views (old school, of course), and I should imagine of no particularly outstanding ability. His candidature proved rather a stumbling block, as there were only three places vacant, but this difficulty was surmounted by giving him an independent role as Military Director. In any case his job would be of secondary importance, since he had no control over troops at the Front.

Whatever his ability may have been and possibly I am maligning him, General Kruten was a keen old man and very conscientious. I remember his tackling me, drawing me on one side and adversely criticising my support of the candidature of Drushkin. 'Sir,' he said, 'you are making a very great mistake — a fatal

169

mistake — in including this fellow Drushkin. You will live to regret it!'

'Why?' I asked.

'Because Drushkin is a Jew. You British do not know what that means, but we Russians do. Never, never, *never* give a Jew power — because he will sooner or later abuse it. Remember this. The Jews have a saying about us Russians and in fact about all Gentiles. They say "It was we who gave you Christ and one day we will give you a king!"'

His words remained in my mind and a moment came when I wondered if he had not been right and I had been wrong.

'After a long series of deadlocks', I cabled, 'I have just succeeded in collecting what promises to be a really useful Committee of Public Safety. Its composition is as follows:

'General Kruten, independently of the Committee in his role of Military Director, but with the right of a voice in the Committee. In the Committee proper, Zimin, Byelov, and Drushkin and two Turkman representatives, one of whom is almost certain to be Haji Murat.

'The combination Zimin, Byelov, and Drushkin is about the best we can possibly get. Byelov is very straight and has the respect of the working classes. Drushkin is indefatigable in his anti-Bolshevik methods and Zimin makes a very good go-between.'

And so we had weathered the crisis. The Committee of Public Safety had come into being and, with the assumed backing and declared goodwill of the British, was soon showing a firm hand.

Confidence was being restored throughout the country. This was very clearly shown by the attitude of the workers' community in Kizil Arvat, who actually expressed a desire to have a detachment of British troops sent there to cope with Bolshevik agitation which was still very active. True, the Turkman question was not yet settled and we should probably still have some trouble with Haji Murat and Ovezbaiev. *But* most important of all there was the phantom of Finance looming up in the background and darkening the whole picture.

If only the Committee had sufficient money to pay the railway workers, everything else could wait. We were now already in January and many of them had not yet received their wages for the second half of November. Added to which it was the traditional holiday time. The workers wanted to buy a few simple presents for their families, instead of which they had not even money enough to buy bread.

The Committee called on me next day and wanted to know what 4.1.19 we proposed to do. What could I say? I had to prevaricate. I had to think out explanations and try and give plausible reasons why they could not expect any definite decision this morning . . . this afternoon and tonight. Tomorrow . . . doubtless there would be news.

Somewhere in Delhi and in Whitehall, generals in brass hats and politicians in frock coats were doubtless deliberating the Trans-Caspian question. At a distance it must have appeared a very small item on their daily programme of post-war problems. . . . Or perhaps they were not deliberating at all. Perhaps the whole question had just been filed, or shelved.

Well, anyway, we had to carry on and the railway had to carry on.

But Zimin was getting weary. Once he let himself go and accused us of fooling them. He said some very bitter words, but checked himself, and apologised. I must excuse his feelings. He had not slept for many nights and was really worried. I patted him on the back and advised him to go and get a good night's sleep. I needed it myself. He almost burst into tears, for he was not at all strong and the strain was telling on him.

I gained a certain respite by discussing details of expenditure and running costs with the Railway Board. I spent several hours wading through schedules and statistics. This looked as though we were at least interested in the railway and it enabled me to escape for a time from the pressing attentions of the Committee.

The least perturbed person of all was Drushkin. He did not come and worry me, for he was far too busy carrying out his 'disarmament campaign'. Aided by a party of militiamen, armed to the teeth and occasionally reinforced by some of our own men, he seemed to be unearthing rifles, pistols and bombs all over the place and was as happy as a terrier in a field chasing rabbits.

The next day brought nothing from Meshed and I was left to face 5.1.19 the Committee once again. I tried my best to cheer Zimin up. He was pale as a sheet and his nervous fingers tore at his brown beard. I often wondered what he would have looked like without a beard.

It certainly gave him a degree of dignity which he might otherwise have lacked, though I must admit that in speech he was always very dignified and he spoke firmly and well. He occasionally smiled, but I never knew him make a joke. The last few weeks had certainly seen very little cause for either smiling or joking.

A diversion was caused by the presence in Askhabad of a deputation of railwaymen from Kizil Arvat. They had called on the Committee in an attempt to obtain some undertaking regarding the payment of their arrears of pay. The Committee had of course not been able to give any assurances and the deputation had thereupon expressed the desire to come and see me. Zimin begged me to receive them.

I did not want to get involved in direct relations with the railwaymen. Though I had already met some of the Askhabad men unofficially, these Kizil Arvat people were strangers to me. Finally, at the urgent request of Zimin, we agreed that if no news came from Meshed that night I would arrange to receive the deputation the following day.

By evening there was still no news from Meshed and Zimin became rather desperate. Drushkin had unearthed another conspiracy to overthrow the new Committee and had found a lot more arms and ammunition. At this rate soon the only people not disarmed would be the Turkmans. Would Drushkin be able to cope with them too, I wondered.

Among the material found in the possession of certain of the arrested Bolshevik agents had been a large quantity of propaganda on the usual lines. Among this was one communication which was rather enlightening. It appeared to have emanated from Baku and described some local strike movement which had broken out there. It declared that the British military authorities had been compelled to come to terms with the strikers and that this went to prove that strikes were the best weapon with which to deal with the British.

Further documents were found addressed to the workers in the railway shops at Kizil Arvat and along the line, urging them to go on strike and thereby drive the British from Trans-Caspia. They contained all the well known terms of abuse habitually levelled against the British and showed clearly that we still had plenty of Bolshevik agents and agitators in our midst. The more Drushkin roped in, the more fresh ones seemed to arrive.

When I assured Zimin for the nth time that I had already reported every detail of the situation to Meshed, he begged me to make one more effort and send a personal appeal to General Malleson direct. I did not see much point in doing this, but Zimin was so insistent that I should make just one more personal effort that I finally promised to do so.

When Zimin had gone, I sat down and wrote out a personal telegram. I knew that I had already covered all the ground and had said everything I could, but I added a few suggestions. These, I thought, might help evoke an answer of some sort, even if it were only an emphatic negative. I was certain that this telegram would make me unpopular with the Mission, but by this time I was long past caring about that.

'Secret and very urgent. The political situation here without money is absolutely impossible. The new Committee of Public Safety has, in the initial stages, proved a great success. Since its formation, the public have been impressed with its energetic measures in disarming the civil population, but most of all by the support accorded it in maintaining order by our troops.

'It is generally recognised that this new government has the confidence of the British and respect for it has grown accordingly. There are everywhere signs of an improved feeling among the working classes, whose hope of receiving their wages has also risen considerably.

'Reports from the Front and from Merv and even from Kizil Arvat show a corresponding improvement in the feeling of the workmen there. The general feeling is, in short, one of expectancy. If the new Committee could only produce the pay required, their position would, by this fact alone, be put on a very firm footing. If they fail to do this, they will fall and the result of their fall will be more odium cast on the British.

'To return to facts, Sir, *the new Committee cannot carry on*. I have done my very best, but nothing I can possibly do, short of some official promise, will keep them together. Unless I can give them some sort of a promise tonight, they will resign, and we shall be in a worse position than ever.

'I have put forth every argument I can possibly think of to tide matters over for a day or two more. The Committee will not remain, however, and they are not to blame.

'The only suggestion I can make is that I pay out all the money I have earmarked for promissory notes. It will do us far more good at this moment than if kept for payment of our notes, for the latter are recognised as good and need no boosting.

'The second suggestion I hesitate to make, as you have already negatived it, viz. the printing of a small number of promissory notes. The mere fact of it being known that they were being printed would inspire confidence and keep the situation going.

'The third suggestion is that you wire some sort of statement inspiring confidence that the wages of the workmen will be paid, fixing some definite date. If you could fix a definite date it would not matter if it were relatively distant, as the fact of its being definite would be sufficient for the working classes. On the strength of this statement alone work would continue on the railway and we should avert the now imminent danger of a strike.

'Fourthly, could not the authorities at Baku do something?

'I sincerely hope you will at least allow me to pay out what sums I still have left with me. It will help a little. I must have an answer tonight, as, if not, I doubt if I can keep things together till tomorrow. Committee is giving me no peace and I have another meeting with them tonight. If I have nothing to reply, my position becomes impossible.

'In conclusion I wish to emphasise that none of the above points has been set forth with a view to keeping the Government on its legs for any particular time, but with the one intention of keeping the railway going for a few days longer and with it to ensure the safety of our troops, who, unless some immediate action is taken, will find themselves in a very difficult situation.'

If I could only get this most vital matter settled and be able to rely definitely on there being no stoppage on the railway within the next two or three weeks, then I should feel that I had done everything that was humanly possible in the circumstances and my one desire would then be to get away from Trans-Caspia as soon as possible. I was disgusted with the constant necessity of lying and prevaricating day after day. I was in fact sick and weary of the whole thing and instead of being proud of my position as Representative of Great Britain, I was heartily ashamed of the ignominious role I was continuously called upon to play.

6.1.19   The next morning Zimin was round early. I still had no news for

174

him, but I told him that I had sent off a long personal appeal to Meshed and that I was now prepared to meet the Kizil Arvat railwaymen. This obviously pleased him.

That afternoon the railwaymen, four in number, came round and I gave them tea — the simplest possible meal, for I wanted them to see that we also were not living in the lap of luxury. As a matter of fact the *samovar* was the only warm thing about the place, for we had run out of fuel and my rooms were so cold that we sat and shivered even in our overcoats.

I spoke to my visitors frankly. I did not ask them what their troubles were, for I knew that as well as they did, but I expressed great regret that they had got into their present condition. I blamed lack of foresight and prodigal expenditure in the early days of the last government, for which some of their own railwaymen were also partly to blame. (Mutters of 'Funtikov' and 'Dokhov'.) I then went on to expatiate on the reasons that had brought us British up to Trans-Caspia in the first place. I rubbed in dozens of reasons why we should never dream of taking over the country and, feeling rather hypocritical, added that the only thing which prevented our going away was a feeling of duty towards the Trans-Caspians.

The money difficulty was very great because of the tremendous distances and lack of communication with India. Here followed a graphic description of the road! Also, we had so many troops on the road, that it was all we could do to get rations and forage for them. (No harm in letting them know that we had plenty of reinforcements within reach!)

The men, who were really very decent outspoken fellows, explained that they were seriously concerned about the steadily increasing activity of Bolshevik agitators, particularly in Kizil Arvat. They themselves did not want to have any more to do with Bolshevism. They had had one dose and that had been quite enough. Furthermore, since many of them had played an active part in suppressing the Bolsheviks during the July revolt and had actually taken part in the shooting of Commissar Fralov, if the Bolsheviks got into Trans-Caspia again their lives would certainly be forfeit. This is why they were so anxious to have a British detachment sent to Kizil Arvat. The local agitators would then be kept in check without them themselves running the risk of becoming further involved.

Without pledging or committing ourselves in any way, I did secure a tacit promise that the railwaymen would not try to force the hands of the Askhabad Committee. I assured them that the latter was really out to help them and that any money it received would be expended on the railway before anything else. The Government was doing its best under very great difficulties. After all, it had only been in existence three or four days and I begged them to give it a fair chance. They saw the commonsense of this and promised to refrain from any action likely to embarrass the Committee.

They agreed with me that it would be far more sensible to continue bearing their present troubles a little longer, rather than lose everything at one swoop by a strike. It was in everybody's interests to keep the railway going and their people working and earning their regular salaries, even if these were paid with some delay. Only the Bolsheviks could gain by a stoppage.

I promised to help in the matter of taking repressive measures against the Red agitators in Kizil Arvat and that I would take up the matter of sending down a British detachment.

As we parted, I asked them to make it quite clear to their friends in Askhabad what we had discussed and the verbal promises they had given me. They agreed to call a meeting that evening and expressed confidence that when their Askhabad colleagues learned of their friendly conversations with me, they would certainly decide to shelve the question of a strike and would co-operate with the Committee as far as possible. We all shook hands and parted in a very friendly spirit.

One thing was certain. The better elements among the railway-men were thoroughly sound and reliable, but one could see that they were being got at mercilessly by the Bolsheviks and were really in need of some active support.

Here was another job for Drushkin, but could he do it without the support of British bayonets? Permission had been given for our troops to be used in aiding the police in Askhabad, but to send them all the way to Kizil Arvat was a different proposition. One had to be quite certain that they would not walk into a trap, but this again was only a matter for careful enquiry beforehand.

That evening I received the long awaited response from Meshed. And what a response!

'My orders leave me no option in the matter. No money whatever is to be paid without the sanction of H.M. Government and no such sanction has been received, nor can I even hold out hopes that it will be subsequently received. I can give no comforting assurances to Askhabad Government and if they feel they must resign tonight I cannot help it.'

Zimin was round almost as soon as I had received the telegram.

'Well,' I said, 'I have had a reply from Meshed. I'm afraid it doesn't take us very far, as they have not yet received sanction from London to make any payments yet, but I have some very good news about the railway workers. They are not going to strike, and they are not going to worry the Committee, but they are going on working until this money question clears up. Now that they have agreed to do this, I want you and your colleagues to take the same reasonable view. . . .' and I went on to tell him in detail all about my talk with the railwaymen and the necessity of taking strong measures to 'liquidate' the Red agitators in Kizil Arvat and gave him no chance to revert to the question of Meshed.

When Zimin had gone — and his departure was a great relief, for the longer he stayed, the more I had to talk to keep him off the one undesirable topic — I read and re-read General Malleson's telegram.

It was certainly blunt and definite enough, but one could not call it exactly helpful. Obviously he could do nothing and knew nothing, but 'if they feel they must resign tonight I cannot help it. . . .' was tantamount to saying that it was all the same to him and he didn't care two hoots what the Askhabad people did. That, at any rate, was what it would appear like.

He did not take the trouble to make any suggestion as to what I should do if they did resign. No mention of any measures to be taken, or interest shown in what the situation might become. Not a bit of help whatever.

Though it was unwise to pin one's faith to any particular factor, with a fluid situation such as this, I could not help placing a good deal of reliance on the attitude of the railwaymen and the promise they had given me. It was the one bright spot in the picture. Even Zimin had seemed much relieved when I told him about it and promised to get Drushkin onto the question of carrying out some 'liquidation' (his own favourite term!) down at Kizil Arvat.

Zimin's feelings and mine were further relieved that evening when we heard that the Askhabad railwaymen had convened a meeting to review the result of their Kizil Arvat comrades' interview with myself. The meeting passed an unanimous resolution not to strike for the present and to give the Committee a fair chance.

The situation was therefore much better. All we wanted now was money. One thing seemed quite definite. Either the British Government would have to pay up, or we would have to get out. From now onwards the issue was a clear one. It was 'Stay and stay indefinitely — or Go'. That was a question which only H.M. Government could decide and doubtless this, among countless other greater problems, was already giving food for very serious thought in the councils of Whitehall.

I only knew that I personally was becoming very stale and weary of the whole thing, and while there could be no question of my giving up in the middle of a crisis I felt that, as soon as we did definitely weather the present storm and see a little daylight ahead of us, I would put in for leave to go home.

If we were definitely going to stay, or even if there were a hope that we would definitely stay, then I would be prepared to carry on for months yet and I did not care how many crises we had, so long as we had a policy. But if we were not going to stay, then this muddling-on from day to day, which was all it was, could only end in one thing — disaster. That was very clear to me and must have been clear to all concerned. I cabled again on January 7th.

7.1.19   'I have thought fit not to convey the contents of your M.1385 of last night to the Committee as the effect of this would be to make the latter resign at once.'

8.1.19   January 8th brought a batch of cipher telegrams from Meshed.

'*Secret* C.G.S. has replied to my telegrams dwelling on the seriousness of the situation and issues the following orders:

"1. Preparations to be made to concentrate the troops at present in the Merv area either at Askhabad or its vicinity, or in the neighbourhood of the Persian frontiers such as Kaahka and Dushak.

"2. Should the situation take an unfavourable turn, you are authorised, if essential, to expend funds or incur liabilities to the extent necessary to secure the co-operation of the railway

178

workers in providing necessary train service for such concentration. You must not consider this to be authority to pay wages or arrears of wages to the railway workmen. Ends."

'General Beatty will work out the necessary scheme and calculate the trains required. No payment to railway workmen is to be made without my previous approval. The whole of this telegram is to be kept absolutely secret.'

General Beatty had just arrived in Trans-Caspia to take up the command at the Front. This at any rate was something concrete at last. The Powers-that-Be were evidently beginning to take notice.

There was a shorter telegram, also in cipher. It was in reply to mine above and read: 'You must exercise your own discretion as to how much you tell the Committee, but on no account hold out misleading hopes, as I do not want to let anyone down.'

The phrase about 'misleading hopes' and 'letting anyone down' touched me on the raw. If anybody had consistently tried to avoid giving misleading hopes, it was myself. As for 'letting people down', if those on the spot had been asked, it would not have been myself they would have accused of 'letting people down'. I replied: 'My intention was in no way to hold out misleading hopes. I suggested refraining from telling the Committee bluntly there was no hope of any money, as to do so directly would mean their resignation. As regards letting them down, in view of the tone of your telegrams today, I wish to point out clearly that neither the Committee nor the general public had any idea of our troops evacuating in the near future.

'If we actually intend withdrawing our support, then I submit we are in honour bound to give some sign of this in our relations with the Committee. I should welcome some very definite instructions from you on this point, as to continue my present relations with the Committee is certainly tantamount to holding out misleading hopes.'

The above telegram may seem somewhat 'crusty' and unnecessarily abrupt when read now, but at the time I felt it was essential to send it. The point was that, quite apart from any sentiment, I sensed a danger that if things were to go at all wrong, I might quite conceivably be held responsible for not having communicated the text of the General's message literally to the Committee.

9.1.19   I asked for 'very definite instructions', but this is exactly what Meshed would *not* give me. Their reply avoided the issue completely and merely gave me a snub. 'G.O.C. desires you merely carry out instructions and avoid jumping at any conclusions. His orders from Government have been communicated to you with a view to your being prepared for all eventualities, but he still has hopes that Government may decide to continue to support Trans-Caspia. To tell the Askhabad Government anything before the decision had been arrived at would ruin all. The whole matter is under reference to London and in the meanwhile we must carry on as best we can.'

10.1.19   Fortunately, next day, other telegrams from Meshed followed and here at last was the news we had all been waiting for so long.

'Authority has now been given me to pay railway staff for the next few weeks pending the final decision of H.M. Government on the whole question of policy. . . .

'Wire at once what is the absolute minimum necessary to keep the Askhabad Government going for the next four weeks. It is useless putting forward extravagant claims, otherwise the whole thing will be negatived . . . Meanwhile you can start printing and signing promissory notes, but no payment whatever is to be made pending further authority from me.

'You should also explain clearly to the Askhabad Government that the difficulties of finance are so great that they must make every effort to get in revenue and make themselves self-supporting, as it is impossible for us to provide funds beyond the next few weeks. . . .

'Do not draw attention to it, but in preparing further promissory notes, make them out for six months, instead of three months. Also make both the English and Russian text on the notes to read, "*Promise to repay in rouble notes at or before the end of six months*". This is with a view to making it clear there is no liability to repay in coin.' (The real reason was obviously that the rouble was dropping steadily in value and the longer we gave it, the cheaper it would become.)

So the financial crisis appeared to have been successfully weathered, at any rate for the time being. Now, however, I had other problems to attend to, for the problem of the Turkmans threatened to come to a head at last.

Turbulent Turkmans

◆

Later that same day, 10th January, I received a phone call from 10.1.19 Haji Murat. He told me what I already knew, that there had been a large meeting of Turkmans and he now explained that a deputation of the tribesmen wished to come and see me. He hoped that I would receive them. Half an hour later they arrived.

There were some forty of them in all, comprising chieftains from the different sections of the Tekke tribes from all over Trans-Caspia. Without exception they were in tribal dress. This consisted in soft leather moccasins and leg wrappings, or in some cases Russian boots, cotton shirt and pantaloons, and over them a long plum coloured *kaftan*, sometimes hanging open down to the knees, but more often girt round the waist with a narrow strap or belt of wrought leather; then, the crowning glory, an enormous *papakha* of black and white or brown sheepskin. The Turkman *papakha* is by far the biggest and most striking male Asian headdress and by adding appreciably to the height of the wearer — Turkmans as a rule are inclined to be tall — gives him a most distinguished appearance.

The house I was using as my combined headquarters and residence was a large one which had been loaned to the Government by its owner, a wealthy Persian. It had been constructed in a modified Persian style, with one large upper room extending down the whole of the back of the building and flanked by a wide balcony or verandah.

The room was the show-piece of the place, or rather the pictures were, for the owner had had a decided *penchant* for nude Circassian dancing girls and had commissioned some western painter to produce a series of these life-size masterpieces. There was nothing impressionistic about them. This artist belonged to the starkly realistic school and his ladies were certainly very lovely and seductive and, during the heat of a Central Asian summer, no doubt calculatedly disturbing. But now we were in the depths of an abnormally rigorous winter and my household was still without fuel or firewood. I wore a wool-lined trench coat all day inside the house and spread it over my bed at night. Even indoors one's breath became visibly vaporised on the frosty air that pervaded the whole building.

I was unable at such short notice to provide seating accommodation for so many unexpected guests. Those from outlying districts had come in by train, but those from the nearer *auls* had ridden in on horseback and had tied up their animals outside the garden gate.

I had them all shown into the big room and as they came crowding in, many of them with daggers protruding from their waistbands, I could not help thinking of Ali Baba and the forty thieves. When they were all assembled, I joined them and mingled with the crowd. I recognised several tribal leaders. Haji Murat and Ovezbaiev were both there and introduced a number of other chieftains, presumably from among their own supporters. None of these spoke Russian but we managed to exchange salutations and compliments in Persian bolstered by my limited scraps of Turki.

It was noticeable that the crowd had roughly divided itself into two sections, the one comprising the followers of Haji Murat and Ovezbaiev and the remainder centred upon Mahtum Quli Khan, with whom were a group of *ak-sakal* or tribal grey-beards. Some of these were very fine looking men with pronounced Mongolian, though in many cases highly intelligent, features. It seemed clear that the older and better type of Tekke supported Mahtum Quli Khan and frankly I was very glad to see this, for it bore out what I had been repeatedly told, namely that, although he was less vocal and less educated than Haji Murat, Mahtum Quli Khan still wielded much greater influence within the tribe.

While I did not know for certain what had prompted this particular visit by the deputation, I made a little speech in Russian and welcomed them, regretting that I could not offer them hospitality, but assuring them that I was greatly honoured by their visit and would hope to entertain them another time in proper tribal fashion. This seemed to go down very well and there were audible grunts of approval, while some of the elders stroked their sparse Mongol beards.

Since Haji Murat and Ovezbaiev were almost the only ones fluent in Russian, they did most of the talking. They explained that while the Turkmans had certain differences among themselves, they were all anxious for some assurance of British support and expressed the hope that we would not continue to stand aloof, but would associate ourselves with internal reform, the improvement of laws and so forth.

Several other leaders, including Mahtum Quli Khan, whose Russian, though intelligible, was not fluent, made little speeches in their own language and finally, after about an hour, the meeting broke up. I saw them to the door in Persian fashion and shook each one by the hand as he left.

Haji Murat and Ovezbaiev lingered until the last, and finally whispered in my ear that they would like to come and visit me privately, so I fixed the following evening. I could see that there was something very much on their minds, but they clearly did not wish to be seen lingering with me in conversation and they followed the others out.

The temperature of the room from all those khalat and sheepskin covered bodies had risen about fifty degrees. I was surprised that none of them seemed to have noticed the paintings on the wall.

I very soon learned the real motive which had prompted the Turkman deputation to call upon me. The whole of that morning they had been holding a mass meeting just outside the town to settle the vexed question as to who should have the two Turkman seats in the Committee.

In allocating two seats, as I have already mentioned, the idea had been that one of these should go to the 'conservative' and the other to the 'progressive' element among the tribesmen. The two candidates the Russian members of the Committee had had in mind were Mahtum Quli Khan and Haji Murat. However, when put to the vote, the two candidates approved by the majority where Mahtum Quli Khan and Oraz Sardar, an interesting result, for it showed clearly that the progressive element was much less influential within the tribe than had been suspected. This decision was not what Haji Murat and Ovezbaiev had expected and they quickly set about securing a reversal. On the plea that Oraz Sardar could not possibly leave the Front and also that certain *auls* had not been represented, they succeeded in getting the decision voided pending the holding of another meeting.

At the first meeting held that morning, both Haji Murat and Ovezbaiev had expressed the greatest contempt for the Russian officials in Askhabad, including the new Committee for Public Safety. Ovezbaiev had been particularly outspoken. He had declared that the Russians were finished in Trans-Caspia and that if it came to a show-down there were enough armed Turkmans in the country to wipe out the Russians to the last man.

Haji Murat was much more restrained. While agreeing that they could deal with the Russians, he reminded the tribesmen that the British were the real power to be reckoned with and that therefore the most important thing was to win over the British to supporting the Turkmans in the Committee. For that reason he thought it a suitable moment to pay a courtesy call upon the British Representative and try and impress him with the strength of Turkman feeling on the subject. He and Ovezbaiev really intended to bring only their own followers, but when Mahtum Quli Khan realised what was in the wind, he decided to bring along his own following as well and the result was a combined deputation comprising both factions.

11.1.19   A second mass meeting held the next day was packed by the followers of Haji Murat and reversed the previous day's findings, with the result that both Haji Murat and Ovezbaiev were elected.

I immediately called Meshed: 'I have just heard that Haji Murat and Ovezbaiev have been elected to represent the Turkmans. The presence of the latter in the Committee, as I have already pointed out, is not only undesirable, but dangerous. He has a very definite policy and from his several conversations with me, I can see quite plainly that he intends playing on the Turkmans' ignorance and pretending he has the support of the British. He talks a lot of rubbish, but it is dangerous rubbish. He is a soldier and his proper place is at the Front.

'I have just reminded the Committee quietly that according to the resolution of the late Executive Committee, candidates must have the approval of the British Mission. I shall negative Ovezbaiev. I will do it tactfully so as not to hurt his feelings, but he must go back to the Front.

'Since the Turkmans seem unable to elect anyone themselves without outside assistance, I am going to ask Mahtum Quli Khan to come in. My meeting with all the Turkmans yesterday convinced me that his influence is far greater than that of Haji Murat or Ovezbaiev, or indeed, of both these two together. Mahtum Quli Khan stands for peace and order and has no progressivist ideas. Trust you approve action.'

'Haji Murat and Ovezbaiev came to see me last night. . . . They *12.1.19* were very argumentative, Ovezbaiev being particularly outspoken, saying that if it was a question of representative government, then the entire government ought to be Turkman. I pointed out that Ovezbaiev's proper place was at the Front. He replied that he could be at the Front as well as hold a place in the Committee.

'Haji Murat was much averse to working together with Mahtum Quli Khan, for the chief reason that the latter stood for the old Russian administration, had absolutely no following and could only be a hindrance.

'Ovezbaiev said that his appointment would probably lead to dissension among the Turkmans and there might be bloodshed. I seized the opportunity to remind him that any disorders of the nature hinted at would be vigorously suppressed by us.

'After talking for two hours, Haji Murat and Ovezbaiev left, very far from satisfied. I personally do not think this will be the end of it and consider it highly probable an attempt will be made to murder Mahtum Quli Khan.

'The latter also came to see me this morning. He admits that he has lost influence to Haji Murat and Ovezbaiev, who are younger and more able than he. Force is on their side, but in the district, away from their direct influence, the Turkmans cling to the old regime and only wish for peace and order.

'Mahtum Quli Khan admits that he has no armed following, but says that if his presence in the Government is desired he is quite ready to take his place. I must admit he seems rather a helpless old man, but he would undoubtedly serve as a satisfactory counter-poise to Haji Murat.

'As for Ovezbaiev, his policy is so tactlessly precipitate that his association with the Government would almost certainly bring things to a head in a very short time. I hear today that he and Haji Murat were yesterday hatching a plot to arrest Dokhov, Karpinski and one or two other Russian officials who have been associated with the control of internal affairs. I expect the move will be to get Oraz Sardar to threaten to resign unless Mahtum Quli Khan is removed. Should he do so, I submit that not too much importance be attached to his threat.'

Realising that he was getting up against the British Ovezbaiev returned sulkily to the Front, accompanied by Haji Murat, who was also very disgruntled. They went straight to Oraz Sardar and pitched a long story of high-handed action by the Askhabad Committee and talked the old Turkman into tendering his resignation. My warning that this would probably happen had prepared our people for it. They tactfully made a fuss over Oraz Sardar; the question was allowed to slide, but in Askhabad we did not give way and Ovezbaiev did not take his seat in the Committee.

Instead he kept up a steady intrigue with Haji Murat. One day he would be at the Front and the next he would disappear into the *auls* and nobody would know where he was. Having failed to get his own way in Askhabad, he set to work on a more ambitious scheme, a hint of which he had himself given me when he had last called on me. This was no less than the formation of an independent Turkman Republic comprising a number of small 'khanates'. He had been attracted to this idea by the fact that the British, though in military occupation of Azerbaijan, had not restored the former Russian regime, but had recognised the de facto independence of the Azerbaijan Republic. If the British could do this on the other side of the Caspian, they might quite well agree to recognise an independent Turkman Republic of Trans-Caspia. And it was to the furtherance of a scheme on these lines that Ovezbaiev now turned his activities.

The Russians, both Red and White, were dependent on the railway, or confined to it. They could not operate and could not even exist save in the immediate vicinity of those two shining steel rails that traversed the desert from the Caspian to the Oxus and down to the Afghan frontier. But with the exception of that narrow steel track, the Turkmans had the whole of the vast interior in which to roam about. The country was really theirs and *in sh'allah* they would take it.

So Ovezbaiev and Co. drew up attractive schemes for parcelling up not only Trans-Caspia but also the rest of Turkistan. Ovezbaiev would have his sphere of influence, Haji Murat would have his and there would be plenty of territory left for Aziz Khan of Tejen, for Allahyar the freebooter (who was supposed to have been hanged, but who was still very much alive), and Junaid Khan the ravager of Khiva. Even the Emir of Bokhara was included in the scheme, doubtless to give it tone.

The first-fruits of Ovezbaiev's far-flung activities were frequent outrages committed on the defenceless Russian settlers in outlying villages. Day after day we would hear of some raid by armed Turkmans who would murder all the men and carry off the girls and women into the *auls*.

I wrote to Colonel Knollys and begged him to see Oraz Sardar and insist that Ovezbaiev be ordered back to the Front and kept there. This time Oraz Sardar issued stronger orders that Ovezbaiev did not dare ignore.

Ovezbaiev came to say goodbye to me before he went away. He was thoroughly disgruntled at my having 'checked his political career', but he was good enough to say that he bore me no personal ill-will.

I knew him fairly well by this time, for he had been round to see me privately on a number of occasions and we had some quite long talks together, on unofficial matters. He declared he found me very 'sympateechny' and liked my English cigarettes. I think he also liked me because I was very outspoken and gave him plenty of sound advice, but without letting him feel there was any racial gulf between us.

He did not hesitate to run down his own tribes-people as a lot of cowardly cut-throats, which was exactly what they were, and he was particularly impressed by the friendly and almost brotherly relations existing between our British officers and their Indian *sepoys*. I told him stories about India and about the North West Frontier. He laughed when I told him we occasionally had trouble with our own tribes-people. 'There's going to be a good deal of that in this country before we've finished,' he said. 'Do not forget that today every Turkman is armed. With the whole of the country in our hands. . . .'

'Except the railway,' I ventured.

'Well, except the railway; but what is the railway, after all? Our ancestors lived without it and in any case we have the whole of the steppe to move about in.'

'That's all very well, Ovezbaiev,' I said, 'but I thought you were progressive and wanted to move with the times? You can't get very far on horseback these days, you know!'

Ovezbaiev remained unconvinced, but he shook hands warmly and took a supply of my cigarettes with him before leaving.

Haji Murat was a different type. He also had benefited by a military upbringing and he too was instinctively an admirer of the Turks, with their common ties of blood and language. He also was ambitious, but he was some ten years older than his younger companion and was more ready to recognise indisputable facts.

He had the greatest contempt for the Russians. Red or White, he regarded them as equally impossible. The British were the deciding factor. With British assistance and under British protection, Trans-Caspia could remain a peaceful country, and the Turkmans asked for nothing better than to live under our rule.

It was possible to discuss things rationally with Haji Murat and we had many interesting conversations together. There were many questions on which we did not agree, but we agreed to disagree. From him I learned a great deal about the different tribal sections of Turkmans, and regretted very much that I had not had an opportunity of visiting the country before the war.

Haji Murat several times invited me to go off into the *auls* with him and, as the Russian members of the Committee would have been greatly shocked and the Mission in Meshed would have 'panicked' had I done so, I shall not say whether I went or not. Officially, at any rate, I can safely say that I never left Askhabad.

Unofficially, many things are possible. I fear that my old Peshawar habits of sneaking into *caravansarais*, hobnobbing with camel-men and generally venturing where self-respecting angels would fear to tread, would now and then prove too strong for me, particularly with an individual like Drushkin about the place. Drushkin could always provide a thrill at short notice if one felt in the mood for it. His henchman Alanya could have told some stories, too, if he had lived, but the Reds saw to it that he didn't.

I was always very careful. If Drushkin suggested that he had a particularly interesting 'crib to crack', or as he would call it a 'liquidation to carry out', and I might like to go along, one could be quite certain that one would be kept well out of harm's way. On such occasions of 'off duty', my place was ably taken by Captain Haines, one of the best and most loyal of good fellows. No British officer, let alone the British Representative, would have been seen on such occasions — merely an extra member of Drushkin's militia bodyguard. So there was no harm in it.

In spite of Drushkin's almost superhuman activities, and in the face of much opposition by the better elements among the railway workers, Bolshevik agitation went on. No sooner had Drushkin's myrmidons 'liquidated' one nest of agitators, than fresh ones started up. He carried out an excellent piece of work in Kizil Arvat, where, supported by a detachment of the Royal Warwicks, he descended upon the town and arrested a large batch of undesirables and seized about one thousand rifles together with ammunition. But it was a hopeless task, for by this time the Bolsheviks at the Front were well aware of the British Government's decision not to permit our troops to advance eastwards beyond their present positions. The Reds felt quite secure and could take their own time over things.

Every day some report would come in describing either the latest outrage by Turkmans, or the activities of the latest arrived Red agitator. The following telegram is indicative of what was happening all round us at this period.

'Conclusive evidence has been found today showing a conspiracy *14.1.19* on the part of a number of local Bolsheviks to overthrow the present Government. The conspiracy included Funtikov, Sedikh, Anisimov, Gladirev and Byelokon. The two last named are Kronstadt sailors. The conspirators have collected a number of arms including bombs, and have also today obtained blank passports with a view to escaping if their plot fails. Active measures are being taken for their arrest tonight.'

The sudden discovery by Drushkin of the Funtikov conspiracy in our very midst naturally caused quite a sensation, in spite of the fact that we were getting quite used to all manner of alarms and excursions.

I had always looked upon Funtikov as a drunken fool, but bigger fools were they who took him into their confidence and included him in their conspiracy. It was his own drunken blatherings that gave him away. Drushkin had been watching him as a cat watches a mouse ever since the meeting at the Railway

Institute. A search of Funtikov's house revealed rifles and bombs underneath the floor.

His companions were all known and were speedily roped in. They were a clumsy crowd, but more rifles and bombs in their possession showed that they meant business.

Drushkin was in excellent form. He never turned a hair and in spite of his nocturnal activities he nearly always looked spruce and well turned out. Whenever he would open his *porte-feuille* and I glimpsed those neatly typed lists and the files of manuscript reports, I thought of the French Revolution, particularly when Drushkin, picking up a list of names and running his finger down it, would say in his quiet voice, 'Yes, I think we will arrest him tomorrow.' Or, 'No, we will leave him for a day or two longer.' Here was Fouquier-Tinville all over.

The arrest of Funtikov caused no little sensation in Askhabad. Firstly, people were beginning to realise the serious danger of the enemy within their midst, and secondly, Funtikov was a member of the Social Revolutionary Party.

The Social Revolutionaries, or the S.R.s as they called themselves, were an old political organisation with tradition and a reputation to keep up. To be arrested was almost second nature with them. (Was not Siberia full of them, or of their bones!) Funtikov's disgrace, therefore, did not lie in his being arrested, but in the fact that he had been guilty of plotting against his own party comrades. In plain Russian he was a *sookin syn*, otherwise a 'dirty dog'.

In the old days he would most certainly have been sent to Siberia. As circumstances over which the Trans-Caspians had no control prevented his being sent there at present, they scratched their heads and decided that since tradition demanded he should be sent somewhere on a long journey, the next best thing would be to ask the British to send him down the road to India. The only alternative would be to shoot him, for they did not like the idea of keeping him in the Askhabad gaol. It was too near home — and one never knew, these days. Nobody seemed keen on shooting Funtikov. At any rate his brother S.R.s did not wish to do so. It would have stained the family escutcheon, so to speak. Drushkin was quite prepared to shoot him — it would have served to keep his hand in — but then doubtless Drushkin had no family escutcheon to worry about.

'Committee asked last night whether you could possibly arrange to take over these prisoners and keep them in Meshed for a time. Nearly all of them have by one crime or another, from murder downwards, rendered themselves liable to criminal proceedings, entirely apart from official offences.

'The Committee is anxious to try them on these grounds, but as their presence under arrest in Askhabad is likely to be the direct cause of more plotting and agitation, they are anxious, if possible, to have them kept in Meshed for a short time until their fate can be settled.

'There are certain reasons why it might be more politic not to shoot them out of hand. Several of them are members of the S.R. party. Some workmen's delegates yesterday expressed the hope that we would, if possible, dispose of Funtikov and Company without shooting them. They admitted that Funtikov and Company were a disgrace to their party, but they felt that the disgrace would be increased if they were shot.'

Meshed replied: 'The times are such that some show of strength and decision on the part of the Committee are absolutely essential. Apart from the fact that it would be most inconvenient to provide guards and escorts for these men, the decision to send them to Meshed would be rightly interpreted as a pitiful display of weakness and fear of taking responsibility on the part of the Committee. There seems no reason why they should not be tried by Court Martial and disposed of one way or the other within forty-eight hours. . . .

'I presume Drushkin has considered question of guaranteeing life of one of those most involved in exchange for giving away the whole conspiracy. Encourage the Committee, if they value their own skins, to be firm in dealing with this matter. Zimin is so weak that I hope his voice will not be allowed to count for much. What is Funtikov doing in this?'

I replied: 'I discussed the question of Funtikov and others with Drushkin this morning. He is also of opinion that it would be more advisable merely to deport and not to shoot these prisoners, as to do so would give rise to considerable ill-feeling on the part of the Social Revolutionaries, who are at present the most reliable political body in Trans-Caspia. I consider Drushkin's opinion sound, as he is by no means weak, and would not hesitate for one moment to shoot all the prisoners if he thought the situation demanded it.

'Further, there is the fact that these prisoners, though important, are nevertheless less dangerous than other conspirators still at large, but whose identity and whereabouts have all been ascertained through one member who was threatened with death if he did not disclose them. The arrest of this further party will probably take place tonight. I understand that one of the fresh lot will have to be shot.'

The sequel to the story is that Meshed steadily refused to take over the prisoners and the Committee could not make up their minds to shoot them. The outcome was that they lingered in gaol in Askhabad until the Reds came in, whereupon Funtikov was promptly shot for the part he had taken in the anti-Bolshevik revolt of last summer. Rather bad luck on Funtikov, but he was not a great loss to humanity.

Debacle

◆

Active operations on the front had now practically ceased, following the decision of the British Government that our troops were not to advance or to engage in operations further east than their present position.

Our troops had settled into winter quarters at Bairam Ali. In the old pre-war days this must have been a delightful little place. Round about was the former Imperial estate, well stocked with small game, including pheasant. In the village itself was the Palace, really a shooting box, built on luxurious lines for the convenience of the Tsar, or other members of the Imperial Family should they ever visit these far-flung corners of their domains.

Our troops had their headquarters in the Palace itself and they could not have found more comfortable and even luxurious quarters in the whole of the country. Some cynically minded Russians were unkind enough to suggest that it was the comfortable quarters which decided the British command not to invite further commitments by advancing further east into the desert.

The enemy were at Charjui. I was about to say they had dug themselves in there, but this was not the case. 'Digging-in' on either side was rendered unnecessary by the presence of those two shining steel rails which so conveniently spanned the desert. For this was a railway war.

Both sides possessed locomotives and rolling stock and both sides lived in their respective trains. Even our troops lived in trains, such of them, that is, who were not residing in the Imperial Palace!

Now there is an art in living in trains. I can speak with some authority on this because I once lived in a closed truck for several weeks in the depth of winter. For many days I had to share the truck with fourteen other people. Such trucks are called *teplushki*, which literally means that they are heated vans. This again suggests that they are artificially heated by stoves, but in practice many of them — my own particular truck among the number — were heated naturally by the warmth from one's body. With fourteen other people in it, my particular *teplushka* was really heated.

The Bolsheviks had other ideas of luxury. They had their women with them. I say their women; I must correct this, for as a matter of fact, most of the women were not theirs at all, at any rate not legitimately. Some of them, it is true, were voluntarily there. Some of them actually took part in the fighting and were occasionally found among the casualties. But many of the others, poor things, were there by force, conscripted wives and daughters of the Intelligentsia of Tashkent and elsewhere.

When the Reds raided a place, or evacuated it, they had a playful little habit — emulated by the Turkmans — of carrying off all the girls and women. The Turkmans used to sell them in their *auls* — an old Turkman custom — but the Bolsheviks took their captures with them on active service.

War is beastly, but it also has its funny side, and quite the funniest side of this railway war was the daily duel of the armoured trains.

So here we have the picture: Bairam Ali with its palatial headquarters and the rest of our people in trains, including such Turkmans as were not away in their *auls* and such Russians as were not in Askhabad or elsewhere. Some twenty miles further on eastwards along the line was the little place called Annenkovo, which was the furthest east to which we were allowed to move, and beyond this was Tom Tiddler's ground. At Annenkovo barbed wire defences had been constructed in the form of a chain of outposts, each within close range of its neighbour and garrisoned by infantry. Cavalry patrols could move about freely between these little posts and of course under the protection of their machine-gun fire if necessary.

Through the centre of these posts ran those shining steel rails, linking Annenkovo with headquarters at Bairam Ali and thence running westwards to Merv, Askhabad and the distant Caspian. In the other direction they also led straight to the enemy's positions, with his collection of trains, a little over a mile away, while beyond him again was Charjui and the great bridge across the Oxus.

The Trans-Caspians possessed at this time three armoured trains, one of which mounted a howitzer taken from the fortress at Kushk and also a field gun and machine-guns. This was the principal 'battle train', the other two being kept in reserve. The Bolsheviks had similar armoured trains, but were believed to have heavier guns. In any case their shooting was execrable, so it made little difference.

The daily operations were very simple. Between our position and the enemy's, the line made a bend and ran through a small cutting, which afforded a certain amount of cover. Armoured trains always liked bends and cuttings, for it enabled them to creep up out of sight of the enemy. Possibly like the ostrich with his head in the sand, they felt more secure. The Trans-Caspian train would advance bravely forth and puff and snort its way down the line to the 'home' end of the cutting. There it would stop just long enough to let off one round and would then promptly go into reverse and make straight for home.

Local etiquette and the rules of the game then required the enemy to wait a little while, and after a reasonable pause their train would perform a similar evolution and fire its daily round at the Trans-Caspians. After watching this operation for a few days one understood perfectly the origin of that old phrase 'the daily round, the common task'.

I must add that the shooting was wild and it was very unusual that any damage was done. The great advantage was that both sides had their bit of fun, there was no discomfort and honour was satisfied.

At night cavalry patrols used to go out and occasionally, more by chance than design, they established contact with the enemy. On one or two occasions patrols of our own cavalry actually ran into superior numbers of the enemy, but they always got away with it after inflicting heavy casualties. In fact the 19th Punjabis and the 28th Cavalry between them were the terror of the Reds and they established a reputation for prowess that will be handed down in the *auls* of Turkistan for generations to come.

But in spite of the comforts of Bairam Ali and the amusement afforded by the daily duel, the situation could not go on like this forever. The Bolsheviks were only biding their time. They could afford to continue playing 'tip and run' with their armoured trains and carousing with their captured women, for they knew that the British would not move out to attack them. It was, indeed, only a question of waiting until the British packed up and went home. Then they would just walk through Trans-Caspia and get their own back with a vengeance. Meanwhile, they could gradually collect reinforcements and they could also send numbers of agitators into the enemy's rear to prepare the way for their coming advance to the Caspian.

As reinforcements they received several thousand Austrian and Hungarian prisoners of war. These wretched people, tens of thousands in number, had been interned in Turkistan prior to the Russian debacle. The Revolution had freed them, but the Bolsheviks had conscripted them. When they demanded to be sent home, the Reds tauntingly pointed towards Trans-Caspia and said, 'That way leads home. You can fight your way there.'

Several thousands of them were put into tattered uniforms, given a rifle, pushed into a train and decanted onto the Annenkovo front. One or two small parties of them had tried to make their way across to our positions. Of these only few individuals got safely across. The remainder were recaptured by the Reds and some of them were shot, or worse still they were murdered by the Turkmans. It was quite common for the cavalry patrols to come across the naked bodies of these wretched fellows, their throats cut and every strip of clothing taken. On one occasion there were women among the victims.

Oraz Sardar and the Trans-Caspian Government were desperately anxious to push the Reds back to the Oxus, where they would have a better chance of holding them when the day came, as come it must, for our troops to withdraw from the country, but both Turkmans and Russians — the latter with a number of outstanding exceptions — were thoroughly unreliable. The Turkmans never had been reliable; the Russians were becoming completely demoralised.

A powerful factor contributing to the demoralisation of the Russians was the refusal of the British Government to permit our troops to co-operate in any advance further along the line. This veto came as a great blow to the Trans-Caspians, who felt that they were being left in the lurch, and in December Zimin had handed to me the following petition with the request that it might be submitted to the British Government.

'On the 17th November last, in a letter to General Malleson, I had the honour to request General Malleson to approach his Government with a view to their sanctioning the co-operation of their troops at present at Merv with our troops in an advance on Charjui.

'I repeat again the reasons which make an early occupation of Charjui so important:

(1) Charjui is a strong and convenient position to hold. It would be no difficult matter for our troops to hold the crossing over the river, particularly since there is no other possible crossing within 200 versts of Charjui. Once in possession of Charjui, our troops, who are weak in both numbers and morale, could stand fast, strengthen their position and reorganise themselves. General Malleson, as a military man, must appreciate better than anyone the advantage of Charjui, and our consequent anxiety to get there.

(2) The occupation of Charjui would also be of immense advantage to us in that it would bring us into direct communication with Bokhara. We have already been told definitely that the Emir of Bokhara and the Bokharan people have suffered so severely at the hands of the Bolsheviks that they will welcome the arrival of troops and our allies the British with open arms, and will afford us every assistance. Of the truth and reliability of this, the Trans-Caspian Government, which is in continuous communication with the Emir of Bokhara, is firmly convinced.

(3) The fear that the appearance of British troops in Bokhara will give rise to a feeling of hostility in Afghanistan is totally unfounded. The Trans-Caspian Government is in constant touch with Herat and the latest reports from there show everything to be perfectly quiet and the prestige of the British to be higher than ever before. If the Afghans remained loyal in spite of German agents while Great Britain was at war, there can be no possible grounds for fearing complications with them now when Britain appears as the most powerful nation in the world.

'The condition of our troops at the Front, however, has become dangerous. After having been stationary for about one month, our army, consisting of ill-disciplined volunteers, worn out both physically and morally, has commenced to go to pieces. Our soldiers and with them a certain portion of the population of the province, hitherto placing all their hopes on the success and assistance of the Allies, are beginning to doubt whether the British really wish to help us, inasmuch as they cannot believe for one moment that the Allies, after having conquered the whole world, and having occupied the Caucasus and Baku, are unable to send to the Trans-Caspian Front a single aeroplane and two heavy guns.

'The Russian troops are dispersing day by day. They number at the present moment not more than 200 men. Meanwhile we have received reports that the Bolsheviks intend making a strong offensive and are bringing over troops from the Orenburg Front for this purpose.

'Our position is serious to a degree. There is no time to lose. If the British Government has decided to help us and wishes to have Russian troops at the Front, it is absolutely essential they should give us this assistance at once without wasting a single moment.

'For this reason the Trans-Caspian Government has ordered me to request you to forward its request to General Malleson with as little delay as possible. Namely:

(1) To ask the British Government once more by telegraph to permit British troops at Merv and at Askhabad to take an active part in operations against Charjui.

(2) To send some fighting aeroplanes to this Front.

(3) To send heavy artillery and ammunition.'

15.1.19   Not until 15th January did General Malleson reply: 'No advance by our troops is permissible beyond Bairam Ali. The situation internally does not admit of garrisons of either Merv or Askhabad being further reduced.'

This came as a stunning blow to the Trans-Caspians. As the Government had stated in their petition, they simply could not understand why Britain, having just emerged victorious from a world war, found it impossible to give them the very limited assistance on which their very existence depended. From now onwards Trans-Caspian morale began to fall off rapidly.

The news that General Milne, Commander-in-Chief of the Army of the Black Sea, would shortly visit Trans-Caspia helped to stem the rot for a short time. Hoping against hope, the Trans-

Caspians tried to persuade themselves that the British Government might at the very last moment show a change of heart.

The day before his arrival the members of the Government all 18.1.19 came to me and begged me almost on their knees to do my utmost to induce the Commander-in-Chief to grant the assistance they had asked for. The issue, they declared, was now a purely humanitarian one. An entire civil population was faced with disaster. The Bolsheviks had long since threatened to wipe out Askhabad with all its inhabitants as revenge for the events of the past summer. Nobody doubted but that they would carry out their threat. The British could easily avert the disaster and they alone could avert it. The Government now appealed to me, not as a government, but as spokesmen of the people, pleading the cause of the entire population. They implored me on my honour to do my best for them, and I promised.

The following morning the Commander-in-Chief's special train *19.1.19* steamed into Askhabad station to the rattle of rifles, as guards of honour, both British and Russian, presented arms and the railway band played the National Anthem.

General Milne inspected the guards of honour and then received me in his railway carriage. He was very kind and asked me a great many questions about the situation in the country. His questions showed that he had a very clear grasp of the whole picture, which I was able to fill in here and there with further supplementary details.

In particular he wanted to know more about the initial stages of our relations with the Trans-Caspians and what obligations we had assumed. On this I was able to enlighten him.

He had evidently heard some adverse reports against the Trans-Caspians and was interested to know what sort of a show they had put up. I defended them on a number of counts and pointed out the serious limitations and handicaps under which they had been working.

General Milne's final question was what would happen if we withdrew our troops? My reply was that without a doubt the Trans-Caspian resistance would immediately crumble and the Bolsheviks would re-occupy the whole of the country. I then mentioned the petition to the British Government for the continued co-operation of our troops and the appeal of the Trans-Caspians on humanitarian grounds and made out as strong a case as I could in favour of our standing by them a little longer.

General Milne seemed satisfied that he now had all the information he required as far as the political aspect of the situation was concerned and, with more saluting and band playing, his special train steamed off again towards Merv.

The Commander-in-Chief paid a very brief visit to the Front and then returned via Askhabad to the Caucasus and Constantinople. Whether he had already come to any decision as regards a withdrawal of the troops was not stated, but something was said about sending guns and ammunition. The Trans-Caspians were given to understand, however, that the decision not to advance further would not be modified and it seemed pretty clear that the fairly near future would see our complete withdrawal from the country.

The news, of course, increased still further the alarm and despondency among the population as a whole, both Turkman and Russian. The Turkmans had no illusions as to their own fate at the hands of the Reds and more than anything they dreaded reprisals against their families in the *auls*. A deputation of leaders submitted a petition to General Malleson for British protection of the tribal regions, but this was, of course, quite impracticable.

Deputations from all classes of the population pleaded for delay in the withdrawal of our troops to allow more time for reinforcements to arrive from the North Caucasus. Several Cossack and Daghestani detachments did come across from the Caucasus, as did also the guns which General Milne had promised. But the psychological moment when their appearance might have turned the scale had passed. The general morale had now sunk too low and the rot had set in.

Instead of staying at the Front, many of the Daghestanis flocked back to Askhabad, where they swaggered about the streets and provoked the working classes to retaliation. The town was filled to overflowing with refugees from down the line and their numbers swelled daily as they fled before the menacing Red wave.

General Malleson returned to Askhabad with a couple of his staff and they took up their residence in the town. But even this had little effect upon the general despondency. It was not a Mission in the rear that was needed, but British bayonets at the Front.

The members of the Government were listless. Red agitators were appearing on all sides. Drushkin continued to struggle manfully with their suppression and his work of 'liquidation' carried on. The Mission backed him to the extent of giving him a personal bodyguard of *sepoys*. But the enthusiasm of his colleagues waned. Many of the members of the first committee were in gaol. Drushkin had put them there.

Feeling turned against Drushkin. He was carrying his zeal to extremes. Arresting, locking up and 'liquidation' seemed to have become a mania with him. The only thing that seriously hampered him was lack of adequate prison accommodation. I began to suspect that he was disposing of his prisoners otherwise than behind bars.

The last time I had a chance to speak with him alone, over the usual glass of tea, his manner was still suave and calm and he still preserved all his self-control. But I detected a glint in his eye which I had not noticed before and I had misgivings. I warned General Malleson that Drushkin was going too far, and his life was no longer safe. He was several times assaulted on the street. Still he carried on. One night a crowd of Daghestanis attacked his house. His Indian guards were compelled to open fire and killed several of the attackers. Then Drushkin lost his nerve at last. He asked to be given protection as far as the Caucasus. The Mission paid him a bonus of several thousand roubles and sent him under escort as far as Tiflis. There he fell sick and died of typhus.

Meanwhile, the main problem troubling the Mission and the British Command was how to ensure the safe withdrawal of our troops from the Front without bringing down a Red attack upon them. The solution was found in a subterfuge. Rumours were judiciously put about, with the certainty of their reaching the Reds, to the effect that the British Command were planning two simultaneous flanking movements — one from Bokhara with the co-operation of the Emir's troops and the other from across the Persian border near Sarakhs, with fresh forces brought up from India.

The plan worked. The Bolsheviks, still extremely sensitive to any possibility of attack by the British and Indian troops, took the threat of this imaginary pincer movement seriously. They also took appropriate measures to counter it. They withdrew units from Annenkovo from where they knew the British were pulled back and left that Front denuded until late in April, by which time the last of our troops had already left the country. The 28th Cavalry and 19th Punjabis crossed back into Persia via the Artyk–Muhammedabad road. The British units, including those in Askhabad, left late on the night of April 14th by train for Krasnovodsk and the remaining details in Askhabad, together with General Malleson and his party, left quietly at a very early hour in the morning and crossed the Persian border before daybreak, thereby bringing to a close the final act of the Malleson Mission in Trans-Caspia.

Before his final withdrawal took place, I had already left the country. My own departure was less ignominious, indeed far less so than my first arrival in the territory, for I was given a special train by the Askhabad Government and was accorded a touching send-off by members of the Committee, representatives of the railwaymen and a deputation from the civilian population, who expressed their 'heart-felt thanks for all you have done for us'. (Or tried to do for them!)

The night before my departure, Haji Murat paid me a farewell visit and on behalf of the Turkmans presented me with an old tribal whip mounted in silver. This, he told me, had belonged to his father, a Tekke chieftain who had carried it at the battle of Geok Tepe, where the Turkmans made their last desperate stand against the invading Russians. The whip, he said, had been in his family for many generations and he begged me to accept it as a token of Turkman gratitude and esteem.*

Our own military had a guard of honour on the station for my departure. The officers had planned to give me a farewell party, but I declined, and all agreed that it was no time for celebration. They thanked me for my co-operation, especially for my efforts to improve the hospital conditions for the Indian sick and wounded. Only from General Malleson I had not a single word of appreciation.

I watched the flat, desolate landscape glide past me with mixed feelings of relief and sadness. For years, since early boyhood, it had

*This whip, one of his most treasured possessions, was stolen from Teague-Jones's baggage over sixty years later during his move from Spain to Plymouth.

been my dream to get to Central Asia. True, I had seen only a small part of it, and that in anything but favourable circumstances, but I still felt the spell of its ancient charm. Perhaps one day I might revisit it under happier conditions, but for the present I had seen enough. The Trans-Caspian dream had begun in tragedy and was ending in tragedy.

Ring down the Curtain!

Epilogue

by Peter Hopkirk

◆

Although the events surrounding the massacre of the twenty-six Baku commissars occupy only a small part of Teague-Jones's narrative, their repercussions, as we know, were to haunt him for the rest of his life. For very soon the Bolsheviks were to seize on the affair and turn it into a *cause célèbre*, with Teague-Jones cast as the villain. Because of what followed, precise knowledge of his subsequent career and movements is difficult to obtain, and I shall confine myself here to the extraordinary events which forced him to change his name and vanish from sight until his death, some seventy years later, in November 1988.

Until the spring of 1919, Teague-Jones does not appear to have been unduly worried about the affair, having been more than 200 miles away from the scene of the murder on the morning when it took place. Moreover, the outcome of the Bolshevik revolution was still far from certain, it being assumed by many that Lenin's power would be short-lived. But then, early in 1919, an article appeared in a Baku newspaper violently accusing Teague-Jones of being responsible for the commissars' deaths. It was written by a Socialist-Revolutionary lawyer named Vadim Chaikin, who claimed to have conducted a thorough investigation of the events leading to the massacre. He quoted Funtikov, by now in an S.R. jail in Askhabad after being toppled from the presidency, as pinning the blame personally on Teague-Jones. According to a sworn statement made by Funtikov, the British officer had insisted to him — against his wishes — that it was 'imperative' that the commissars be shot, and had afterwards expressed satisfaction that this had been carried out 'in accordance with the aims of the English mission'.

In April 1919, Joseph Stalin, himself of Caucasian origin, entered the fray on the Baku commissars' behalf, denouncing the British as 'cannibals' for their alleged role in the murders. From that moment onwards charges of British implication, all of them based on Chaikin's wholly uncorroborated 'evidence', began to proliferate, to the increasing concern of the British Foreign Office, not to mention of Teague-Jones himself, who was by then back in London on leave before returning to his peacetime career in the Indian Foreign and Political Department. But worse was still to come. In March 1922, Chaikin repeated his allegations against Teague-Jones, in greater detail, in a 190-page book published in Moscow. In it he demanded that Teague-Jones be brought before an international tribunal to face war crime charges. He also challenged Teague-Jones to sue him for libel in a British court if he disputed the 'evidence', volunteering to come to London to appear in the witness box.

Chaikin's allegations were particularly valuable to the Bolshevik propaganda machine, since he himself belonged to the rival camp within Russia, the Socialist-Revolutionaries, and could therefore be said to be disinterested in the commissars' fate. However, as a Socialist-Revolutionary he had good reason for seeking to pin the entire responsibility for the murders on the British — and especially on their representative nearest to the spot — for this would exonerate his friends on the Askhabad Committee from blame. If this was his hope then he failed, for no sooner had the Bolsheviks ousted their rivals and gained control over the Trans-Caspian region than retribution was unleashed on everyone even remotely connected with the affair. Even Chaikin was to get his come-uppance, as Teague-Jones had forecast, though not for many years, by which time he had served his purpose.

But in the meantime the Bolsheviks continued to step up their campaign against the British, whose intervention in the civil war they bitterly resented, and whose world-wide power they saw as the principal obstacle to their dream of global revolution. After reading Chaikin's book, Trotsky now took up the cudgels on behalf of the Baku commissars, who were already being hailed in Moscow as martyrs in the struggle against imperialism and foreign intervention.

Dedicating his own book, *Between Red and White*, which dealt with events in the Caucasus, to the Baku commissars, and accepting all Chaikin's uncorroborated charges as proven, he too pinned the blame for the murders squarely on the shoulders of the unfortunate Teague-Jones, further alleging that he had acted with the full 'knowledge and approbation' of the British military authorities in Trans-Caspia. Although Trotsky's statement contained a number of obvious errors of fact (including mixing up General Malleson with another British general), this now became Moscow's official line on the massacre. Painters, film-makers and other propagandists vied with one another to portray direct British involvement in the execution, often going far beyond what even Chaikin alleged. One celebrated painting of the execution scene by the revolutionary artist Isaac Brodsky shows no fewer than five uniformed British officers present. Two of them can clearly be seen urging members of the firing squad to shoot the captive commissars, who are depicted striking defiant attitudes.

Precisely when Teague-Jones decided to change his name and vanish from public view is uncertain, for in Britain this can be done by statutory declaration before a Justice of the Peace or a Commissioner for Oaths, with no legal requirement to register it anywhere or advertise it in the newspapers. Thus the declaration itself is the sole evidence of the change. It seems likely, however, that Reginald Teague-Jones became Ronald Sinclair shortly after Trotsky's alarming denunciation of him in May 1922. After all, it was no secret that the Bolshevik death squads had both a long arm and a long memory — as Trotsky himself was to discover in 1940 when living in exile in Mexico. It also appears that for certain official purposes Teague-Jones continued for a while to use his original name.

Foreign Office records show that in June 1922 Teague-Jones, who was then in London on leave, was asked to make a thorough study of Chaikin's charges, since these formed the basis of Trotsky's and all other allegations, and answer these in full. In August 1922, the Foreign Office was still addressing him as Captain Teague-Jones, and writing to him in connection with the Baku massacre at 29, Castletown Road, London, W.14, although by now he had almost certainly changed his name. Not long afterwards he appears to have moved to a new and secret address, not referred to in the files or in his correspondence with the Foreign Office. From then on their letters were addressed to him care of his bank, though still to Captain Teague-Jones. Although on extended leave at the request of the Foreign Office while they tried to resolve the Baku affair with Moscow, and also while his own future was decided, Captain (now Major) Teague-Jones was still officially on the payroll of the Indian Government. To have merely substituted the name of Ronald Sinclair for that of Teague-Jones in all official correspondence would not only have defeated the purpose of his change of name, but would also no doubt have caused utter confusion in Whitehall and Delhi. Disappearing, apparently, is no easy matter when one is in the throes of unfinished official business. For the time being, it seems, he maintained two identities simultaneously, though his secret was known only to those few who needed to know.

In November 1922, Teague-Jones produced an official 1,500-word rebuttal of all Chaikin's charges, denying any personal involvement in either the decision to shoot the Baku commissars or in their actual execution. Repeating largely what he had written in his journal, and which appears in this book, he reported that Funtikov, the S.R. President, had confided to him that he had sent a special emissary — his fellow committee member Kurilev — to Krasnovodsk to make the arrangements for the execution. 'To the best of my belief,' Teague-Jones wrote, 'the murders were actually carried out by Kurilev and a party of men sent by the Krasnovodsk authorities.' He further denied that either General Malleson or any other British officers had advocated the killings, adding that Malleson had wanted the captured commissars eventually sent under escort to India (to serve, if need be, as hostages for the safe return of British officers held by Moscow). It was only after the massacre, he insisted, that he had learned of it. 'The execution', he wrote, 'was carried out secretly by the Russians without informing the British. Had it not been for the fact that I dragged the information from the drink-sodden Funtikov, I should have known nothing about it until some time afterwards.'

Teague-Jones concludes by declaring that he reserved the right to institute libel proceedings against Chaikin, whom he describes as a 'thoroughly unscrupulous and dangerous political adventurer', at such time 'as there shall be a civilised and responsible

207

government in Russia.' The final version of his reply, which was formally addressed to the Under-Secretary of State at the Foreign Office, and dated November 12, 1922, was passed to the Soviet Commissariat for Foreign Affairs together with the observation that the allegations against Teague-Jones were considered by H.M. Government to be 'baseless' and 'founded in deliberate misstatements'. There the matter rested, as it has done to this day, neither side being prepared to give ground. Anyone wishing to examine Teague-Jones's rebuttal of the charges, which is far too long and complex to summarise here, will find the full text reproduced in Command Paper 1846 (Russia No. 1, 1923). A copy of this can be seen in the Public Record Office at Kew, together with Chaikin's contentious book (in Russian). The principal correspondence surrounding the Baku affair, and Teague-Jones's involvement in it, is to be found in file numbers Fo 371 8204, Fo 371 8205 and Fo 371 9357, which cover the period 1919–23.

Although there is not the space to go into it any further here, anyone comparing Teague-Jones's account of the massacre given in this book (taken directly from his journal) with that stated in his official rebuttal will notice one important discrepancy. In the former he records that Malleson was not keen to relieve the Askhabad Committee of the captured commissars because it was 'very difficult to find the necessary guards to send them down to India'. Malleson suggests instead, somewhat ominously, 'that the Trans-Caspian authorities should find some other way of disposing of them'. Yet in his official rebuttal, written some two years later, he declares that Malleson *did* want the commissars sent to India. Indeed, on September 18, 1918, two days before their execution, Malleson telegraphed Simla to report thus: 'Askhabad Government is being asked to hand over the above mentioned leaders to me for dispatch to India as their presence in Trans-Caspia is most dangerous at present time when probably fully half Russians are preparing to turn their coats once more at the slightest sign of enemy success.'

On September 23, however, he telegraphed to report that the commissars had been shot. Too late, their messages apparently crossing, the Chief of the General Staff in Simla telegraphed Malleson advising: 'It is essential that you should take over at once the Bolshevik prisoners . . . to hold as hostages.' The full text of

208

these telegrams and other related ones can be seen in the India Office Records (Fire series L/MIL/17/552 *et seq*). On the face of it, therefore, it would appear that the British authorities did not wish to see the commissars executed, at least not while they might still serve a useful purpose. Why then, in his journal, does Teague-Jones give an entirely different impression by quoting Malleson as suggesting that the Askhabad Committee 'should find some other way of disposing of them'?

Aware of this apparent discrepancy, Teague-Jones explains in his rebuttal that it was the 'semi-intoxicated' Funtikov who had assured him that Malleson, through the S.R. representative in Meshed, had declined to take over the prisoners, declaring that the Askhabad Committee would have to 'make its own arrangements'. It was at the now-notorious meeting, at which the fate of the commissars was to be decided, that Funtikov first announced this, and it appears that Teague-Jones took it at face value. In his rebuttal, the latter insists that Malleson's orders were therefore 'deliberately suppressed or misquoted'. Only one construction, Teague-Jones concluded, could be put on this — 'namely that the Socialist Revolutionaries were determined to have the prisoners executed'. Funtikov and Kurilev, he added, were foremost in advocating this. 'The arguments continued endlessly, and finally I left the meeting before anything had really been definitely decided,' he wrote. Only on the following evening did he discover from Funtikov what the meeting had finally decided, whereupon he immediately wired Malleson to warn him of what had happened. Three more days were to pass, however, before he learned from Funtikov that the Baku commissars had been 'quietly shot'.

Teague-Jones's explanation for this discrepancy may not satisfy everyone. But now that his posthumously published narrative, together with other material of his in the Imperial War Museum, is available for comparison, it will no doubt be closely studied by scholars interested in the intervention period. This may well throw up renewed controversy, for there are still plenty of unanswered questions surrounding the Baku commissars' deaths. Soviet scholars reading the available material, including that in the Foreign Office and India Office records, are likely to claim that Teague-Jones and Malleson got together to hide the truth of what really happened between Askhabad and Meshed. Indeed, in a letter to the Foreign Office written in the summer of 1922, Teague-Jones says that he must consult Malleson before replying to the Russian charges. This seems reasonable enough, if only to discover the reason for the discrepancy noted above, but a Soviet scholar might well interpret it rather differently. Nor is that the only discrepancy, for in the typescript of Teague-Jones's *Adventures with Turkmen, Tatars and Bolsheviks*, referred to in my introduction, he even suggests he was not present at the fateful meeting after all. That discrepncy I shall have to leave to others to explore, since my space is limited.

For those who wish to pursue further the uncertainties surrounding the deaths of the commissars, there are two other first-hand accounts of British activities in Trans-Caspia at that time. One is an article on their fate by General Malleson himself, entitled *The Twenty-Six Commissars*, which appeared in the *Fortnightly Review* of March 1933. He also gave a lecture to the Royal Central Asian Society on January 24, 1922, entitled *The British Military Mission to Turkistan, 1918–20*, which was reprinted in the society's journal. The other first-hand account of Malmiss is *The Transcaspian Episode*, by Colonel C. H. Ellis, one of Malleson's officers, which was published in 1963, and which speaks highly of Teague-Jones.

The official Soviet view of British activities in Trans-Caspia at that time, and Teague-Jones's role in these and in the massacre of the Baku commissars, can be found in Leonid Mitrokhin's *Failure of Three Missions*, published in Moscow in 1987. Drawing on British documents now in the National Archives of India, he claims that the activities of Malmiss 'marked the beginning of the planned seizure of all Turkistan' by the British, and that this was 'preceded by subversive work carried out by a ramified network of British secret agents', who included Captain Teague-Jones and Colonel F. M. Bailey. Needless to say, he holds Teague-Jones responsible for the deaths of the Baku commissars. However, despite his impressive array of footnotes and sources, he adds very little to what we already know, most of the documents he draws on being also available in the India Office Library and Records. Mitrokhin, in common with other Russian scholars, blames the present troubles in the Caucasus in part on British intervention there in 1918–20. A further book is promised shortly, according to Moscow, which will contain 'a great deal of new material' on the subject.

The individual who has probed most deeply so far into the Baku massacre and Teague-Jones's role, if any, in it, is Brian Pearce, a Russian scholar. My own interests in the affair — for a book on British, German and Turkish intelligence activities in Persia, Afghanistan and the Caucasus — owes much to his pioneering scholarship, not to mention his valuable advice. Unfortunately his own research into the subject has appeared only in highly specialised journals, though if anyone should be encouraged by a publisher to unravel further the life of Reginald Teague-Jones it is surely he. Because Teague-Jones is merely one of a number of individuals who interest me, my own pursuit of him has necessarily been limited mostly to the Foreign Office and India Office archives. However, in addition to this, and to Brian Pearce's published material, I have the benefit of what Teague-Jones's publisher, David Burnett of Gollancz, has turned up from his own sources. These include past conversations with Teague-Jones, whom he got to know when working on his travel book — *Adventures in Persia* — which dealt with a journey by car from Beirut to India in 1926, as well as discoveries which Burnett has made subsequently.

The first clue suggesting that there might be more to Teague-Jones's disappearance than simply fear of Bolshevik vengeance came to light shortly after his death. Burnett, who at that time had no idea that his author was anyone other than Ronald Sinclair, was going through his manuscripts, papers and photographs trying to piece together his career for an obituary in *The Times* when he came upon a large, brown manila envelope of the type once used in Whitehall. Written on it in pencil were the words MAJOR SINCLAIR, MI5. At the time it merely confirmed what Burnett already knew — that Sinclair had once been involved in intelligence work. The envelope was empty and there was no way of dating what appears to be a piece of internal mail.

It was only subsequently, when Ronald Sinclair's real identity was revealed in a second obituary in *The Times* (written by myself), that the full significance of his find struck Burnett. Teague-Jones had not merely changed his name to escape Bolshevik wrath, but also — with his cover blown by his activities in Trans-Caspia — so that he could continue to work for British intelligence. His exceptional skills and experience were too valuable to lose at a time when Bolshevism was seen as a grave threat, especially to British

India. Working for MI5, he would almost certainly have been employed in monitoring Comintern activities and shadowing suspects, a task for which he was singularly well qualified, with his fluent Russian and other languages, his familiarity with Bolshevik tactics and his pre-war experience of subversive movements in India.

It would appear, moreover, that he was also sent on clandestine missions overseas for his Whitehall chiefs. This would explain some of his travels in the Middle East and Far East between the wars. It might even explain the real purpose of his journey through Persia by car in 1926. Ostensibly it was to investigate, on behalf of a small group of British companies, the opportunities for trade. However, it seems rather more likely that he was sent to determine the extent of Soviet penetration there. Persia was considered to be particularly vulnerable at that time, and its proximity to India, which Moscow was known to covet, made it vital for the authorities in London and Delhi to know what was going on there. Teague-Jones's credentials for such a task, including fluency in Persian and familiarity with the country, could hardly be bettered. His knowledge of commerce, on the other hand, was virtually nil. However, if his real purpose was to investigate Soviet activities in Persia, he could not have chosen a better cover, for his journey was to take him to a large number of towns and villages from Tabriz in the north to Zahidan on the frontier with India. It also gave him a valid pretext for asking innumerable questions in a region where such behaviour invites immediate suspicion.

All this, of course, is speculation, and it is unlikely that the truth will ever be known, for the intelligence services do not discuss such matters, even when they happened so long ago. Furthermore, despite the 30-year-rule releasing official records, many of the inter-war intelligence files are still closed, although the World War II ones are available. Some intelligence-related files of the period have also been withdrawn from the India Office Records as being 'too sensitive', in official eyes anyway. Such reticence, which has been criticised by an all-party Commons Select Committee, does not make it any easier to follow the inter-war career of Captain Teague-Jones. Just to confuse matters, there was another Captain Sinclair engaged in intelligence work at that time. He was Captain Hugh Sinclair, R.N., Director of Naval Intelligence, who in 1923 was appointed head of the Secret Intelligence Service, Britain's spy network, better known as MI6.

Although there may be further clues to Teague-Jones's movements following his disappearance still to come to light, the Foreign Office and India Office records fall silent at around this time. However, in a letter to the Foreign Office written in 1922, at the height of the Bolshevik campaign against him, he makes an interesting personal disclosure. He refers to the anxiety of his wife over the fate of her parents. For it may not come as a total surprise to the reader to learn that he had married the Russian girl, Valya Alexeeva, whom he first met on the boat from Krasnovodsk to Baku in the summer of 1918. They had fallen in love, for those were heady times, and he had arranged for her escape from Baku, which was about to fall into the hands of the advancing Turks. Their marriage, sadly, was not destined to last, due in part no doubt to the severe strain they now both found themselves under, not to mention their very different backgrounds. According to one confidential source, Valya worked for many years for the British intelligence services, though in what capacity is uncertain. Teague-Jones in the meantime remarried. This time it was to a German girl named Taddy. There were no children by either marriage. Many years later, as we shall see, Valya was to come briefly back into his life.

One intriguing question is just how Teague-Jones, now Sinclair, coped when, as he inevitably must have done, he ran into pre-war or wartime friends who knew him by his old name. Did he look blank and say: 'I'm sorry, but you must be mistaken. My name is Ronald Sinclair. I must have a double'? Or was word discreetly passed around his former friends and colleagues that for good reason Teague-Jones had ceased to exist, and that to recognise him or talk about him would be to put his life at risk? Certainly his colleagues in MI5 and MI6 would have been aware of who he was — as too would the mandarins at the Foreign Office and India Office. Indeed, according to Brian Pearce, when Teague-Jones changed his name the India Office requested (of whom, he does not say) that no publicity be given to it, 'so far as the law allows'. Although Pearce does not give his source for this, as he does for everything else, the latter may refer to the legal process by which his name was to be changed. As we have already noted, there is more than one way of doing this. Changes by Deed Poll, for example, must be published in the *London Gazette*, but those made by statutory declaration avoid any publicity. Alternatively, it might merely have meant that Fleet Street editors were asked to ignore it.

Inevitably Teague-Jones's activities during the inter-war years are shrouded in secrecy, though there could just be people still around who, as very young men, worked with him, or knew him, in the 1930s. But being of the generation which took the Official Secrets Act more seriously than some of their successors, they are unlikely to come forward and talk about him now. However, a little bit more is known about his movements in World War II and afterwards. In 1941, at the age of 52, he was posted to the British Consulate-General in New York as a Vice-Consul. There, according to a source close to him, he was engaged throughout the war in intelligence work of various kinds, although officially he was designated head of the commercial department.

Shortly after the war he retired, moving to Miami Beach in Florida with Taddy in 1953. Nine years later, perhaps finding their British pension inadequate for living in the States, they moved to Spain, where they remained until the mid-1980s. His wife's failing health — she had Parkinson's disease — necessitated their return to England, where shortly afterwards she died. On learning of his loss, his first wife Valya, now in her eighties, made contact with him. He was then living in a private retirement home in Plymouth, enjoying excellent health, considering his age, his war-wound and the strain of his subsequent experiences. Nor, as we shall see, was he hard up. Valya, he was dismayed to discover, was living alone and in extremely straitened circumstances in London. He at once invited her down to Plymouth to live, at his expense and in her own room, in his retirement home, so that he could be with her to the very end, which was clearly not far off.

It was Valya herself who unwittingly provided a clue to their secret past, although no one realised its significance at the time. Every morning Teague-Jones would make his way over to the block where Valya lived, and would sit for hours holding her hand and talking gently to her. Always she addressed him as 'Reggie', not 'Ronnie' like everyone else, something which puzzled Anne Randall, on the staff of the home, who looked after him devotedly until his death, in his hundredth year, some months after Valya succumbed to pneumonia. It was only then, when she learned of his real name and his extraordinary past from his obituary in *The Times*, that she grasped the significance of Valya's 'Reggie'. His death also yielded one further surprise, that he was a wealthy man, for he left more than £500,000.

So far as Teague-Jones himself was concerned, he took his secret to the grave, his cover being blown only after his death. But he left behind him many unanswered questions. One would like to know, for example, much more about his early life, including his years as a schoolboy in St Petersburg, where, during the 1905 Revolution, he was nearly crushed to death by a mob. One would like to know too what precisely happened that night in Askhabad when the fate of the Baku commissars was decided, and what role, if any, Teague-Jones played in this. Could he have prevented it? Did he try to prevent it? Did Malleson not even wish to prevent it? The answers to these three questions will almost certainly never be known, now that Teague-Jones, the last living witness, is dead. Finally, one would like to know about those missing years, from his disappearance in the summer of 1922 to his appointment, in 1941, as Vice-Consul in New York. Here the prospects for a determined researcher or biographer would appear more promising.

Perhaps a final word should be devoted to the twenty-six Baku commissars, with whose deaths Teague-Jones's name, fairly or unfairly, will always be linked. After the massacre, it will be recalled, their corpses were tossed unceremoniously into a communal grave and hastily covered up. Two years later, in September 1920, after the Bolsheviks had regained control over Baku, they were disinterred and shipped back across the Caspian to the Azerbaijani capital, where they were reburied in a square named after them.

Today a large monument stands on the spot to commemorate their martyrdom. In the middle of it burns an eternal flame cupped in the hands of a worker whose head is bowed in mourning. Each hour a requiem, specially written in their memory, is played, while every year, on the anniversary of the massacre, they are officially honoured by the city. Also in the square is a red granite relief depicting the execution scene, the defiant figures facing the firing squad symbolising Courage, Moral Conviction, Undaunted Spirit, and Faith in the Cause. At intervals around the square are individual busts of all twenty-six commissars. Elsewhere in the city the homes of two of their leaders have been turned into memorial shrines, while the personal possessions of others can be seen in the main history museum. There are numerous other reminders of the twenty-six men, including a station and a district named after them. Nor will the tour guides allow one to forget them, especially if one is British, although I have not been back there since relations with Moscow began to improve.

But before one dismisses all this as tedious propaganda, and regardless of whether there should be any British guilt over their brutal deaths, one thing should be remembered about these men which cannot be said of most Bolsheviks, and certainly not of Lenin. The Baku commissars, led by Stepan Shaumian, firmly rejected the use of terror as a means of winning or holding on to power, sincerely believing that this could be achieved by democratic means. During their brief period of rule in Baku, not one member of the anti-Bolshevik parties was arrested, let alone executed — something which for Stalinist historians later castigated them severely. Had they been as ruthless as their foes were prepared to be, then they would almost certainly not have perished. But it was their moderation and idealism which made them easy prey for their revolutionary rivals, and which led to their tragic fate beside the railway track on that September morning in 1918.